Anne's Bohemia

MEDIEVAL CULTURES

SERIES EDITORS
Rita Copeland
Barbara A. Hanawalt
David Wallace

*Sponsored by the Center for Medieval Studies
at the University of Minnesota*

Volumes in the series study the diversity of medieval cultural histories and practices, including such interrelated issues as gender, class, and social hierarchies; race and ethnicity; geographical relations; definitions of political space; discourses of authority and dissent; educational institutions; canonical and noncanonical literatures; and technologies of textual and visual literacies.

For other books in the series, see p. 194

Anne's Bohemia

Czech Literature and Society, 1310–1420

Alfred Thomas
Foreword by David Wallace

Medieval Cultures
Volume 13

University of Minnesota Press
Minneapolis
London

Published by the University of Minnesota Press
111 Third Avenue South, Suite 290
Minneapolis, MN 55401-2520
http://www.upress.umn.edu

Library of Congress Cataloging-in-Publication Data
Thomas, Alfred.
    Anne's Bohemia : Czech literature and society, 1310–1420 / Alfred Thomas ; foreword by David Wallace.
        p.   cm. — (Medieval cultures ; v. 13)
    Includes bibliographical references and index.
    ISBN 0-8166-3053-4 (hardcover : alk. paper). — ISBN 0-8166-3054-2 (pbk. : alk. paper)
        1. Czech literature—To 1500—History and criticism.   2. Czech literature—Social aspects.   3. Literature and society—Czech Republic—History.   4. Bohemia (Czech Republic)—Social conditions.
I. Title. II. Series.
PG5005.5.S62T48   1998
891.8'609001—dc21   97-44613
                                                                 CIP

Printed in the United States of America on acid-free paper

The University of Minnesota is an equal-opportunity educator and employer.

10 09 08 07 06 05 04 03 02 01 00 99 98   10 9 8 7 6 5 4 3 2 1

For J. S. W.

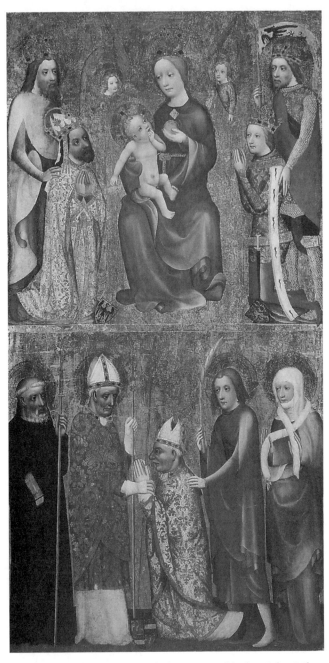

Frontispiece. The Votive Panel of Prague Archbishop John Očko
of Vlašim (after 1370). Reprinted with permission of the National
Gallery, Prague, Czech Republic.

Contents

✛

Contents

Illustrations

Foreword

❖

David Wallace

In organizing what turned out to be the crucial protest march of the 1989 "Velvet Revolution," student leaders chose the date November 17: the fiftieth anniversary of Hitler's Special Action Prague, which saw 9 student leaders executed and 1,200 students sent to the concentration camp at Sachsenhausen. Such consciousness of relatively recent history combined, as the march unfolded through the city, with claims to identity rooted in a deeper past: for the urban spaces or linked townships of Prague—one of the most beautiful of European sites—were decisively developed in the Middle Ages. The university that nurtured the protesters of 1939 and 1989 was founded by Charles IV, Holy Roman Emperor, in 1348. In the same year, Nové Město (New Town) was founded on the east bank of the Vltava to accommodate a rapidly expanding, predominantly Czech-speaking population of rural immigrants. Staré Město (Old Town), north of Nové Město, gained rights for a town hall in 1338 (and for the university ten years later). Here, and at Malá Strana—the "Small Side," the town that had grown up across the river beneath the Prague castle complex—German was the most favored language. During the twelfth century, the Jewish community of Prague—which was to develop a long and brilliant history—expanded into the area now known as Josefov (north of Staré Město); the remarkable Staronová Synagoga (Old-New Synagogue), still standing today, was one of Prague's first Gothic structures.

Today this vibrant, multicultural medieval past is being recuperated and reinterpreted as the new Czech Republic attempts to reorient itself within new European and internationalist frameworks. It would, of course, be foolish indeed to mistake medieval Bohemia for the modern Czech Republic: to forget that this very new republic includes North and South Moravia, to forget about the Slovaks. But there has never been a time when any responsible account of this region could afford to be less than vigilant about matters historiographical, political, and ethnic. Any new account must begin, as Alfred Thomas begins, by acknowledging the constraining political interests at work in any production, past or present, of the Bohemian past.

Anne's Bohemia is the first book in English on Czech and Bohemian literature and society, 1310–1420. Those of us who have tried to explore this tantalizing subject without knowing Czech have hitherto had to rely on German scholarship (a distinguished scholarly tradition, with its own particular agendas), encyclopedia entries, stray articles, and uneven translations. This book will interest anyone who cares about European culture, past or present; it will be of especial importance for students of medieval England, for two main reasons. First, Anne of Bohemia, daughter of Emperor Charles IV, traveled to England in 1381 to marry Richard II. As Richard's friends and favorites fell in a series of political crises, Anne — who was the same age as her husband — assumed increasing importance as his longtime companion and political collaborator. On numerous occasions (some of them commemorated by manuscript illuminations), Anne knelt before Richard to plead for various parties who had incurred the royal displeasure. The staging of such appeals added a flexibility to Richard's kingship without compromising its authority: the woman at his feet was, after all, an emperor's daughter. Chaucer, a member of the king's affinity, devoted a great deal of creative energy to exploring the potential of wifely eloquence, particularly that part of eloquence that might dissuade irascible, powerful men from following their more violent, vengeful impulses. In *Troilus and Criseyde,* Chaucer compliments Queen Anne ("Right as oure first letter is now an A," line 171) by subtly equating her current social preeminence ("now an A") with the preeminent beauty of his Trojan heroine (line 172); in the *Legend of Good Women,* he is commissioned to compile a new work and "yive it the quene...at Eltham or at Sheen" (F496–7). The cosmopolitanism of Anne and her Bohemians, whose cultural links with France and Italy were particularly strong, complement Chaucer's celebrated internationalism in ways we have yet to investigate. It seems quite possible, for example, that Chaucer learned as much about Petrarch and incipient Italian humanism from Bohemians in Westminster as he did from Italians in Genoa, Florence, and Milan.

Second, England and Bohemia were linked in unique and complex ways through the exchange of texts, ideas, and personnel associated with Lollardy and the Hussite movement. Anne Hudson, in her patient and ultimately monumental reconstruction of the Lollard textual corpus, spent a lot of time in Czech libraries. Two of the three extant manuscripts of the increasingly famous *Testament of William Thorpe* are of Bohemian provenance; one of them is still to be found in Prague (Metropolitan Chapter Library O.29). The very survival of much Wycliffite writing is due, in no small measure, to the efforts of Bohemian scholars who, sympathetic to the English Reformist movement, came to Oxford with the express purpose of copying Wyclif's texts and carrying them back to Bohemia. In England, meanings ascribed to Wycliffite writings and Lollardy have, from the outset, been colored by the self-legitimating initiatives of monarchical regimes: first the Lancastrians and later the Tudors (and latterly the Victorians, who sparked the revival of Wycliffite scholarship). Hussitism, too, has been recruited to serve a variety of class-based, ethnic, and nationalist agendas (summed up best, perhaps, by Ladislav Šaloun's lowering statue of Hus, unveiled on the five hundredth anniversary of his death by burning, which still dominates Prague's Old Town Square). Thomas's work, following Hudson's, should help further the complex, unfinishable task of restoring medieval religious movements to the Middle Ages. Thomas makes his distinctive contribution here not by studying Hus, but rather by seeking to recover those particular traditions of textual culture by which Hussitism was preceded, transmitted, and surrounded. And in doing this, he delineates a specific textual/historical phenomenon that makes further comparative study of Czech and English cultures seem especially promising: the gradual but decisive displacement of Latin by the vernacular as the definitive language of both orthodox and heterodox self-expression.

Within this greater comparative framework, Thomas encourages us to consider more specific textual conjunctions at a variety of social levels. In Bohemia as in England, selective idealization of peasantry may be read as part of a critique of urban, artisan, and mercantile cultures. Czech verse romances, derived from German originals, offer instructive points of comparison with the English tail-rhyme corpus (derived from the French); anti-Semitic strategies employed by the farcically dramatic *Ointment Seller* might be compared with those of the Anglo-Irish *Croxton Play of the Sacrament*. The Czech *Life of Saint Catherine*, Thomas argues, powerfully synthesized international courtliness and lay devotion in ways that invite comparison with the Middle English *Pearl*. And the complex political allegories of *The New Council*, in which the Lion King is treated to the advice of various animals, finds an analogue in Chaucer's *Parliament of Fowls*. This serves to remind us that Chaucer's missing "book of the Leoun," alluded to in the "retracc'iouns" that conclude his *Canterbury Tales* (10.1087), need not necessarily have been based on a *Dit du Lyon* by Machaut or Deschamps.

Such openings to future comparative work might usefully augment current efforts, ongoing at Charles University and elsewhere, to redress the eastward orientation imposed upon Czech culture in the years before 1989. At the same time, they need not simply aspire to draw Czech culture back into the traditional boundaries of a greater European, and beyond that western, culture. Life in the Czech Republic, as any visitor may tell, plays out excitingly and unpredictably between east and west. Wenceslas Square may now look (at first glance) like Times Square, but the Charles Bridge (designed by Peter Parler and completed circa 1400) seems determined to resist, for the most part, pressures of creeping commercialization. At U Fleků, the celebrated medieval beer hall, teenage "language students" crowd in where once townspeople sat and drank; the waiters find themselves caught between the impulse to interrupt the singing and the obligation to respect the logic of a new socioeconomic order. Such dilemmas give rise to strains of humorous reflection analogous to those that proved such a memorable, enabling part of the 1989 "Velvet Revolution" (and, indeed, of the 1992 "Velvet Divorce"). This book does not seek, then, to speed the process of triumphalist Europeanist teleological closure. It seeks, rather, to ground appreciation of remarkable cultural affinities—connecting Anne's Bohemia, Anne's England, and the rest of Europe—in a new sense of likeness and difference.

Acknowledgments

❖

M uch of the credit for the present form of this book must go to Rita Copeland and David Wallace who had the courage and idealism to live up to the rubric of their Minnesota Medieval Cultures Series and support new scholarship on noncanonic literatures. Rita encouraged me, at an early stage of the project, to define my audience while David pointed me in a comparatist direction. The University of Minnesota Press editors Lisa Freeman and Robin A. Moir then lent me the kind of important practical support that allowed the book a rapid transition toward completion. Finally, Anne Running has been an excellent copyeditor.

Among my Slavist colleagues at Harvard University, I would like to thank William Mills Todd III for agreeing to read an earlier draft of the manuscript and for making helpful suggestions for its improvement; Michael S. Flier for his useful comments on texts and images; and Horace G. Lunt for sharing his expertise on the early Slavs and the Great Moravian Empire. I would also like to thank my readers Jan Čermák (Prague) and Eva Hahn (Munich) for their helpful and detailed comments on my manuscript. Among the many medievalist colleagues who have offered insights and suggestions over the last three years I should mention Joseph Goering, Eleazar Gutwirth, Jeffrey Hamburger, Anne Hudson, Ruth Mazo Karras, Richard Newhauser, Derek Pearsall, Ferdinand Seibt, František Šmahel, Jane H. M. Taylor, Jiří Josef Veselý, and Jan Ziolkowski. I would also like to mention the students who participated in my Survey of Czech Literature course at Harvard (1994–96). While not specialists in medieval literature, their intelligence, enthusiasm, and perspicacity have been a source of delight and stimulation. Lastly, I thank James S. Williams, who has given me so much personal support in the last few years, even from afar. I dedicate this book to him.

Several chapters of *Anne's Bohemia* have been read as scholarly papers or have appeared in article form. Chapter 3 was presented at the panel "Gender, Race, and Ethnicity in the Middle Ages" at the International Congress on Medieval Studies held at Western Michigan University, Kalamazoo, May 1996; a reduced version of chapter 4 was read at the conference "Obscenity: Social Control and Artistic Creation in the European Middle Ages," held at Harvard University, May 13–15, 1995, and was subsequently published in German translation as "Frauen, Juden, und Deutsche: Aussenseiter in dem alttschechischen *Unguentarius*" in *Bohemia* 38, no. 2 (1996); a modified form of chapter 5 appeared as "*Imitatio Christi*: A New Perspective on the Fourteenth-Century Czech *Verse Legend of Saint Procopius*," in *Die Welt der Slaven* 39, no. 2 (1994): 344–55; chapter 6 was read as a paper at a conference entitled "Christ among the Medieval Dominicans" at Notre Dame University, September 6–9, 1995; and part of chapter 7 was read as "The Reception of Arthurian Literature in Medieval Bohemia" at The Eighteenth International Arthurian Congress, Garda, Italy, July 21–27, 1996.

Abbreviations

AFP	*Archivum Fratrum Praedicatorum*
AfSlPh	*Archiv für slavische Philologie*
ANTS	Anglo-Norman Text Society
ČČH	*Český časopis historický* (Czech Historical Journal)
ČČM	*Časopis českého muzeum* (Journal of the Czech Museum)
EETS	Early English Text Society
FMLS	*Forum for Modern Language Studies*
FRB	Fontes Rerum Bohemicarum
LF	*Listy filologické*
MGH	Monumenta Germaniae Historica
MHB	*Medievalia Historica Bohemica*
SATF	Société des anciens textes français
SlR	*Slavische Rundschau*
SSR	*Scottish Slavonic Review*
VKČSN	*Věstník královské české společnosti nauk* (Bulletin of the Royal Czech Society of Sciences)
WdSl	*Die Welt der Slaven*
ZfSl	*Zeitschrift für Slavistik*
PMLA	*Publications of the Modern Language Association*
SEER	*Slavonic and East European Review*

Quotations from the *Alexandreida* without a letter refer to the Saint Vitus Fragment. The other fragments are denoted by the following letters:

B	Budějovice Fragment
Š	Šafařík Fragment

A Note on the Use of Czech Proper Names

❖

In order to facilitate the understanding of the anglophone reader, I have tended to use the English or (where none exists) the German form of Czech personal names (e.g., Wenceslas instead of Václav, Ulrich instead of Oldřich), except when I am making a distinction between Czech fictional characters and their German prototypes (e.g., Jetřich Berúnský and Dietrich von Bern). Place names, however, retain their Czech, rather than German, forms, since these tend to be more familiar to English speakers (e.g., Kutná Hora rather than Kuttenberg).

Anne's Bohemia

Toward a Comparative Study of Medieval Czech Literature

On December 18, 1381, the fifteen-year-old Anne of Bohemia made the crossing from Calais to Dover in Kent with her extensive entourage. Several weeks earlier she had left Prague, the city of her birth, and had made her way across western Europe to England. She interrupted her journey in Brussels, where she stayed for a month as the guest of her paternal uncle, Wenceslas, duke of Brabant. On her arrival at Dover Anne was met by her future husband, King Richard II of England. In those days the journey between the coast and London was long and tiring, so the young couple rested in the *camera regis* of the Royal Lodge at Ospringe near Faversham, whence they continued to Leeds Castle to spend the Christmas holidays. Richard and Anne were married in Westminster Abbey on January 20, 1382. Two days later, Anne was crowned queen of England.[1]

The marriage was apparently a happy one: Richard was devoted to his new wife and rarely left her side. Traditionally, scholars have emphasized her docile qualities as a dutiful and loyal wife. But considering Richard's later infatuation with the international court culture, he must have found his young bride a source of cosmopolitan glamour, a precious jewel with which to adorn his own fledgling court. As a member of the late-fourteenth-century international "jet set," Anne read and spoke several languages fluently (French, German, Czech, and Latin). Moreover, her pedigree was impeccable. Her father was the deceased Charles IV, Holy Roman Emperor and king of Bohemia (r. 1346–78), and her half brother Wenceslas IV (r. 1378–1419) was king of Bohemia and king of the Romans. At this time "Bohemia" was a byword for chic: the so-called Bohemian "beautiful style" in panel painting, sculpture, and jewelry represented the height of European fashion. A cursory glance at Anne's crown, exquisitely wrought by French craftsmen and now in the *Schatzkammer* in Munich, gives us a glimmer of the dazzling impression she must have made on the English court.

London may well have struck Anne as somewhat tawdry and provincial by comparison with Prague, the city where she had spent her childhood. Her father, Emperor Charles, had transformed the Bohemian capital into the administrative center of the empire and a growing metropolis with a population of thirty-five thousand. Charles was a man of boundless energy who, unlike his imperial predecessor Lewis of Bavaria, preferred diplomacy and building to conflict and war. He was a zealous collector of religious relics, which he housed — along with the crown jewels — in his residence at Karlstein Castle near Prague (see Figure 1); a passionate builder who erected the Gothic Saint Vitus Cathedral and the stone bridge across the Vltava River; an urban planner who laid out the so-called New Town of Prague; and a great sponsor of learning who founded the oldest university in central Europe at Prague in 1348. At his cosmopolitan court, French, German, Italian, Latin, and Czech mingled as languages of refinement and edification. The distinguished Italian humanists Petrarch and Cola di Rienzo, the painter Nicholas Wurmser of Strassburg, the builder Matthew of Arras, and the architect-sculptor Peter Parler came to Prague from different parts of Europe, adding an international luster to the imperial capital.

Thanks to the pioneering scholarship of Gervase Mathew, the extent of the Luxembourgs' influence on Richard II's court has been appreciated for some years now. On the Luxembourg side of the family, Anne's great-grandfather had been the patron of Dante; her grandfather, King John of Bohemia (r. 1310–46), enjoyed the secretarial services and poetic gifts of Guillaume de Machaut; her father corresponded with Petrarch, who, on a visit to Prague, likened the enlightened emperor and his courtiers to the ancient Athenians; and her uncle, Wenceslas, duke of Brabant, was the illustrious patron of Jean Froissart and Eustace Deschamps.[2]

Less familiar to anglophone medievalists, but no less significant in shaping Anne's intellectual pedigree, was her Bohemian ancestry. Count John of Luxembourg had strengthened his claim to the Bohemian throne by marrying Elizabeth Přemyslovna, the last surviving member of the Slavic dynasty that ruled Bohemia from the earliest times to the year 1306, when her brother, Wenceslas III, was assassinated at Olomouc in Moravia. The unusually high rate of literacy among the female members of this family is of great significance in understanding Queen Anne's precociousness. Her ancestor Saint Agnes of Bohemia, who founded the first Franciscan monastery in the Bohemian Lands, had corresponded in fluent Latin with two popes and Clare of Assisi, from whom she solicited advice about the everyday running of her religious house in Prague. Agnes's great-niece, Abbess Kunigunde, was one of the greatest female patrons of the arts in late medieval Europe and possessed a large library of books. Queen Anne, according to Wyclif's *De Triplici Vinculo Amoris*, owned copies of the New Testament in Latin, German, and Czech, a claim that was eagerly exploited by Lollard propagandists.[3] All this evidence points to a strong tradition of female literacy in the Bohemian royal house.

It is the principal object of this book to bring Anne's Bohemia to the attention of an English-speaking audience by placing in their social context key works of fourteenth- and early-fifteenth-century Czech literature written between 1310 and 1420, dates coterminous with the reigns

Figure 1. *The Scene of the Relics*, mural in Saint Mary's Church, Karlstein Castle, Karlstein, Czech Republic.

of the three Luxembourg rulers John, Charles IV, and Wenceslas IV. In undertaking this project, I have intentionally eschewed writing a compendious "history" of medieval Czech literature, since two studies of this kind already exist.[4] I offer instead close readings of salient texts, a focus that inevitably means that not every genre in medieval Czech literature will receive the attention it deserves. Exclusively theological works, for example, do not loom large in the following pages, a deficiency I hope to make up at a later date; and the less original translations from Latin have had to yield space to adaptations from German and Latin that offer deeper insights into the local Bohemian context.

Just as English outstripped French as the language of courtly and popular entertainment and edification between 1300 and 1400,[5] so did the Czech language begin to vie with German and Latin. This complex multilingual and multicultural situation has been generally overlooked as a consequence of the historiographical tendency to treat Anne's Bohemia as a platform upon which imperial and dynastic politics were staged, with the Holy Roman Emperor as the central protagonist and Prague as the principal setting. Studies such as these have been invaluable in helping us to appreciate the achievement of Emperor Charles in raising his capital to such magnificent heights.[6] But this exclusive concern with dynastic politics overlooks two fundamental issues pertaining to Czech literature and culture: the horizontal relationship between the royal court and the provinces and the vertical relationship between different classes.

In the course of this book, I shall be referring not only to Prague but also to several significant provincial centers of cultural patronage, for example, Hradec Králové in eastern Bohemia, where Wenceslas IV's consort, Queen Sophie, held her regional court and which gave rise to the important *Hradec Králové Codex* (c. 1380s). This city was one of the important points of origin of the Bohemian reform movement, which, in the fifteenth century, exploded into rebellion and revolution. Another important regional cultural center was Olomouc. Thanks to the efforts of Chancellor John of Středa (bishop of Olomouc between 1374 and 1380), this Moravian city became a burgeoning center of humanist learning in the late fourteenth century, a process interrupted only by the Hussite Wars.[7] Moravia had long since preserved a high level of cultural achievement. During the reign of John of Luxembourg, Elizabeth Rejčka (1288–1335), widow of Wenceslas II, had established a brilliant court at Brno that eclipsed that of the royal court at Prague. Elizabeth was a great patron of the arts who commissioned no fewer than nine beautifully illuminated manuscripts for the devotional use of the Cistercian nuns at the convent of Aula Sanctae Mariae, which she founded on June 1, 1323.[8] Since those days, Brno had remained the regional capital and court of the margraves of Moravia, a title traditionally held by the king's younger brothers. Charles IV's brother John Henry and Wenceslas IV's brother Jošt both resided there.

A third important area of provincial cultural activity was southern Bohemia, a region dominated from the thirteenth to the seventeenth century by the powerful Rožmberk family. Although firm evidence for this family's direct involvement in Czech literature is difficult to establish,[9] there can be no doubt that the Rožmberks were generous patrons of the arts. Both Peter I and his son Peter II supported the family foundation, the Cistercian monastery of Vyšší Brod, and embellished its church with the famous altarpiece that is now in the National Gallery in Prague. In the bottom right-hand corner of the Nativity scene from this cycle of nine panel paintings, a kneeling Peter I offers a model of the Cistercian monastery to the Virgin and child (see Figure 2). Peter II continued in

Figure 2. *The Nativity,* Master of the Vyšší Brod Altar, National Gallery, Prague, Czech Republic.

his father's benevolent footsteps by bequeathing valuable books to the Augustinian canons at Třeboň.[10] In the fifteenth century, a female member of the same family named Perchta (1429–76) achieved note—even notoriety—as an eloquent and prolific correspondent with her father Ulrich and brothers Henry and John (see chapter 2).[11]

The mobile relationship between the royal court and the provinces is clearly not peculiar to medieval Czech literature; for example, it is very much the subject of current scholarly debate in Middle English studies. In a recent article, Michael J. Bennett argues that it has become accepted practice in the last few years to focus on the cultural situation in the English provinces to the extent of denying the existence of a court culture in London altogether.[12] Echoing Elizabeth Salter's assessment of English culture at a somewhat earlier date, Bennett maintains that there is no straightforward opposition to be found between provincial and court culture in late-fourteenth-century England.[13] In the later years of his reign, when London became more and more unsympathetic to his vision of an absolute monarchy, Richard II removed his court for a period of time to York and traveled extensively around the northwest Midlands, where, Bennett proposes, the alliterative romance *Sir Gawain and the Green Knight*—that masterpiece of international courtliness—may have received a viva voce airing.

This fluid relationship between the capital and the countryside also holds true for fourteenth-century Bohemia. Charles IV was an indefatigable traveler within his kingdom of Bohemia and within the empire. Wherever he went, the imperial court went with him. We can imagine that the verse *Life of Saint Catherine* might have been read aloud at Charles's peripatetic court. It may have been through this itinerant route that the legend ended up in a provincial manuscript analogous to the famous Cotton Nero MS, which contains all the alliterative masterpieces of the *Gawain*-poet.

More important still, the lines of contact between Prague and the provinces were a vital means of literary, philosophical, and ideological transmission. The aforementioned John of Středa, bishop of Olomouc, was also chancellor of Bohemia and a close associate of the emperor's; Peter I and Peter II of Rožmberk both occupied the prestigious office of Lord High Chamberlain and, in this elevated capacity, attended important state ceremonies in Prague (for example, Charles's coronation in 1346). Needless to say, there was a constant, two-way traffic between Prague, the center of royal and imperial power, and Brno, the capital of the margraves of Moravia.

An important feature of this two-way traffic between the capital and the countryside was the crucial role played by the university at Prague as a center and disseminator of new ideas from abroad.[14] John Hus is obviously the most famous example of a Czech from the provinces who came into contact with the writings of Wyclif at Prague, but he was not the first person to profit from the university. Having studied for a few years at Prague, the nobleman Thomas of Štítné went home to southern Bohemia, where he wrote progressive works in Czech for the edification of his daughter Agnes and other unlettered young women.

The second fundamental deficiency facing contemporary scholarship of medieval Czech culture is the reluctance (especially in the post-Communist era) to address the vertical relationship between classes in the transmission of literature. As I argue in chapter 2 (on female readers and writers), class and gender are intricately linked in the complex process of growing lay literacy throughout the fourteenth and fifteenth centuries. The important (albeit sometimes exaggerated) phenomenon of female literacy among the Hussites would have been impossible had not royal princesses and noblewomen enjoyed similar privileges in the fourteenth century. We might speak here of a trickle-down process whereby an elite of educated women at court grew, across the course of a century, into a significant number of female adherents of the preacher John Hus centered around the Bethlehem Chapel, the earliest home of preaching in the Czech language. Perhaps one reason that scholars in Communist Czechoslovakia ignored or played down this trickle-down process is that it is closer to a capitalist paradigm of monetary relations ("trickle-down economics") than a classical Marxist model of economic exchange.

Although many of the challenges facing students of medieval Czech literature are analogous to those confronting their Middle English counterparts, there are also imporant areas of difference. The biggest difference is that less scholarly attention has been paid to the field of medieval Czech studies. There is, for instance, no Czech equivalent to the Early English Text Society, and the Old Czech dictionary, begun in the last century, is still incomplete. But the greatest challenge facing the intrepid Bohemist are the ideological assumptions that have come to dominate the discipline since its infancy in the nineteenth century. Like its sister discipline, Czech historiography, medieval Czech studies have been handicapped by a partisan legacy of patriotic and Protestant ideology, which has prevented an objective reconstruction of the medieval past. The great nineteenth-century historian Francis Palacký (1798–1876) saw medieval Bohemia as a site of ethnic conflict between Germans and Czechs that culminated in the "progressive" Hussite Revolution of the fifteenth century. Palacký's teleological view of medieval Bohemian history as a prelude to Hussitism has exercised an enormous influence on Czech historians and literary historians ever since. It has also found a popular mediator and supporter in the figure of the philosopher-president Thomas G. Masaryk (1850–1937). For Masaryk the Hussite Revolution witnessed the first manifestation of Czech *humanita* — a rather nebulous creed defined roughly as the commitment to democracy and the human spirit — which Masaryk saw as the key to the "meaning" of Czech history.

Masaryk's understanding of Hussitism as an early example of campaigning for human rights and democracy was based on later Enlightenment principles of liberty, equality, and fraternity and had little in common with the essentially religious and nationalist underpinnings of the Hussite Revolution. Masaryk's views were later attacked by the Catholic historian Josef Pekař (1870–1937), a prominent member of the empirical school of Czech historiography founded by Jaroslav Goll (1846–1929) and Antonín Rezek (1853–1909). Pekař drew attention to the unhistorical, a priori tendency of Masaryk's ideas and placed the emphasis on nationalist and religious factors in the formation of Hussitism.[15]

Where Masaryk and Pekař saw humanism and nationalism, respectively, as the key to the Czech past, the Marxist school of critics that dominated Czech scholarship between 1948 and 1989 inevitably emphasized class conflict. Needless to say, the more fundamental applications of this creed degenerated into a simplistic distinction between "low" and "high" culture and "reactionary" and "progressive" trends, a distinction that overlooks the fluid horizontal and vertical relationship between social groups and the crucial role played by orthodox and heretical religion in linking these groups.

Burdened, then, by a tradition that has insisted on finding the "meaning" of Czech history,[16] historians and literary historians alike have tended to be overly narrow, introspective, and programmatic where a more comparative, objective approach would have shed a clearer light on the Czech cultural situation in the fourteenth and fifteenth centuries. Comparing the situation in England and Bohemia, for example, constitutes a particularly valuable exercise, since significant lines of diplomatic and intellectual contact existed between these countries in the late fourteenth century. In both countries lay literacy was on the increase and the vernacular was maturing into a vibrant literary language; a struggle for power was being fought between a centralizing monarchy and a belligerent nobility; and reformist ideas were being transmitted from academic circles to the laity via the vernacular, ideas that contributed to the English Peasant Uprising of 1381 and the Hussite upheavals of 1419 and 1422.[17] Admittedly the development of these countries did not follow paths that were absolutely parallel in either the fourteenth or the fifteenth centuries. One major area of difference was the early use of the vernacular as a mouthpiece for the cause of the Czech-speaking nobility in its ancient power struggle with the kings of Bohemia, a tradition exemplified by the xenophobic *Dalimil Chronicle* (see chapter 3). It was as a partial consequence of the Czech ethnic identity forged by writers in the fourteenth century that Hussitism assumed a polarized ethnic, as well as religious, character. As Anne Hudson succinctly puts it, "Whilst Hussitism became identified with the incipient movement toward a recognition of national identity, Lollardy did not."[18] In England the Lollard rebellion of 1414 was crushed by Henry V, whereas, in Bohemia, the

Hussites defeated several armies sent by the emperor Sigismund and the pope to eradicate the heretical movement. Yet even in the fifteenth century some similarities can be found: in both lands, a period of peace and détente was followed by a time of protracted military conflict.

In order to attempt a viable comparative study of medieval Czech literature, we need first of all to reconstruct the social context in which late medieval Czech literature arose. There are three main factors involved in this process: ethnicity (in particular, the relationship between Czechs and Germans), class, and gender. As chapter 2 seeks to demonstrate, women were prominent as readers and even writers, first in the royal family and later in aristocratic circles, as literacy spread outward and downward from the court. The anonymous *Life of Saint Catherine*, discussed in chapter 6, is a good example of an important text whose social reception has not been studied in a sufficiently serious fashion, apart from the vaguest speculation that it may have been written by someone within the court circles of Charles IV for the benefit of a noble audience. My close reading of this text, which draws as much as possible upon relevant material in other vernacular literatures, attempts to deduce from all the textual and extratextual evidence available the kind of author we are dealing with and then hypothesizes about a possible audience. I conclude that this audience consisted of noblemen and women, and that the intellectual and affective profile of the virgin-martyr offered by the text was meant to serve as an imitative model to women on how to combine their social roles as thinking and corporeal beings.

Even in the rare instances of texts whose authors are known to us by name—such as *The New Council*, discussed in chapter 8—complex problems of reception remain unresolved. *The New Council* underwent two redactions, only the second of which is extant. Here we have an author undergoing a gradual change of social identity from courtier and royal insider (in the 1380s) to a rebellious outsider by the beginning of the 1390s. Commensurate with this modified identity is a changing reception from a relatively large, homogeneous courtly audience for the first redaction to a small group of disaffected co-rebels in the noble *fronde* of 1394. As Paul Strohm claims in his subtle discussion of the "social Chaucer," the last decade of the fourteenth century witnessed a complex transformation in the reception of texts and their audiences as power shifted from a weakened individual to a group of powerful and disaffected magnates.[19]

A further challenge faced by the would-be comparatist is the need to overcome the taxonomic division into "pre-Hussite" and "Hussite" studies of Czech history and literature. Conscious of the artificial nature of this dividing line, the present study will focus upon the period 1310 to 1420, dates that encompass the Hussite Revolution but are not defined by it. The dichotomy "pre-Hussite" and "Hussite" is inconsistent with my conclusion that the social and cultural forces that led to the Hussite

Revolution formed part of a century-long process of gestation. The readings of *The Dalimil Chronicle, The Ointment Seller,* and the verse *Legend of Saint Procopius* (see chapters 3, 4, and 5, respectively) all point to the construction of a Czech ethnic identity in the fourteenth century that formed the basis of the political alliance between the Czech-speaking gentry and the peasantry during the Hussite Revolution. *The Dalimil Chronicle* was a particularly important catalyst in the creation of a patriotic (and xenophobic) distinction between Czechs and Germans, a legacy we see reflected, for instance, in *The Younger Prose Legend of Saint Procopius,* considered briefly in chapter 5, and in the Hussite *Dispute between Prague and Kutná Horá,* discussed in chapter 9.

The reign of Charles IV represents a powerful example of the religious continuity between reform and revolution in fourteenth- and early fifteenth-century Bohemia. The emperor himself was partly responsible for providing the impetus to the reform movement that preceded the Hussite Revolution of the next century. He personally invited the Austrian Augustinian canon Konrad Waldhauser to preach in Prague and even tolerated the fiery sermons of the former Dominican Milíč of Kroměříž, although his tolerance was sorely tested when Milíč audaciously compared him to the Antichrist in 1369.[20]

Not only has scholarship concentrated too exclusively on Hussitism to the neglect of the preceding period; it has also tended to focus upon the reformist trends in fourteenth-century Bohemia to the detriment of traditional religion. The consequence of this one-sided approach is a rather simplistic picture of the relationship between Czech literature and society in the age of the Luxembourgs. If scholars have highlighted the reformist strain in a work like the verse *Legend of Saint Procopius,* they have failed to isolate an analogous orthodox animus in the verse *Life of Saint Catherine.* I argue in chapter 6 that this work — far from representing a mystical and romantic world, as scholars have argued — was conceived with the practical need to reinforce orthodox beliefs in a noble audience increasingly vulnerable to anticlerical opinions emanating from reformist pulpits in Prague churches. The highly physical *imitatio Christi* that the virgin-martyr Catherine undergoes — especially her flagellation prior to execution — is peculiar to the Czech version. As David Aers has discussed in connection with late medieval English writings, such corporeal evocations of Christ's suffering humanity were intended to reinforce orthodox beliefs in the audience.[21] Christ's body was the agency of ecclesiastical authority in matters of faith, and its suffering was an expression of the church's enormous control over people's lives.

Dubbed *rex clericorum* by William of Ockham, the pious and orthodox Charles IV surrounded himself with priests like Ernest of Pardubice, archbishop of Prague; John of Středa; the Dominican John Moravec (his personal confessor); and the Alsatian Dominican John of Dambach (his court theologian). But in fourteenth-century Europe, there was frequently a fine line between orthodoxy and heresy, as the example of the former Dominican friar and member of the imperial chancellery Milíč attests.[22]

The vernacular saints' lives examined in chapters 5 and 6 reveal the extent to which the religious conflict between conservatives and reformers was already under way fifty years or so before an anonymous Dominican from southern Bohemia attacked the Hussite supporters of John Wyclif in his treatise *Invectio satirica in reges et proceres viam Wiklef tenentes* (1414) and the Dominican friar Peter of Úničov began his well-documented assault on Hus and the Utraquists in Prague, at the Council of Constance and at the University of Bologna.[23] *The Older Prose Legend of Saint Procopius*, written by an anonymous court Dominican at the instigation of the emperor sometime in the 1370s, highlights the sacramental importance of penitence and warns its audience against the envy of radical critics. On the other side of the ideological divide, the anonymous author of the verse *Legend of Saint Procopius* anticipates the nationalism of Hussitism by idealizing Procopius, abbot of the Sázava Monastery, as a virtuous Czech peasant and by demonizing his Latin opponents as devious Germans.

If we consider the cultural situation in England at about the same time, we find a similar conflict between orthodoxy and reform, between works like Langland's *Piers Plowman*, which influenced some of the leaders of the Peasant Uprising of 1381,[24] and the Dominican Roger Dymock's antiheretical treatise *Liber contra duodecim errores et hereses Lollardorum*, written for Richard II in 1396. Like Charles IV, Richard II was orthodox in matters of faith: two of his personal confessors, Thomas Rushook and John Burghill, were Dominicans,[25] and he favored Dominican preachers and read the daily hours after the Dominican use.[26] In 1410 Nicholas Love sent Archbishop Arundel his English translation of the pseudo-Bonaventuran *Meditationes Vitae Christi* for approval. The archbishop not only endorsed its scrupulous orthodoxy but encouraged its dissemination in lay circles, a sign, as Anne Hudson has astutely pointed out, that the English church establishment now realized that it had to appropriate the tool of the heretics — the use of the vernacular — if it was to win the doctrinal battle for the hearts and minds of the faithful.[27]

The deployment of the vernacular rather than Latin as a tool of heresy and orthodoxy helped to shape the form and direction taken by Czech literature in the second half of the fourteenth century. The reformist mood of sermons preached by Waldhauser and Milíč in Prague can be felt in several works contained in the *Hradec Králové Codex* — including the verse *Legend of Saint Procopius* — and in the theological writings of Thomas of Štítné. These reformist texts provoked a reaction from conservative elements at the court, a reaction that Charles almost certainly encouraged in the form of translations and adaptations from the Latin. Even though some of Charles's pet projects were disinterested works of scholarship, like the great encyclopedia known as *Claretus*, with its Czech-Latin glossary compiled by Bartholomew of Chlumec,[28] other commissions, like the prose *Passional* based on *The Golden Legend*, the verse *Life of Saint Catherine, The Older Prose Legend of Saint Procopius*, and the prose *Life of Christ* (adapted from the pseudo-Bonaventuran *Meditationes Vitae Christi*), were probably written by court Dominicans with the express purpose of combating heretical tendencies in the upper levels of Bohemian society.

The policy of using the vernacular to spread and combat reformist ideas inevitably led to a proliferation of lay literacy as traditionalists and reformists found Czech a valuable tool for the spreading of propaganda. It is not surprising, therefore, to find the first translations of books of the Vulgate being undertaken as early as the 1370s. The first Czech Bible was probably the work of several authors; one of them, who translated the Book of Tobias and the Acts of the Apostles, was the same Dominican who translated the Old Czech *Passional* and *The Life of Christ*.[29] The reformist preacher Milíč also had a hand in translating the Czech Bible; this was followed in the 1390s by a German translation of the Bible—the lavishly illuminated Wenceslas Bible—commissioned by the rich Prague burgher Martin Rotlöw and dedicated to Wenceslas IV.[30]

We can assume that the circulation of these biblical translations would have been tightly controlled and carefully circumscribed. If Anne of Bohemia possessed personal copies of the New Testament in German, Czech, and Latin, it was possible only because her religious education would have been carefully monitored by her tutors and confessors in Prague. Not surprisingly, attempts to uncover Wycliffite sympathies within the queen's household have fallen on barren ground.[31] At her father's and brother's court, Anne would have been exposed only to the most scrupulously orthodox works, like *The Life of Saint Catherine*, with its traditional veneration for the saints, sacraments and holy images (see chapter 6). Richard and Anne's shared commitment to orthodoxy is an important part of the deep affinity that existed between them. I do not think that this connection has been sufficiently emphasized by scholars in England and elsewhere.

If Charles sponsored the translation of the Gospels into the vernacular, his motives in doing this, as in everything else he achieved, were a complex mixture of idealistic and practical considerations. Charles identified deeply with the language of his Slavic ancestors and emphasized his spiritual and familial descent from Saint Wenceslas, the patron saint of Bohemia. But by espousing the Czech language he was also co-opting the favored political medium of the nobility, whose support he needed to strengthen his dynastic claim to the Bohemian kingdom. Thus Charles's decision to bring Czech into the orbit of the other court languages (French, German, and Latin) was a calculated policy to defuse the traditional deployment of the vernacular as a vehicle of antimonarchical ideology. It was also inspired by religious needs: as we have seen, Czech was becoming the medium of ideological contestation between reformists and traditionalists in society at large.

Charles must have learned some fundamental political lessons about monarchical rule at the French court, where he spent his formative years. It was there that he first acquired his appreciation of the political and ideological importance of the cults of the saints in creating a strong centralized monarchy. In addition to his own autobiography (the so-called *Vita Caroli*), Charles wrote a Latin homily to his Přemyslid ancestor Saint Ludmilla and a vita of her grandson Saint Wenceslas in the guise of a courtly knight. The historical Wenceslas I had been concerned to preserve the political survival of his dukedom by means of nominal feudal payments made to the German emperor, a pacifist policy that led to his overthrow and murder by his warlike brother Boleslav I. Charles emulated his saintly ancestor's pacifist policy by preferring negotiation and diplomacy to warfare and overt military conflict.

It seems quite plausible that this *pax carolina* helped to inspire Richard II's policy of détente with France in the 1390s. The famous Wilton Diptych, painted for Richard around 1390–95, provides a visual example of the ideological affinity between Charles and Richard. Art historians have already explored the iconographic and stylistic evidence of Bohemian influence on this beautiful diptych: for example, the figure of the Virgin and child, before whom the king kneels in adoration, recalls the "beautiful style" of contemporary Bohemian sculpture,[32] and Anne's personal device is evoked through the scattered branches of rosemary among which the white hart reposes on the reverse side of the panel. But what art historians have failed to consider are the ideological ramifications of the Bohemian connection with Richard's court. These are manifested less through iconographic symbols and motifs than through relationships and identifications between the figures in the painting. A cursory comparison of the Wilton Diptych with the Bohemian Votive Panel of Archbishop John Očko of Vlašim (c. 1371) suggests that Richard's profound identification with his pacifist predecessors Edmund the Martyr and Edward the Confessor may have been modeled on Charles IV's cult of his holy ancestors, the martyrs Ludmilla and her grandson Wenceslas (see frontispiece).[33] Just as Richard kneels before the Virgin Mary and the Christ child, surrounded by his patron saints Edward the Confessor, Edmund the Martyr, and John the Baptist, so in the Bohemian panel Charles IV and his son Wenceslas genuflect before the Virgin and child, flanked by their respective patron saints, Sigismund and Wenceslas. On the lower level of the same panel John Očko of Vlašim is surrounded by Saints Vitus, Ludmilla, Adalbert, and Procopius, first abbot of the Sázava Monastery and a central figure in the Old Church Slavonic liturgy, which Charles restored to its former prestige and prominence after its abolition by Duke Břetislav II in 1097.

If there was indeed a *pacifist* affinity between Richard and his father-in-law, the reasons for it are not simply romantic or mystical but intimately tied to Richard's political and dynastic ambitions in the mid-1390s to succeed his father-in-law as Holy Roman Emperor.[34] To this end, it made perfect sense for the English king to emulate his illustrious father-in-law's piety. Particularly significant in this connection were Richard's efforts to arrange the canonization of his murdered great-grandfather Edward II. If this attempt had been successful, it would have provided the king with a saintly figure from within his own (Plantagenet) family. Having been crowned *rex Romanorum* in 1346 and eager to be elevated to Holy Roman Emperor, Charles was able to demonstrate to his old tutor and mentor Pope Clement VI his descent "from the roots and the lineage of the most blessed father Wenceslas, duke and patron of Bohemia."[35]

Czech Literature from 1310 to 1420

Chapter 1 traces the emergence of vernacular culture in the Bohemian Lands in the twelfth century, when the Czech kings began to patronize German language and culture as part of their larger political ambition to become key players in the politics of the empire.[36] By the end of the thirteenth century Czech had already developed into an articulate and resourceful medium for the expression of the nobility's beliefs and the construction of their political identity. Central to this identity was a profound identification with the Czech language and a concomitant antagonism toward German speakers within the ecclesiastical and the court establishments. This xenophobia is reflected in *The First Cycle of Legends* (c. 1306), a series of vernacular saints' lives in verse based on *The Golden Legend* by Jacobus de Voragine. Texts such as these were instrumental in forging a distinctive ethnic identity that ultimately motivated many members of the nobility to identify with the martyred Czech preacher John Hus (1369?-1415). In this complex fashion, religious dissent, ethnic enmity, and class solidarity against a centralizing monarchy all played their part in creating one of the most momentous religious and social upheavals of the later Middle Ages.

By the first half of the fourteenth century, the Czech literary language began to make significant inroads into the culture as an articulate medium of religious and political ideas in centers of learning like the Augustinian monastery at Roudnice (founded for the sons of Czech-speaking families in 1337) and the Benedictine Convent of Saint George at the castle in Prague, especially under the aegis of Abbess Kunigunde. At this time we also find the beginnings of a secular literature written in Czech, like the *Alexandreida* (c. 1290–1300) and *The Dalimil Chronicle* (c. 1308–10). Here questions of ethnicity, gender, and class all come into play in the formation of the Czech literary language: the Augustinian house at Roudnice was founded as an ethnic counterbalance to what was until then the dominant influence of Germans in the upper echelons of the Bohemian church; the presence of a Czech-language prayer on the Host alongside Latin texts in Kunigunde's personal breviary was clearly related to the female cult of the Eucharist at this period; and the composition of *The Dalimil Chronicle*—a highly partisan history of Bohemia from the perspective of the gentry—must be seen in the context of conventional class conflict between the nobility and the kings.

In this study I will be arguing that class, ethnicity, and gender are equally important and interrelated constituents of Czech literature in the age of the Luxembourgs. In most works of medieval Czech literature written during this period, women are represented as objects of male power rather than as subjects in their own right. But late medieval Bohemian women were also important readers and writers who made a significant contribution to the development of medieval Czech literature. Chapter 2 explores how female literacy trickled down from the court and noble households to the lower levels of society and thus contributed to the involvement of laywomen in the Hussite reform movement. The devout and literate women who gathered around the pre-Hussite preachers (like Matthias of Janov) later thronged to the Bethlehem Chapel. Such women owed their literacy to the example provided by royal princesses like Agnes of Bohemia, Abbess Kunigunde, and Anne of Bohemia.

Chapter 3 examines *The Dalimil Chronicle*, which contains the first comprehensive political program of the state seen from the standpoint of the lower nobility. Central to its intention is the promulgation of a Czech ethnic identity distinct from that of the German and Polish nations. This ethnic identity is constructed by differentiating between the Czech and German speakers of Bohemia, the latter having established a significant presence in the kingdom first as farmers in the border areas and later as artisans exploiting its great mineral resources of gold, silver, and copper. This German minority became so important to the economic interests of the Czech kings that their presence began to arouse resentment from the nobility, the selfsame class that had facilitated their arrival in the first place. Chapter 3 explores how the advancement of Czech ethnicity in *The Dalimil Chronicle* is contingent—as are all forms of identity—on the prior existence of the Other, which encompasses not only ethnic outsiders like Germans but also those newly literate women able to express themselves in the vernacular. In this way, Czech ethnic identity—as represented in the first Czech history of Bohemia—is exposed as a construct intended to perpetuate the power of a patriarchal minority over the rising influence of literate women as well as foreigners.

In addition to Germans, Jews also constituted a significant minority in late medieval Bohemia. The reign of Charles IV was a period of relative peace and prosperity for them, although they were customarily subjected to mockery in the population at large and even persecuted in the years preceding and following Charles's rule. Chapter 4 examines how the anonymous author of the religious farce *The Ointment Seller* utilizes obscenity to enforce a distinction between unmarked insiders (Czechs) and outsiders (Jews and Germans). As in *The Dalimil Chronicle*, the anonymous author of the play excludes the female from the imaginary community, equating old women and prostitutes with Germans and Jews through the shared imagery of lower body parts (the vagina and the anus).

The subject of chapter 5, Saint Procopius, is an interesting example of a local saint whose cult was a source of ideological contestation between the reformers and traditionalists. *The Older Prose Legend of Saint Procopius*, which was written by an anonymous court Dominican at the emperor's instigation, emphasizes the orthodox values of penitence and obedience to authority. The anonymous author of the verse legend, however, stresses the saint's Christlike avowal of poverty and his earthly ministry, significantly excluding the list of posthumous miracles detailed in the Latin source. In this important respect, the verse legend exemplifies the reform-minded *imitatio Christi* familiar to English readers from Langland's *Piers Plowman*.[37] But the author of the legend also gives the saint's *imitatio Christi* a specifically Bohemian form by making the saint a heroic fighter against German control of the Sázava Monastery and by turning the historical nobleman into a Czech-speaking peasant. The verse legend survives as a unique copy in the *Hradec Králové Codex*, which also contains devotional works and satires aimed against the vices of artisans and city magistrates. These recall the similar attacks on fraudulent bakers, butchers, and cooks in passus III of the B and C versions of *Piers Plowman*.[38] As in Langland's great work, the cobblers, butchers, bakers, and magistrates excoriated in *The Satires of the Artisans* provide a negative contrast with the idealized peasant Procopius.

In addition to honoring Bohemian saints like Procopius, Ludmilla, and Wenceslas, Charles IV also encouraged the cults of foreigners like Saint Vitus and Saint Catherine of Alexandria. A Czech version of the latter's vita represents the high point of medieval Czech literature and stands worthy of comparison with the courtly masterpieces of the English *Gawain*-poet (see chapter 6). Like the alliterative English poem *Pearl*, *The Life of Saint Catherine* represents the perfect fusion of vernacular lay piety and international courtliness. As an epic tale of courage and piety, *The Life of Saint Catherine* would have appealed both to knights and ladies of the court. Departing from the conventional view of this text as quintessentially mystical and apolitical,[39] I argue that it was written very much with political and social—as well as religious—considerations in mind. Like many works of medieval mysticism, the legend was intended to instill ideological and religious conformity—particularly into women—at a time when heresy was commonly equated with female waywardness.[40]

I suggest that the anonymous author may have looked to the emperor's third wife, Anne of Schweidnitz, as his patron, just as Anne of Bohemia was the intended recipient of Chaucer's *Legend of Good Women*, as well as the real-life surrogate of the character Alceste (as David Wallace suggests).[41] The Czech *Life of Saint Catherine* includes what may be a significant allusion to the empress's namesake, Saint Anne, where there is none in the Latin source. Christ's grandmother was popular in the late Middle Ages as the patron saint of childbirth, a topic clearly on Petrarch's mind when he wrote a short treatise *De laudibus feminarum* for Empress Anne (newly delivered of a baby girl). Petrarch states that Anne's sex is noble not only for its childbearing capacity but also for its intellect, for its manifold virtues, and for the glory and accomplishments of the empire.[42] Such praise for women as mothers and thinkers comports with the curious dovetailing of somatic and intellectual motifs in the verse *Life of Saint Catherine*, further evidence that it was written for an audience with the dynastic need for healthy offspring and with the humanist belief in the high value of female literacy.

Consistent with its appeal to educated women like Empress Anne, *The Life of Saint Catherine* grafts the secular language of the romance and the lyric onto the saint's life to produce a hybrid "hagiographic romance."[43] This synthesis would appear to reflect the anonymous author's status as a clerical courtier and his audience's familiarity with chivalric romances. Charles IV was somewhat traditional in his policy of recruiting clerics into his household and depending heavily upon their advice. The likely author of *The Life of Saint Catherine* was one of the Dominican clerics who also served as diplomats and counselors to the emperor. As Richard Firth Green states, members of the royal chamber in the late Middle Ages were expected to combine everyday activities of diplomacy and administration with the social function of poets and entertainers.[44]

An important consequence of the blend of courtliness and piety found in Caroline Bohemian culture was the development of a Czech chivalric romance genre, which diverges significantly from its western European archetype. The romance *Duke Ernest* (c. 1350) recalls *The Life of Saint Catherine* in its subtle synthesis of secular romance and religious sensibilities. By the reign of Wenceslas IV (r. 1378–1419), however, chivalric verse and prose romances of German courtly provenance were assuming a more secular form (see chapter 7). Inevitably, not only the language but also the ethos of the German models underwent a profound "acculturation" as they were transmitted to a later and noncourtly Czech audience. The Czech verse romances thus witness to the leisure moments of a pious lower nobility with an appetite for secular stories of love and adventure but with an aversion for the courtly sensibility and mores enshrined in the original versions. In their piety and simplicity these popular works are strongly reminiscent of the Middle English tail-rhyme romances dating from about the same period. That few of the verse romances survive should not surprise us when we consider that the genre was accepted late in Bohemia (during the reign of Wenceslas IV) and suffered an inevitable eclipse during the Hussite Wars. Only following the restoration of peace in the second half of the fifteenth century did these secular works reappear in a few Bohemian codices.

Chapters 8 and 9 of the book examine the final great efflorescence of medieval Czech literature during the rule of Wenceslas IV, an ineffectual ruler whose reign saw the beginnings of the political and religious turmoil that would culminate in the Hussite Revolution. An interesting analogue to Chaucer's *Parliament of Fowls* from this period is the political-allegorical *New Council* (1394) by the high nobleman Smil Flaška of Pardubice (c. 1340s-1403). The original version of this series of forty-four animal counsels to the Lion King, written between 1378 and 1384, was intended as an instructive *speculum principis* for the new king. The later (extant) version, however, is colored by the author's resentment toward the king's perceived encroachment on baronial power. Whereas the earlier *Council* consisted solely of positive counsels, *The New Council* combines old and new ones that allude scathingly to the king's love of public baths, alcohol, songs, and tournaments. (We find a similar criticism of alleged royal excesses in the grievances leveled against Richard II by the Lords Appellant in 1387.) In chapter 8, I argue that this paradoxical amalgam of benevolent and satirical counsels was not the consequence of the author's consciously ironic stance but the effect of his ideologically ambivalent status as a courtier-turned-outsider. Analogously, in contemporary England, Geoffrey Chaucer was changing from the purely courtly author of *Troilus and Criseyde* to the ironic chronicler of the diverse social world mirrored in *The Canterbury Tales*.[45]

Another variation on the theme of conflicted identity is the prose dispute *The Weaver* (c. 1407/9), a meditation on the loss of a beloved written by an anonymous author at Hradec Králové, the regional court of Wenceslas IV's consort Queen Sophie. Chapter 9 argues that the debate between Misfortune and Ludvík Tkadleček ("Weaver") concerning the respective vices and virtues of the latter's girlfriend Adlička (who has jilted him and disappeared) dramatizes the well-known tension between the authorial *personae* of clerk and courtly lover familiar from the poems of Machaut, Froissart, Petrarch, and the English *Gawain*-poet. But unlike these writers, the Czech author is both unwilling and unable to reconcile the aesthetic and didactic discourses in his work. Courtly love is placed in the balance and found wanting by Misfortune, who is given the last word in the dispute. Unlike its German analogue *Der Ackermann aus Böhmen, The Weaver* is thus less a metaphysical *cri du coeur* than a discursive debate between courtliness and didacticism, a subtle barometer of Wenceslas IV's failure to achieve what his father, Charles

IV, and his brother-in-law, Richard II of England, had succeeded in realizing: a court culture in which the secular and the sacral dimensions of kingship could be reconciled.

If *The Weaver* represents the breakdown of this synthesis of courtliness and lay piety, its Middle English analogue *Pearl* may be said to exemplify its most perfect consummation. Richard II's aspiration to forge a court of peace at the intersection of the heavenly and earthly domains is beautifully encapsulated in the intermingling of courtly love and mystical piety that characterizes the masterpiece known as *Pearl*.[46] It is likely that the achievement of Chaucer and the *Gawain*-poet derives more than we have hitherto suspected from Queen Anne's crucial role as a representative of international court culture in England. (One is even tempted to speculate whether *Pearl* might have been intended as a veiled elegy on her death in the summer of 1394.) As this book hopes to make clear, Anne's presence on English soil and her brief reign as queen of England provided a strong impetus for the rise of international court culture in London, for English religious reform (especially through the translation of the Gospels into the vernacular), and for the realization of a deeply sacral vision of English kingship. The presence of all these elements in late-fourteenth- and early-fifteenth-century English culture owes a great deal, I suggest, to Anne's Bohemia.

CHAPTER 1

Prologue

Literature in Old Church Slavonic, Latin, and Czech before 1310

From the fifth century A.D. there was a westward migration of Slavs into territory formerly occupied by Germanic tribes, principally Goths, Burgundians, Vandals, and Langobards.[1] In the first half of the sixth century the Langobards still occupied present-day Moravia, while remnants of the Markomanni tribe moved, along with their Germanic neighbors, southwest toward the Danube and into Bavaria. In the mid–sixth century the Avars from central Asia occupied present-day Hungary and subjugated the Slavic and Germanic populations of the area. In 568 the Langobards moved into northern Italy, thus making room for the Slavs to enter the present-day Bohemian Lands from the north. The earliest inhabitants of the Bohemian Lands had been the Celts, who developed a high degree of civilization as builders of the so-called *oppidas* (fortified centers) and as manufacturers of iron instruments and ceramics. Bohemia has preserved in its name that of the original Celtic tribe, the Boii. But the Celts' position in the region had been weakened by attacks by the Romans, who penetrated as far as Trenčín to the southeast, and by the Germanic Markomanni and the Quadi tribes.

From the beginning of the sixth century to the middle of the ninth century, the Slavic population was already settled, living from farming and cattle breeding. Land and cattle were the communal property of the tribe, which formed a collective in both production and consumption. Fortified villages that were seats of tribal chieftains formed independent centers sparsely scattered through the land. In the seventh century, from which we have more definite written evidence, this original collective society was already in decline. An important factor in this disintegration was the introduction of slaves as a new labor force. The slaves had to carry out most of the heavy work, which had been done in the past by the free members of the tribe. The tribal system changed into the clan system. Pastures, forests, and some fields were still communal for the whole clan, but the clan chieftains appropriated the best land of the clan. In this way, collective property passed into the private ownership of individual families. This development went a step further, toward the formation of a primitive state organization, which was the result of two factors: the efforts of individual chieftains to preserve and enlarge their power vis-à-vis other clans, and the voluntary association of clans for the purpose of defense against invaders, in particular the Avars to the east and the Franks in the west.

The first primitive "state" organization on Czech and Slovak soil was the short-lived empire formed by the Frankish merchant Samo in the early seventh century. Probably a loose military association of Slavic clans, Samo's empire provided a bulwark between the Avars and the Frankish kingdom, whose attack it repulsed in 651. It was, however, a temporary formation and did not survive Samo's death in 658. After the destruction of the Avars by Charlemagne in 796, the Slavs in central Europe inevitably came under the influence of the Frankish Empire; and following the tripartite division of the Frankish Empire in 843 (in accordance with the Agreement of Verdun), they had to acknowledge the political dominance of the East Frankish kingdom under Charlemagne's grandson, Louis the German.

By the eighth century the Roman Catholic Church had established itself as a powerful evangelizing presence in central and southern Germany, thanks largely to the pioneering work of Saint Boniface (d. 754). By 800 the Bavarian Church—the foundation of which dates from 716 with the establishment of a bishopric independent of Frankish control—was strong enough to undertake its own missionary activity among the Slavs. This missionary work was combined with an effort to bring the converted population under the subservience of the empire. By the 830s, several Moravian chieftains had been baptized according to the Roman rite, and in the year 845 fourteen Czech chieftains and their retinues arrived in Regensburg to receive baptism there, since Bavaria had its own bishopric and Prague did not.[2]

What has come to be known as the Great Moravian Empire, which probably developed along the Danube and its tributaries in the first half of the ninth century, was the first real state in the region.[3] It arose in what was the most fertile, economically the most advanced, and strategically the most advantageous area, and it formed an important bulwark between the East Frankish Empire in the west and Byzantium in the east. Christianity, with its monotheistic idea and advanced organization, undoubtedly played the role of catalyst in the process of state formation. Yet such influence carried a price: its first ruler, Mojmír I, had to choose whether to place his burgeoning empire in the western or eastern sphere of influence. In order to resist this political pressure from the East Franks, Mojmír's successor, Rostislav, turned to Byzantium for help and asked Emperor Michael III for priests to come and evangelize the region. If the reasons for the Constantine-Methodius mission of 863 were primarily political, it still had an enormous cultural and spirtual importance, laying the foundation of a liturgical Slavonic language and literature.[4] Old Church Slavonic became the third liturgical language, side by side with Greek and Latin, and appears as one of the oldest European languages in written form, long before French and Italian. Yet, although of fundamental importance for the East Slavs, the work of Constantine and Methodius and their followers was only an episode in the development of Czech medieval culture. Under the pressure of economic and social factors, the Czechs did not adapt Byzantine civilization, but turned toward western civilization.

At the beginning of the tenth century Great Moravia collapsed under the concerted onslaught of the nomadic Magyar tribes and the forces of the East Frankish Empire, and the center of development moved to Bohemia. There, in the second half of the tenth century, changes in production took place that deeply influenced social structures. After the violent liquidation of the remaining clans, the Přemyslids established themselves as the ruling family in the land. In the middle of the tenth century the Bohemian state was consolidated and a working agreement was established between the dukedom and the German Empire. Nominally, the rulers accepted Bohemia in fief from the German emperor, but in practice the land was independent. It played an important part as an ally of the empire, and in 1085 the Czech duke, Vratislav II, was rewarded for his service to the empire by receiving the royal crown with the titles of Bohemia and Poland.

An important factor peculiar to the Bohemian situation was the colonizing policy of the Přemyslids and other feudal lords. In the tenth century Bohemia and Moravia had probably some 250,000 inhabitants and most of the land was not cultivated (forests extended up to thirty kilometers from Prague). In order to enlarge the number of their subjects, the rulers and their feudal lords began the colonization of the Bohemian Lands by German peasants prior to the twelfth century.[5] The German settlers had to pay for the land but enjoyed many privileges; eventually the land became their hereditary property. Their settlements were mainly in fortified villages in the frontier region, but several German colonies were planted in the middle of the Bohemian Lands.

With the development of technology the Czech kings, wishing to exploit the country's rich mineral reserves of silver and gold, invited miners and skilled artisans from Germany to found royal towns as centers of mining, the most important of which were Kutná Hora, Stříbro (literally, "Silver"), Příbram, Levoča, Kremnica, and Košice, all located in the heart of the country. The power that this royal monopoly on mining gave the kings allowed them to strengthen their own position at the expense of the feudal lords. To make things more polarized still, the royal court embraced German culture and language, so that a linguistic-ethnic wedge was driven between the kings and their magnates, a divide the latter exploited for their own political benefit by propagating works written in Czech rather than German.

By the tenth century a Bohemian national church began to emerge to consolidate the state power of the Přemyslid family. Its earliest national saints were the martyrs Ludmilla (860–921) and her grandson Wenceslas. Although both were murdered for purely political and dynastic reasons, later hagiographers writing in Old Church Slavonic and Latin claimed that they died for the cause of Christianity, thereby reinforcing the links between the Bohemian state and the Roman church. Duke Wenceslas (907–929/935) had aroused resentment because of his peaceful policy toward the German emperor. He undertook to pay a tribute of 500 silver pieces and 120 oxen, a formality that prevented the complete germanization of Bohemia. Wenceslas's bellicose brother Boleslav—not a pagan, as claimed by the later hagiographers, but a Christian—had Wenceslas murdered at the baptism of the former's newborn son in Stará Boleslav (929?). Wenceslas was later canonized and in time became the patron saint of the Bohemian Lands.

Boleslav succeeded his brother as duke (r. 929/35–967). His son and successor, Boleslav II (r. 967–99), achieved the unification of Bohemia by the massacre of the rival tribe, the Slavniki. In 973 A.D. a bishopric was established in Prague, thereby ending Bohemia's dependency on the see of Regensburg. In Bohemia the clergy did not form a special estate; all church property was in the hands of the duke and other feudal lords, and the priests were in fact officials of the duke. In the rest of western Europe the church hierarchy had independence in ecclesiastical matters and owned considerable profits and benefits.

Bohemian Old Church Slavonic and Latin Hagiography

With the fall of the Great Moravian Empire under Magyar assaults at the beginning of the tenth century, exiled monks of the Cyrillo-Methodian tradition settled in Bohemia during the reign of Duke Spitihněv (d. 915); there they continued to practice the Old Church Slavonic rite and culture.[6] It was at this time that the growing cult of the murdered Duke Wenceslas first found literary expression in Old Church Slavonic: the so-called *First Church Slavonic Life of Wenceslas*—written shortly after the events—is important because it was written in Bohemia and is of extremely early provenance, a supposition supported by its careful avoidance of direct censure of Boleslav (probably the ruler at the time) and its crude demonization of the Jews as the alleged murderers of Christ. By contrast, the smoother hagiographic mode of *The Second Church Slavonic Life of Wenceslas* suggests that the cult of Saint Wenceslas was already well developed by the time it was written. This time, the legend blames Boleslav unequivocally for his brother's murder, while drawing a transcendental analogy between the assassin's diabolical deeds and Wenceslas's Christlike virtue.

Old Church Slavonic literature eventually found a home in the Bohemian Lands at the Monastery of Saints Mary and John the Baptist on the Sázava River, founded by the Benedictine monk Procopius in 1032–33 on land granted by Duke Ulrich (Oldřich). Here the Cyrillo-Methodian tradition and its Byzantine orientation were perpetuated and religious texts were translated from Latin into Old Church Slavonic. But the days of Sázava as a center of culture were numbered. In 1096–97 the Latinist Břetislav II (r. 1092–1100) forbade the use of the Slavic liturgical language at Sázava, its monks were expelled, and a German abbot was installed.[7] Thus Latin literature was firmly established in the Bohemian Lands by the beginning of the twelfth century. This consisted not only of memoranda and other ecclesiastical documents but also important lives of the saints, in particular those of Ludmilla and Wenceslas. The first Latin *Life of Saint Wenceslas* was written shortly after the death of Boleslav I (d. 967), at about the same time as the Latin *Life of Saint Ludmilla (Fuit in provincia Boemorum)*. A particularly important life of both Wenceslas and Ludmilla — *Vita et passio sancti Wenceslai et avie eius Ludmilae* — was written by a Czech monk known as Christian (Kristián), probably in the tenth century, although this dating is disputed by some scholars.[8]

Cosmas's *Chronica Boëmorum*

From the religious field the use of Latin spread to secular literature. Monasteries kept simple chronicles known as "annals." These legends not only recalled Bohemian history from the beginning but also contributed to an early form of national consciousness, especially the *Chronica Boëmorum* (1110–25) by Cosmas, dean of the Prague Chapter (1045–1125).[9] Cosmas started to write his chronicle when he was over sixty years of age. He was married and had a son who is mentioned in the chronicle. (At this period Catholic priests were still allowed to marry.) He was an experienced and important cleric who took part in several diplomatic missions to Hungary, Germany, and Italy. The most important single factor in his education was that he studied at the famous Latin school at Liège.

Cosmas upheld the Roman rite and was firmly against the Old Church Slavonic liturgy. He was a strong supporter of the duke, the bishops, and the rights of the Prague Chapter. In his chronicle he hardly mentions the Slavonic liturgy at all. His chronicle is a great artistic work and the first conscious mouthpiece of the Czech nation and the Přemyslid regime. The idea of the Czech nation is contrasted purposefully with the German and Polish nations. Cosmas places extremely articulate speeches in the mouths of the dukes, speeches that represent the first program of the state. The chronicle exercised an important civilizing influence and laid the foundation of public opinion. He condemns barbaric excesses (such as the massacre of the Vršovci tribe) and was the first to point out the judgment of moral values.

But the chronicle is also important for its artistic and linguistic content. Cosmas was well trained in stylistic questions, dialectic, and rhetoric. His prose is very rhythmical, changing to verse (dactylic hexameters) when he gets excited about a particular topic or theme. Moreover, he possessed an enormous knowledge of Latin literature and classical authors like Vergil and Ovid, whom he quotes liberally. In spite of his international learning, Cosmas was very much a Czech: he was familiar with the old traditional folk legends from the prehistory of Bohemia, and it can be readily seen that he thought in Czech. In his work Czech names are always transcribed and declined according to the context. He quotes Czech sayings and proverbs, translating them into Latin (unlike any other chronicle in this respect). Cosmas's chronicle served as a model to adaptors and translators in subsequent ages.

Hospodine, pomiluj ny!

Eventually, the Czech language began to make minor inroads into the religious culture of early medieval Bohemia. Although Latin remained the dominant language of the church until the Hussite Revolution in the fifteenth century, Czech began to play a limited role in the cultural life of the country. The oldest surviving song in the Czech language is *Hospodine, pomiluj ny!* (Lord, have mercy upon us!).[10] It is first attested in a collection of prayers by the preacher Milíč (c.1380s) (MS University Library [Prague] XVII F 30, 96a) and in an essay on the structure and composition of the poem attributed to the Benedictine John of Holešov (dated 1397), which also includes musical notation. According to tradition *Hospodine, pomiluj ny!* was written by Saint Adalbert, who became bishop of Prague (from 956 to 977). Adalbert later carried out missionary work in Poland, where he was martyred. The song appears to be a Czechified version of an Old Church Slavonic original and therefore is considered to be the first extant text in the Czech language. Although its use was originally linked with the Sázava Monastery, the home of the Slavonic liturgy from 863 to its destruction by the pro-Latinist Břetislav II in 1097, its status as a Czech work meant that it survived the anti-Old Church Slavonic destruction at the end of the eleventh century. This claim is supported by the fact that Cosmas, a rabid enemy of the Slavonic liturgy, speaks favorably of a *cantilena dulcis* ("sweet song") sung at the election of Duke Spitihněv II (1055–61); this probably refers to *Hospodine, pomiluj ny!* The title, which is also the opening phrase, is a translation of the Greek phrase *kyrie eleison,* which begins the Catholic and Orthodox Mass. But in its expanded form it soon became detached from its liturgical setting and from its Old Church Slavonic context and was often used for state ceremonial occasions, such as welcoming King Wenceslas I back to the Prague castle from a military campaign and Wenceslas II from exile in Brandenburg. The hymn was revived in the fourteenth century by Charles IV, along with everything else written in Bohemia. Charles included it in ceremonial functions, and it is still sung in Czech Catholic churches today. Although the opening and final phrases derive from the

Mass, the song as a whole is less theological than materialistic. The essential concern is for life here on earth. It reflects the common fears of war, attack, misery, and famine and seeks to appease an angry God. The directness of the language, the unornamental style, and the lack of metaphor or elaborate imagery parallel the unadorned style of the Romanesque rotundas of the period.

The Hymn to Saint Wenceslas

The twelfth century witnessed a momentous change in western religious thought, which the distinguished historian R. W. Southern has described as a "humanist" renaissance that placed a new, positive emphasis on the dignity and reason of human nature formed in the image of God.[11] Prior to the twelfth century, the church had presented mankind as sinful, erring, and ignorant, incapable of any valid thought or deed and continually in need of God's merciful intervention in human affairs. We glimpse this bleak vision of the world in the anxious invocations for God's mercy in *Hospodine, pomiluj ny!*

Coincident with the emphasis on man's immense potential for good works based on his reasoning powers and his divine image arose a new vision of the Godhead itself. Influential medieval churchmen like Saint Anselm of Canterbury, Saint Aelfred of Rievaulx, and Saint Bernard of Clairvaux began to redefine the traditional austere image of God, as well as their own roles as spiritual leaders of monastic communities. A fresh vision of Christ's humanity—his incarnation, birth, and death—supplanted the older image of a distant, almighty judge and ruler. Christ ceased to be the *Pantocrator* of Byzantine tradition and became a more accessible, vulnerable figure.

With the spread of monastic foundations eastward, this new vision of God was eventually reflected in the religious culture of Bohemia and Moravia. In the splendidly illuminated *Vyšehrad Codex*, probably commissioned for the coronation of Vratislav II in 1085, Christ is still represented as the omnipotent ruler. In *The Ostrov Codex*, compiled a century or so later, we discover a new image of Christ crucified, his drooping face expressing human suffering and his arms supporting the weight of a bruised, bleeding body. Maternal imagery in the same codex expresses this humanity even more forcefully, indicative both of the growing veneration of the Virgin Mary and a new affective vision of Christ as father, brother, and mother.[12]

The growing cult of the murdered Wenceslas easily appealed to an age obsessed with the idea of a human, suffering Christ. As popular devotion to the saint grew, so did the number of texts written in his honor increase. Most of these were composed in Latin and were limited to the sung celebration of his office at the Cathedral of Saint Vitus in Prague, but one of the earliest extant religious songs about him, *The Hymn to*

Saint Wenceslas, was written in Czech. Although the earliest attestation of this vernacular hymn is in the *Cronica ecclesiae Pragensis* (1370s) by Canon Beneš Krabice of Weitmile (d. 1375), it can be dated on the basis of its language to the twelfth century, when Wenceslas had already become the patron saint of the Bohemian Lands.[13] The hymn is also preserved in many subsequent song and hymn collections from the fifteenth and sixteenth centuries, both Catholic and Protestant.

The song represents a great step forward in terms of both spiritual feeling and language. Unlike *Hospodine, pomiluj ny!*, it contains original metaphors such as the kingdom of heaven as a royal court, a parallel we can see in the wall paintings in the rotunda of Saint Catherine at Znojmo in southern Moravia (c.1136). In the late thirteenth or early fourteenth century two more verses were composed and added, one addressed to the Virgin Mary. (By this time the cult of the Virgin Mary had reached Bohemia from Italy.) It is possible that these extra verses were composed during the imprisonment of the young Wenceslas II and the occupation of Bohemia by Brandenburg troops following the defeat and death of his father, Přemysl Ottokar II, in 1278. This was a difficult period for Bohemia and lasted twenty years; hence the appealing nature of the song and its frequent use during future political upheavals, especially during the ruinous Hussite Wars.

The Song of Ostrov

Another song that partakes of the medieval humanization of Christ is *The Song of Ostrov*, so named because it is preserved in a collection that originally belonged to the Benedictine monastery of Saint John the Baptist on the Island (*ostrov*), located on the Vltava River at Davle near Prague.[14] The song is included in a Latin codex, which also contains a Latin psalter, hymns, and prayers. It can be dated to the years 1260–90 largely on the basis of morphology. The song has four strophes, each of which has the following structure: 8*a* 5*b* 8*a* 5*b*. Each strophe consists of two couplets, each line thirteen syllables long with a break after the eighth syllable. Each stanza creates a syntactic and thematic whole. The strophic structure is not the form of spoken verse in Old Czech poetry, but the form of sung verse, verse prayers, and songs, of compilations that tended to be set to music, not necessarily realized, of course. We do not know for certain whether *The Song of Ostrov* was meant to be sung or not, because no musical notation has come down to us. The thirteen-syllable line with a break after the eighth syllable suggests the influence of Latin liturgical compositions and hymns. The Bavarian Easter play *Ludus de adventu et interitu Antichristi* (c. 1160) was a possible source of influence. This play was a 13-syllable line of 6 + 7 and 7 + 6 divisions. But the 8 + 5 combination appears to be unique to the Czech author. Although no direct foreign model has been found for the rhythmical structure of the song, it must have been conceived and written under the general influence of Latin monastic poetry, as is attested not merely by the structure but also by the thematic content.

Typical of the age's general preoccupation with Christ's humanity, the song narrates the events of his earthly life from his birth to his glorious resurrection without referring to him by name. The opening line "Slovo do světa stvořenie" paraphrases the beginning of Saint John's Gospel: "In principio erat Verbum et Verbum erat apud Deum, et Deus erat Verbum" — the mystery of the divine Logos (lines 1–2), the divine intention to redeem mankind after the Fall (lines 3–4), the annunciation of the Virgin Mary (lines 5–6), Jesus' descent from the line of King David (lines 7–8), his betrayal by the Jews (lines 11–12); his death (lines 13–14), and his glorious resurrection (lines 15–16). Because of the conclusion, the song is generally thought to be an Easter poem, or possibly an Advent poem.

The Prayer of Lady Kunigunde

The Prayer of Lady Kunigunde marks the high point of Gothic literature in Czech.[15] It is a mystical celebration of the Incarnation and the mystery of the Eucharist. It is named for Lady Kunigunde because of its oldest extant record in a manuscript of offices, prayers, and hours that belonged to Kunigunde (1265–1321), daughter of Přemysl Ottokar II and the abbess of the Benedictine Convent of Saint George at the Prague castle. The breviary in which the prayer is contained has no date. The codex has been shown to be by the same scribe who has eleven other manuscripts preserved in the convent archive. The unknown scribe was still active, according to two dated manuscripts, in the years 1318 and 1319. But he was clearly in the service of the convent as early as 1302, when Kunigunde became abbess. He was one of the most diligent scribes, whose head was Canon Beneš, scribe of the beautifully illuminated *Passional of the Abbess Kunigunde*.[16]

The manuscript version does not come from the pen of the writer himself but from a scribe whose language shows that it belongs among the oldest surviving works of Czech literature. The primitive style of orthography proves that the scribe's model belonged to the older orthographical system. Thus it can be dated as early as a decade or so prior to Kunigunde's return to Prague in 1302 (c. 1290). The verse and rhyme structure are among the boldest constructions of Old Czech poetry — consistently maintained eight-syllable monorhyme quatrains. The monorhyme quatrain is unusual in previous and contemporaneous Latin poetry of the Middle Ages, so perhaps it is the original choice of the Czech poet himself. Even though he uses only grammatical rhymes (usually two-syllable but occasionally three- and four-syllable, too), we can admire the poet's rhymes, especially in those places where two or three strophes employ the same rhyme one after the other. The poem can be divided thematically into four parts: part 1 (lines 1–16) is a glowing hymnic welcome to Christ coming down from heaven in all his glory into the Incarnation; part 2 (17–24) gives thanks with songs of praise for his goodness past and present and especially for the miraculous gift that is received in the Host at the altar; part 3 (25–88) provides a poetical explanation of the dogma of the Incarnation and the transubstantiation of the received Host; and part 4 (89–152) appeals to Christ for spiritual strength, true confession and forgiveness of sins, the rejection of the devil's temptations, a life of divine grace pleasing to God, unification with God's will, and a happy hour of death and eternal bliss in heavenly glory.

The author obviously had a deep knowledge of Latin hymnography and hymns by Saint Thomas Aquinas (d. 1274) from his offices of the Mass, written to celebrate the feast day of Corpus Christi inaugurated by Pope Urban IV in 1264. The Czech poem does not paraphrase these poems but competes with them independently, for example, *Lauda, Sion, Salvatorem* and *Hostia, veritas et vita,* the work of the Scholastic theologian John Pecham (d. 1292). The Czech poet surpasses at times these works with the boldness of his metaphors and epithets, especially by his pathetic eloquence, which emerges most of all in the introductory and concluding strophes of the poem.

The poem was probably intended for private prayer by the abbess and was not for public recitation. At the end of the prayer there is a notation in Latin: "Here name A or whomsoever you wish, living or dead." Such reminders were and are common for prayers to be said after the receiving of the Host. Another Latin prose prayer follows immediately ("In presentia sanctissimi corporis et sanguinis tui"), a prayer clearly intended for Kunigunde herself, since members of her family are mentioned (her aunt Agnes, her father, and her mother, also named Kunigunde). It is likely that the Czech prayer was included in the breviary at the abbess's express wishes since she was known to be very devout and learned.

The poet was also very learned. Apart from his knowledge of Aquinas's works, there is a reference to Saint Augustine in line 56 as an authority on the receiving of Communion. There are also traces of the powerful cult of the Virgin Mary (20, 1 and 24, 3), who is invoked as an important intercessor for human salvation, and echoes of the courtly love code in the image of Christ as a beautiful lover (28, 3) hidden from view in the form of the Host (9, 1). Such details suggest that the anonymous author conceived the poem specifically for Kunigunde, a princess familiar from youth with secular romances as well as religious literature. Because of the obvious influence of mysticism in the poem and the central eucharistic themes, one should perhaps look for the author of the poem among the members of the Czech Dominican friars. It is known that the abbess had lively intellectual and cultural contacts with the order of preachers, for example, Meister Eckhart, the famous German mystic, and the Czechs Domaslav and Kolda of Koldice (d. 1327?). Kolda, lector of the Dominican Church of Saint Clement at Prague, composed a courtly parable entitled *De strenuo milite* (On the invincible knight) for Kunigunde's richly illuminated *Passional.* (This manuscript will be discussed in greater detail in chapter 2.)

The First Cycle of Legends

There must have existed lyric poems of high merit before the composition of *The Prayer of Lady Kunigunde,* as it could not have been created—sophisticated and mature work that it is—without being the outcome of some sort of literary development in Czech literature. A similar situation holds true for the so-called *First Cycle of Legends,* verse lives of saints and apocryphal lives of Judas and Pontius Pilate influenced by the popular Latin *Legenda aurea* and so named to distinguish them from a later, second cycle dating from the second half of the fourteenth century.[17] Whether the texts that remain were the work of several poets or one poet is unresolved. In any event, only fragments survive, a small part of the original corpus. These include "The Legend of the Passion" (124 lines extant, only half of the original subject matter); "The Legend of Judas" (281 lines extant); "The Legend of Pilate" (106 lines extant); and "The Legend of the Virgin Mary" (28 lines extant, about half of the original). The longest surviving work from the cycle is "The Legend of the Apostles" (624 lines), only half of the original, which was more than 1,000 lines long.

From the historical point of view, the most interesting work is "The Legend of Judas." At one point the anonymous author remarks on the short life of the last Přemyslid king, Wenceslas III, who was murdered at Olomouc on August 4, 1306. The perpetrator's identity remains a mystery. The author blames the Germans for the crime, addressing them indirectly as "treacherous tribe," a biblical expression analogous to the topos of the Jews as the alleged murderers of Christ. Apart from revealing anti-German sentiment in Czech authors of this time, *The First Cycle of Legends* is also important from the linguistic point of view, since it reveals considerable originality in diction, rhyme, and meter.

The Alexandreida

Dating from about the same period as *The First Cycle of Legends* or a little earlier (1290–1300) is a secular epic known as the *Alexandreida.*[18] Even though a secular poem, the *Alexandreida* is akin to *The First Cycle of Legends* in its temperament, language, and style. It relates the life of Alexander the Great (356–323 B.C.), who was one of the most popular heroes of the Middle Ages.[19] The earliest version of Alexander's life appeared in Egypt (second century B.C.) and was written in Greek (Callisthenes). On this book the Pseudo-Callisthenes was based, which was translated several times into Latin. It forms the first part of the sources. The second tradition—beginning with the version of Quintus Curtius Rufus (first century A.D.)—is more sober than the Greek tradition, which is highly ornate and overdone. The Czech poet used Gautier of Châtillon's Latin version (c. 1178–82) as his source, although he also knew Pseudo-Callisthenes and Rufus.[20] Yet he worked independently. Compared with other Alexanders—especially the long-winded German version by Ulrich von Etzenbach, the court poet of Přemysl Ottokar II—the Czech author shows great originality, conciseness, and inventiveness.[21] The other authors, especially Gautier, used a stylized classical apparatus. For example, the dawn before battle is described with the use of classical conceits ("chariots of the sun"). These elements are absent from the Czech version, as are mythological allusions and conceits.

A typical feature of the Czech version is the strong moralizing tendency. The author punctuates the narrative with gnomic triplets. There are many of these. Some are taken from Cato's *Distichs* (a popular Latin textbook in the medieval grammar schools consisting of rhyming couplets), some are reminiscent of folk sayings, and some were probably invented by the author himself, for example:

A bad wheel screeches the most,
a small snake hisses the loudest,
and a little churl is most churlish.[22]
(Lines 216–18)

These triplets show the moral attitude of the poet, but are also important for style and structure. They serve the role of the chorus in Greek drama, marking a change in the action and mood; they frequently punctuate or frame the narrative into self-contained exemplary sections.

Czech scholars have assumed that *The First Cycle of Legends* and the *Alexandreida* were written by the same person or by a group of writers sharing the same stylistic techniques and religious view of the world. This assumption begs important questions of reception as well as authorship. Postwar Marxist critics presented the *Alexandreida* as the first example of "secularization" in medieval Czech literature and the beginning of a "progressive" trend in Czech literature as a whole. The problem with the first term is that it fails to distinguish between the genre of the work and the overall spirit that pervades it; the problem with the second is that it is anachronistic. In the case of the *Alexandreida,* a secular genre is treated in a profoundly religious, even homiletic, manner. What does this appropriation of a secular subject matter—the heroic deeds of an antic hero popular at the European courts—to a religious sensibility indicate about the anonymous author and his audience? Given the subject matter of the text and the fact that it is written in the vernacular, it is likely that the author, who was either a cleric attached to an aristocratic household or a literate nobleman, was writing for the edification of a secular audience deeply religious in its view of the world and spiritual in its perception of chivalry.

This ideology contrasts sharply with the secular vision of chivalry encountered in Ulrich von Etzenbach's German *Alexander,* written for a royal and courtly audience. Since Ulrich's text probably predates the composition of the *Alexandreida,* it is worth speculating whether the composition of the former influenced the composition of the latter in a negative fashion. Certain phrasing in the Czech poem suggests an anticourtly and anti-German animus, although the more vociferous of these may be later interpolations and do not necessarily reflect the spirit and intention of the original author. But if we consider the work as a whole—as far as its fragmentary and incomplete status will permit—we may be forgiven for concluding that the *Alexandreida* was antipathetic to the purely secular ideals of knighthood celebrated at the royal court at Prague. For one reason or another, the *Alexandreida* was well known throughout the fourteenth century, and its gnomic style was emulated in *The New Council* and even parodied in *The Ointment Seller.* More important, its religious vision of knighthood reflected an ideology quite distinct from that of John of Luxembourg's secular court. Although Charles IV tried to bridge this ideological gap by creating a religious court culture, his efforts did not survive him. The story of his son's reign is not only one of religious polarization; it is also one in which the values of the court and the values of the nobility would become mutually hostile and antagonistic.

✤

A Literature of Their Own
Women Readers and Writers in Medieval Bohemia

Czech scholarship has always understood the important role played by women in the life of medieval Bohemia.[1] But—as in the popular monograph *Wives and Lovers of Czech Kings*[2]—medieval women are more usually regarded as wives, lovers, and mothers rather than as subjects in their own right. In fact, some of the most accomplished works written in medieval Czech and Latin were commissioned by female readers. In this chapter, I will trace a long line of female literacy in Bohemia, from Saint Agnes's correspondence with Saint Clare of Assisi in the thirteenth century to the noblewomen of the early modern period who wrote letters to their family members. As we shall see, the important phenomenon of Czech women writers in the National Revival and the equally central role of women's writing in contemporary Czech literature have their roots in an ancient and illustrious pedigree of medieval and early modern female literacy.

Women Readers and Writers in Medieval Bohemia

The principal role played by women writers in the medieval and early modern period was that of correspondents, which usually assumed the form of seeking or giving advice on religious or secular matters to clerics, rulers, and relatives.[3] But women of the intellectual stature of Radegund, Hildegard von Bingen, Héloïse, Catherine of Siena, and Christine de Pisan—to name only the most important medieval exponents of the *ars dictaminis*—were the exception rather than the rule, a fact not altogether surprising when we consider that in the Middle Ages women were generally perceived as intrinsically lecherous, feeble-minded, and garrulous, the instigators of man's expulsion from the Garden of Eden, as delineated in chapters 2 to 3 of Genesis. From the time of the apostle Paul, whose letters form about half of the New Testament and who transformed Christ's teachings into a systematic set of beliefs, women were presented in a negative light. The second-century writer Tertullian linked all women with Eve: "*You* are the Devil's gateway. *You* are the first deserter of the divine law. . . . *You* destroyed so easily God's image, man. On account of *your* desert, that is death, even the Son of God had to die."[4] Women's speech was seen as especially threatening to male well-being, and the most effective way to enjoin female silence was to deny them access to education more readily available to men.[5]

Misogynistic discourse enjoyed great prominence in the monastic movements of the eleventh and twelfth centuries and spared only a few early medieval women, mostly queens or great aristocrats.[6] In the second half of the twelfth century, however, the role of women in the history of salvation came to be evaluated in a less negative fashion, partly as a consequence of the growing cult of the Virgin Mary.[7] The church's new openness was motivated by the pragmatic desire to counter the burgeoning heretical movements that provided a spiritual haven for female religious excluded from the official church hierarchy.[8]

One of the new monastic movements popular with women were the Franciscans. Saint Francis received Saint Clare and her first companions in person into his newly founded monastic movement. Most of the holy women associated with the Franciscans in the thirteenth century came from Provence and Italy, but these Mediterranean regions did not have a monopoly on female lay piety.[9] In Poland Queens Salomea (d. 1268) and Kinga (d. 1292) joined the Order of Poor Clares as widows, and in the Bohemian Lands so did Saint Agnes of Bohemia (1211–82).[10] Saint Agnes was following in the saintly footsteps of her ancestor Ludmilla, the first Christian martyr in the region.[11] In 1233 Agnes founded and became the first abbess of the Convent of the Poor Clares at Prague (Na Františku). She had important connections in the church and corresponded (in Latin) with Pope Gregory IX and Clare of Assisi in order to strengthen links between the Bohemian branch of the Franciscan order and its spiritual home in Italy.[12] Agnes's letters to Clare have not survived but Clare's four letters to Agnes are still extant.[13] They reveal that Agnes was eager to emulate the Franciscan way of life and that she asked for clarification about the Poor Clares' rules on fasting as a prelude to establishing a similar rule for her own foundation in Prague.

Although writing *by* women was highly restricted in the Middle Ages and tended to be practiced by female religious like Agnes, writing *for* women was not uncommon in an age of powerful lay and religious female patronage. Responding to direct commission or prompted by their own position as confessors to women, male religious frequently wrote with female needs in mind. The oldest surviving manuscript of Bohemian origin—the *Wolfenbüttel Codex* (before 1006)—is a copy of Gumpold's Latin *Legend of Saint Wenceslas*. It was made by order of Emma, the wife of Duke Boleslav II (967–99). This lady is depicted on the title page of the codex, kneeling before Saint Wenceslas, who is being crowned by Christ.[14] Another example of a work written by a male religious on behalf of a female patron are several love letters purportedly sent by Queen Kunigunde (d. 1285) to her husband, Přemysl Ottokar II, while he was away from Prague waging a military campaign. These epistles are contained in a collection of letters attributed to Master Bohuslav, the queen's personal scribe. They were probably never sent and were more likely intended as models of the *ars dictaminis* for trainee scribes to emulate. But their profoundly passionate and personal content suggests that they may have been inspired, if not dictated, by Queen Kunigunde herself.[15]

By far the most celebrated patroness of the arts in medieval Bohemia was Queen Kunigunde's daughter and namesake, Lady Kunigunde, abbess of the Saint George Convent at Prague (1302–21).[16] By tradition the abbesses of the prestigious Benedictine Saint George Convent at the Prague castle (founded 920) were daughters of the kings of Bohemia. Kunigunde (1265–1321) is the most important and justly celebrated of these incumbents, a great book owner and patron of the visual arts. On September 8, 1276, Kunigunde entered the convent of the Poor Clares founded by her great-aunt, Saint Agnes. In 1291, at the age of twenty-seven, she relinquished the religious life to marry the Polish duke Boleslaw Mazowius, by whom she had two children, a daughter named Eufrosina and a son named Wenceslas. The marriage was later annulled by the pope when the Polish-Bohemian alliance ceased to be important. By 1302 Kunigunde was back in Prague, where she preferred to live and where she spent the rest of her life as abbess of the Saint George Convent. Here she began to patronize book illustrators and writers and associated with a group of mystics. The most prominent of these was the Dominican Kolda of Koldice, court theologian to her brother, Wenceslas II, and lector of the Church of Saint Clement in Prague.

The Dominicans had been active at the court of Prague as confessors and counselors since the reign of Kunigunde's father, Přemysl Ottokar, and Kunigunde was in close touch with some of them. Apart from Kolda of Koldice, we know of at least one other Dominican, named Domaslav, who may have been the author of *The Prayer of Lady Kunigunde*. Kolda and Kunigunde were friends of the famous German mystic Meister Eckhart, a central figure in the burgeoning movement of female spirituality. Kunigunde's close association with Kolda of Koldice and Domaslav thus forms part of a larger European phenomenon of the Dominican cultivation of female piety.

Kunigunde commissioned from Kolda at least two of the five mystical Latin works preserved in the so-called *Passional of the Abbess Kunigunde*. This beautifully illuminated manuscript (now housed in the University Library of Prague, XIV. A. 17) contains thirty-six parchment leaves, each 29.5 × 25 cm. It is composed of several Latin texts and is not a passional in the strict sense of the word. It contains the following works: a parable known as *The Brave Knight* (*De strenuo milite*, leaves 2–9), which includes a prologue, a parable, and an explication; a dialogue between the Virgin Mary and Saint John (leaves 11–17); a treatise by Kolda entitled *On The Heavenly Mansions* (*De mansionibus celestibus*), attached to which are the anonymous *Nine Heavenly Joys of Kunigunda* (leaves 30–31), *The Speech of Pope Leo on the Suffering of Christ* (leaves

32–34), and *The Dialogue between Mary Magdalene and Mary* (leaves 34–36). The conclusion to the prologue of *The Brave Knight* (leaf 2) is dated 1312. At the end of the treatise *On the Heavenly Mansions* and the *Nine Heavenly Joys of Kunigunde,* Kolda informs us (leaf 31) that he wrote the parable of *The Brave Knight* in 1312 and the treatise *On the Heavenly Mansions* in 1314, both at the request of Kunigunde. All the other works in the *Passional* are anonymous.

The parable *The Brave Knight* is based in part on a story from the *Gesta Romanorum* and tells of how a brave knight (an allegorization of Christ) is betrothed to a beautiful lady (the Soul). This lady is abducted by an evil rival (the Devil) and hidden in a dark dungeon. After thirty-three years (Christ's earthly life span), the brave knight returns, kills the rival, delivers the lady, and is reunited with her.

The religious allegory of a lady (the Soul) abducted by the Devil from her true spouse (Christ), with whom she is finally reunited, may also be intended as a biographical allusion to Kunigunde's enforced shuttling between the monastic cell and the marriage bed and back again in accordance with the political and dynastic ambitions of her family.[17] Seen in this hard light of reality, the story emerges as less abstractly allegorical than it might otherwise seem. We glimpse the immense restrictions faced by medieval women whose sole escape from an unhappy marriage — at least if they were wealthy — was enclosure in a convent.

A more allegorical interpretation of the story is the function of heavenly bodies as symbols to articulate the relationship between Christ and the Soul.[18] The Bridegroom Christ is identified as the Sun, the Bride as the planet Venus. The anonymous illuminator and the scribe, the Benedictine canon Beneš, describe her as the "star of the sea," a reference both to Mary as the morning star and to Eve as the evening star. Joseph of Arimathea represents the Moon, Adam the Earth, and the thief, who abducts the bride, is a demon of darkness, representing the constellation of the Underground Serpent. The cosmological symbolism of the parable clearly derives from the Platonic myth of the soul's deliverance from the earthly cave and its journey to the sun (God).

Added to the cosmological symbolism is the chivalric metaphor of Christ as knight. The illuminations that accompany the parable also represent Christ as a warrior, corresponding to the reference in the text to the "noble knight of royal descent," an allusion to Christ's ancestor King David of Israel. The representation of Christ as knight is appropriate to Kunigunde's royal status as the daughter of Přemysl Ottokar II, a crusader who attempted to convert the Baltic pagans. Kunigunde's brother, Wenceslas II, led similar expeditions to the pagan north. Significantly, the brave knight depicted in the fourth illumination of *The Brave Knight* bears a lance and a shield emblazoned with a crusader's cross, a recognition of the evangelizing fervor of the abbess's father, as well as an allusion to Saint George, the patron saint of the Benedictine convent of which Kunigunde was the spiritual head. Moreover, Kolda and Kunigunde would have both been familiar with the courtly romances popular at her father and brother's court. In one of these—the German Alexander-romance by Ulrich von Etzenbach—the eponymous Greek hero is presented as a Christian crusader and fashionable knight who indulges in jousts and protects the honor of ladies. This spirit of *courtoisie* pervades Kolda's parable and suggests a great deal about his status as a courtier and Kunigunde's elevated stature as a royal princess of the late Přemyslid court.

In distinction to the early centuries of Christianity, the later Middle Ages emphasize the humanity of Christ. Whereas in the early church Christ was venerated as almighty God, in the later period it was his Passion that inspired Christological writings and treatises. The theme of Christ as brother and lover of mankind was developed by Saint Bernard of Clairvaux in the twelfth century and Saint Francis of Assisi in the thirteenth. By the early fourteenth century, the two most human phases of Christ's earthly mission—his humble birth in a stable and his cruel death on the cross—dominated the sensibility of religious people. The interest in Jesus' childhood is reflected in the library of Abbess Kunigunde; it contains two apocryphal works on this theme: the pseudo-Matthew Gospel and a meditation on Jesus' birth according to Saint Thomas.[19]

The tradition of presenting Christ in the secular terms of the knight and the lover dates back to the twelfth century. Frequently this mode of presentation reflects the literary tastes of female readers of romances. The twelfth-century Middle English prose treatise *Ancrene Wisse*, a guide of conduct for three anonymous anchoresses, presents Christ as a chivalric lover and clearly assumes that the female audience was familiar with romantic conventions.[20] Although the theme of Christ as lover is also found in male monastic theology, for instance in the sermons of Saint Bernard of Clairvaux, it tends to remain abstractly allegorical and is not literalized, as it is for women. Since medieval women were identified with emotions and with the body, it was deemed appropriate to couch devotional works intended for them in more affective and corporeal terms. Part of this line of thinking was the female association with Christ's humanity. The Benedictine Convent of Saint George at Prague was famous for its cult of the Passion, a tradition that reached its highest point of refinement during Kunigunde's incumbency as abbess.

A good example of the convent's cult of the Passion is the allegorical excursus that follows Kolda's parable *The Brave Knight*. Extrapolating from the reference to the weapons utilized by the knight to reach and deliver the lady from her incarceration, Kolda draws an analogy between these chivalric accoutrements and the instruments of Christ's Passion. The first of these is the sword that the knight unsheathes to fight his way back to his beloved. This corresponds to the knife used to circumcise Christ's body at birth. Just as the brave knight is wounded on his lady's behalf, so is Christ incarnate scarred for the sake of mankind's redemption. The second instrument of Christ's Passion is the scourge with which he is beaten at the post. Here Kolda interweaves allegorical quotations drawn from the Old and New Testaments with his own emphasis on physical pain and suffering. Christ bears the blows and wounds of the nails in order to redeem our sins and to heal our spiritual bruises. After being crowned with thorns and pinned to the cross, a lance pierces his side, whence flow blood and water. The blood signifies Christ's redemption of mankind, while the water denotes the sacrament of baptism, which washes away human sin.

Throughout his commentary on the Passion, Kolda consistently refers to the courtly parable of the brave knight as if bearing in mind the affective-somatic expectations of the female reader. Christ endures the wounds made by the nails for the sake of his betrothed. Stripped of his robe and pinned to the cross, he is likened to a lover asleep in bed. His robe is sacrificed to clothe his poor betrothed stripped naked by the evil rival. When he falls into the sleep of death, he descends into hell, whence he delivers his betrothed from the darkness of her incarceration. The last instrument of the Passion is the ladder placed against the cross to remove the body of Christ, corresponding to the ladder that takes us from earth to heaven, made possible by Christ's Passion and Resurrection. What is so significant about the parable and its commentary is its successful synthesis of physical detail and courtly elements, both of which were considered integral aspects of the piety of a royal patroness.

The anonymous eucharistic Czech *Prayer of Lady Kunigunde* is contained in the abbess's private breviary. It is immediately preceded by the Latin prayer *Ave vivens hostia, veritas et vita* and is followed by a collection of Latin prayers intended to be read before and after Holy Communion. These prayers reflect the central importance at the Convent of Saint George of the feast of Corpus Christi. The Czech poem is the work of an anonymous author and is an independent variation on the theme of the Eucharist that displays a close knowledge of such important eucharistic hymns as *Lauda, Sion, Salvatorem*.

There is a close thematic and symbolic symmetry between the parable of *The Brave Knight* and *The Prayer of Lady Kunigunde*. In the former, the reader is invited to identify with the lady, an allegorical representation of the female *anima* liberated from the snares of hell by the chivalric Christ. In the latter, she is aligned with *anima* welcoming Christ as her royal spouse as he descends from heaven and takes the mystical form of the bread and the wine on the altar. Although the feminized persona of the soul does not necessarily imply a female reader or auditor, it does coincide with Kunigunde's gender. What clearly began as an allegorical gendering of the soul welcoming the Bridegroom

Christ in the form of the Host developed later into an association of women with eucharistic piety. As Caroline Bynum has discussed, medieval women of all walks of life "were inspired, compelled, comforted and troubled by the eucharist to an extent found only in a few male writers of the period."[21]

The principal rhetorical feature of the poem is *circumlocutio*, reminding us of the earlier meditation on the Incarnation, *The Song of Ostrov*, in which Christ is not mentioned by name but is identified by the salient details of his life, death, and resurrection. In the second strophe of *The Prayer of Lady Kunigunde*, Christ is associated with light, a parallel to the neo-Platonic conceit of God as the sun in *The Brave Knight*. This conceit is subsequently expanded into an explication of the paradoxical mystery of Christ's body: "Of this we have the sun as evidence: when we think of it, we see many rays but know only one sun" (strophe 15).[22] The strong appeal to visual imagery to explicate subtle doctrinal difficulties may be explained as the author's desire to provide a graphic illustration of complex theological issues for a female reader untrained in the niceties of dogma.

A further symbolic and thematic correlation between the parable of *The Brave Knight* and the *The Prayer of Lady Kunigunde* is seen in the references in the latter to Christ as lover. In strophe 9, Christ is presented as mystically present in the bread and as a lover of the courtly code who shields his face from the gaze of the beloved: "In the form of the bread you conceal yourself, / decking yourself in divine radiance."[23] In strophe 28 (line 4) we have a significant allusion to Christ's physical beauty. Both of these references imply a female audience and look forward to the Czech *Life of Saint Catherine*, in which Christ is envisioned as a beautiful bridegroom with long golden hair.

The close thematic and symbolic affinities between the Latin parable *The Brave Knight* and the anonymous Czech *Prayer of Lady Kunigunde* point to Dominican activity at the court culture of Prague in the early fourteenth century. Uniting these texts is the human and sacramental body of Christ, which reflects equally the vision of the male author and the receptive sensibility of the female reader. To understand the complex representation of Christ as knight and lover we should overlook neither the male writer nor the female reader, since we can understand the former's intentions only by taking into account the latter's expectations. The same holds true for the *imago Christi* in the images and texts discussed above. If we look closely at the Mystical Embrace from *The Passional of the Abbess Kunigunde* (see Figure 3), what strikes us is the physical and spiritual intimacy of Christ and Mary, son and mother, man and woman. Just as the Bohemian Dominican authors could not represent Christ in the way they did without considering the courtly taste and sensibility of their patroness, so does the image of the incarnate Christ

Figure 3. *The Mystic Embrace, Passional of the Abbess Kunigunde,* University Library, Prague, Czech Republic.

closely resemble the female body that bore him. As they embrace, these holy figures merge as one, their limbs entwined below the capacious folds of their garments, their heads encircled by the same holy radiance.

Less well known than Kunigunde but just as impressive in some ways was her sister-in-law, Elizabeth Rejčka (1288–1335), widow of Wenceslas II, who presided over a brilliant court at Brno.[24] Elizabeth maintained a scriptorium there from 1316 to 1323 that produced eight illuminated codices. These were presented as gifts to the Cistercian nuns of the Brno Convent of the Virgin Mary (Aula Sanctae Mariae), which Elizabeth founded on June 1, 1323. The two-volume Lectionary of Queen Rejčka (now in the National Library in Vienna, Codex 1772–1773) contains a note indicating why such expense was lavished on liturgical books. It says that the queen wanted the book so that she and her family would always be remembered, alive or dead, no matter to which monastery the book might be given.[25] Visual evidence of this desire to be remembered is also provided by miniatures in six codices representing Elizabeth in various attitudes of piety. In one she kneels at a desk with an open book on it, surrounded by her beloved Cistercian nuns.[26] But there was also a political reason for such munificence: Elizabeth intended her court at Brno to outshine that of King John of Luxembourg at Prague, which it certainly did.

Toward the end of the fourteenth century, several European writers initiated a debate on the misogynistic attack waged against women since the time of the early church. Around 1380, Giovanni Boccaccio compiled a long list of famous and praiseworthy women entitled *De mulieribus claris*, describing women from classical history who were exemplary for their loyalty, bravery, and morality. This was the first such list since Plutarch's *Mulierum virtutes*, and served as the model for scores of similar treatises by men and women from many countries over the next three hundred years.[27] This profeminine reassessment of women's qualities pervaded European court culture in the second half of the fourteenth century. The great Italian poet Petrarch, who visited Prague, wrote an epistle in praise of women entitled *De laudibus feminarum*, which he addressed to Charles IV's third wife, Anne of Schweidnitz.[28] Petrarch was clearly responding to an earlier letter sent to him by the empress upon the occasion of the birth of a daughter. Petrarch commiserates with the empress upon the unfortunate birth (since a son and heir was hoped for) and proceeds to praise his correspondent for her intellectual powers as well as her role as the mother of the future emperor. As we have seen, an important momentum in the direction of female literacy had already been provided by Charles's matrilineal ancestors Saint Agnes and Abbess Kunigunde. In fact, we may even speak of a continuum of learned women in the royal family of Bohemia.

Just as the late Přemyslid kings had favored the Dominicans as confessors and cultivators of female piety, so did the pious and theologically conservative Charles IV include several prominent Dominican friars in his inner circle. The royal confessor was a Czech Dominican named John Moravec, who may have been commissioned by the emperor to write a Czech *Life of Christ* based on the *Meditationes Vitae Christi* by an anonymous thirteenth-century Italian Franciscan.[29] In the manuscript fragment Muzeum 433 of this text the author addresses a female patron named Elizabeth of Bezdražice. Highborn women were equally renowned for their cultivation of saints' lives. At the end of the Czech verse *Life of Saint George*, the scribe mentions that it formerly belonged to a "lady Elizabeth" (*domine elyzabet*), whose identity may or may not be that of Elizabeth of Bezdražice.[30] Not only were women becoming more prominent as patrons of pious literature; they were also increasingly the subjects of such works. *The Life of Saint Catherine,* written in verse in an East Moravian dialect sometime between 1360 and 1375, was probably intended for female as well as male courtiers.[31] The legend has been traditionally associated with the person of Emperor Charles, who promoted the cult of this saint in Bohemia following his victory at San Felice against the Italian League on Saint Catherine's feast day, November 25, 1323.[32] It is plausible that the emperor commissioned this work from one of the Dominicans active at his court, possibly John Moravec. Although the authorship of *The Life of Saint Catherine* remains a matter of speculation, John is as viable a candidate as anyone else in the imperial circle. As a university professor, he would have been familiar with the latest profeminine humanist trends from Italy. The author's double emphasis on the saint's intellectual virginity and maternity is certainly reminiscent of Petrarch's *De laudibus feminarum.* The elevated language and the sophisticated knowledge of courtly discourse are virtually unique in medieval Czech literature and point to a man of great erudition familiar with court life. The concrete representation of Christ as a beautiful lover, Catherine's affective response to her celestial spouse, and the courtly treatment of her *imitatio Christi* are all in the tradition of Kolda's *The Brave Knight* and further suggest a partially female audience.

The Life of Saint Catherine presents several stylistic and thematic parallels to the Czech courtly love lyric, which dates from about the same period (or perhaps a little later), in particular the shared use of epithets of endearment and the incorporation of color symbolism in the description of the virgin's flagellation. The hundred or so Czech songs that have survived from the second half of the fourteenth century can be divided into secular and religious categories, although some of them, like the Marian "Letter M" or "A Bundle of Myrrh" — with its lovely evocation of verses from the Song of Songs — combine secular and spiritual motifs.[33] As in the case of *The Life of Saint Catherine,* the authors of the courtly love lyric are anonymous and may have been affiliated with the court, where they would have come into contact with the Petrarchan lyric (especially evident in the most accomplished of the corpus, "The Song of Záviš").[34] If the question of authorship is a vexed one, so is the problem of the audience. What is clear is that the audience was educated and intimate with the intricacies of the courtly code, since the love lyric does not reveal the popularization characteristic of the Czech verse and prose romances.[35] It is also probable that this audience consisted partly of educated women, since the authorial voice or narrator frequently addresses an implied female auditor. This conclusion would comport with what we know about the female reception of the courtly romance and the courtly love lyric in other countries like France and Germany.

Further evidence of female literacy in late medieval Bohemia can be gleaned from the representation of women in works of Czech literature and painting from the second half of the fourteenth century. In the chivalric verse romance *Tandariáš and Floribella* (c. 1380), the assertive and independent-minded heroine Princess Floribella consoles herself with reading when her lover leaves her and sets out on a series of knightly adventures, whereas her German counterpart Flordibel resorts to the more conventional practice of prayer. In the Annunciation panel of the Vyšší Brod Altarpiece (c. 1360), the Virgin Mary, dressed in the gorgeous garments of a queen and wearing a crown, is reading two books, one placed on an elegant marble lectern, the other balanced on a velvet cushion (see Figure 4). At the moment of the angel's divine intervention, Mary is absorbed in the second volume, perhaps a vernacular translation of the

Figure 4. *The Annunciation*, Master of the Vyšší Brod Altar, National Gallery, Prague, Czech Republic.

Vulgate. In another Annunciation scene, this time from the private missal of John of Středa (after 1364), a fashionably dressed courtier-angel kneels on one leg as he delivers a sealed envelope that announces the imminent birth of the Savior. Mary is seated before one book open on a lectern, with a second closed volume in her right hand. Both these Annunciation scenes are unusual in representing the Virgin with two books, an indication of the bilingual education of the abbess Kunigunde and Anne of Bohemia.

According to contemporary accounts by Wyclif and Hus, Queen Anne possessed copies of the New Testament in Latin, German, and Czech.[36] As a princess of the royal house of Luxembourg—the patrons of Machaut, Froissart, and other great continental poets—Anne's presence in England helped to foster a cosmopolitan climate at the court of Richard II.[37] The fact that Geoffrey Chaucer addressed *The Legend of Good Women* to Queen Anne suggests that he was conscious of her reputation as a learned woman.[38] The only letters of Queen Anne that survive were both written in French, but this was common practice in the Middle Ages, and only in the fifteenth century did royal personages in England begin to dictate their letters in English. One of these letters dictated by Anne was addressed to Michael de la Pole concerning the queen's desire to appoint a new royal escheator in the county of Lincolnshire and proposing that Roger Toup be named to the office.[39] This letter suggests that Anne was very much a skilled and active businesswoman and not just the passive petitioner for clemency that many historians have claimed her to be. Her concern to safeguard the royal privilege of escheatage (the practice whereby the property of deceased owners without heirs passes automatically to the Crown) recalls her brother Wenceslas's extensive use of the same royal prerogative in Bohemia.

There is little reason to doubt that if Anne of Bohemia was already proficient in Latin, German, French, and Czech by the time she came to England at the age of fifteen, she would have had little trouble acquiring at least a passive reading knowledge of English in the years that followed. Most important, her ability to read the Gospels in German and Czech (as well as in Latin) provided an example to the English to have their own translation of the Vulgate. In what is probably an apocryphal story invented by a Lollard propagandist, Thomas Arundel, archbishop of Canterbury, is said to have noted in his sermon at the queen's funeral in 1394 how happy she was to have the four Gospels in English "with the doctoris [glosses] upon hem."[40] The important point about this anecdote is not its historical accuracy but its mythic potency for a generation of English Lollards. The links between London and Prague created by the marriage between Anne of Bohemia and Richard II also helped to strengthen the intellectual contacts between the universities of Oxford and Prague founded by Charles IV in 1348. These contacts paved the way for the free exchange of ideas between Wycliffite Oxford and Hussite Bohemia in the early years of the fifteenth century.[41]

The profeminine humanism that characterized the royal court at Prague and the university soon began to percolate down to the lower levels of Bohemian society. Thomas of Štítné (c. 1331–1401), a member of the regional gentry who studied at the University of Prague, acquired unusually tolerant views on the role of women and communicated them to his family in the provinces. After completing his studies, Thomas returned to his hometown in southern Bohemia and began to write works in Czech for the religious education of his daughter Agnes and other young women. Among these didactic works were the *Six Books about General Christian Matters*, *Conversational Talks* (conversations with children on the basis of Christianity written in the form of a didactic dialogue), and *Talks for Sundays and Holy Days*. Thomas also translated selections from the popular *Visions of Saint Bridget of Sweden* for the edification of his daughter. In the preface to this work by the famous Swedish mystic (c. 1300–1373), Thomas follows his Latin model faithfully in asserting the right of woman to an equal place in the eyes of God: "And have not women been prophets through whom God has worked wonderfully and done great things: Judith, Esther, the widow Anna, the Sibyls?"[42] Thomas was favorably disposed to the reformist preachers Waldhauser and Milíč, whom he mentions in his writings. Imbued with her father's up-to-date ideas, Agnes of Štítné moved to Prague in the fall of 1401. Here she bought a house near the Bethlehem Chapel, later to become the most important center of preaching in the Czech language and the power base of the Hussite reform movement, in which Agnes took an active part, along with many other female members of the nobility.[43]

Although the Hussite Revolution accelerated the rate and widened the range of female lay literacy in Bohemian society, it did not initiate it. As we have seen, an important impetus had already been provided by the time-honored tradition of female literacy at the royal court of Prague. Moreover, the Hussite Revolution significantly narrowed the number of languages accessible to women as Czech became the sole language of devotional practice. It is beyond doubt that the Hussite reform movement appealed to women on all levels of society, from the nobility down, for the obvious reason that the Catholic Church traditionally restricted women's activity in most areas of religious life except the cloister. Among the nobility were Anne of Frimburk, the wife of the royal master of the mint Peter Zmrzlík of Svojšín; the wives of Henry Škopek of Dubá, John of Chlum, Henry Lefl of Lazaň; and many others.[44] In spite of their husbands' disapproval, many noble ladies gravitated to the Bethlehem Chapel, founded for preaching in the Czech language in 1391 by the knight Hanuš of Milheim with the help of the Prague merchant Kříž. Among these women were Elizabeth of Kravař, the wife of Henry of Rožmberk, and

Anne of Mochov, wife of John of Kamenice (the Younger). Anne became one of the most fervent supporters of the Hussite movement in southern Bohemia and was viciously attacked by the anonymous Dominican author of *Invectio satirica in reges et proceres viam Wiklef tenentes* as an instigator of heresy.[45]

The most prestigious female supporter of the Bethlehem Chapel was Queen Sophie of Bavaria (d.1428), consort of Wenceslas IV. When her husband sent letters to the antipope John XXIII and the College of Cardinals protesting against the prohibition of Wycliffite books in Bohemia, Sophie included a protest of her own couched in forthright and indignant language.[46] Queen Sophie was clearly an enthusiastic reader of Czech literature: among her posthumous effects were discovered eleven books, one in German (the rest presumably lost) and ten in Czech, including a psalter, a copy of the satirical *Decalogue* (uniquely in the *Hradec Králové Codex*), and a romance of the life of Alexander the Great.[47]

In spite of the extensive involvement of many women in the Hussite movement, some of the most prominent reformers inherited a misogynistic attitude toward women, including Hus himself, who tolerated them only as important supporters of the reform movement.[48] Such ambivalence toward women characterizes the important prose dispute *The Weaver*, probably composed for the regional court of Queen Sophie at Hradec Králové. In this debate between the profeminine courtly writer Ludvík Tkadleček (Weaver) and the antifeminine Misfortune we have an accurate mirror of late medieval attitudes to women and the prevailing discourses on and about women in Bohemian society. In France a similar debate was raging between the Franco-Italian humanist writer Christine de Pisan, who attacked the misogyny of *Le Roman de la Rose*, and its defenders, led by Jean de Montreuil, dean of Lille.[49]

Of Hussite women's writing nothing has survived. But there is some secondhand evidence that female adherents of the new faith were actively engaged in propagating its tenets through the written and spoken word. John Hus wrote several of his Czech works for pious women, in particular, the treatise entitled *The Daughter (Dcerka)* and certain of his epistles written in Czech.[50] In 1378, a female servant of the Šternberk family named Kačka (Kate) was interrogated by the church authorities in Prague on the charge of taking the Host too frequently, preaching, and composing her own prayers. She admitted to her interrogator that she had composed one prayer and promised to send a copy of it, along with a book in her possession, to the authorities.[51] Another example of female writing is mentioned in a letter sent to the Hussites by Stephen of Dolany in which he paraphrases a booklet named *Little Books (Knížky)*, written in Czech by an anonymous Hussite woman who defends Hus against the Catholic Antichrist.[52] The Czech chronicler and translator of *The Travels of Sir John Mandeville*, Lawrence of Březová, refers to a letter of protest written by a woman concerning the appointment of Táborite officials and sent in July 1421 from the community of Saint Peter at Poříčí in the New Town to the magistrates of the united Prague townships.[53]

An excessive concern with female Hussite writing has deflected scholarly attention from the important correspondence of Perchta of Rožmberk (1429–76), granddaughter of Henry of Rožmberk (d. 1412) and his Hussite wife Elizabeth of Kravař (d. 1444). Her father was Ulrich of Rožmberk (1403–62), a powerful landowner and passionate anti-Hussite. Perchta was married at a young age to a member of another important Bohemian noble family, John of Lichtenstein (d. 1473). An extraordinary series of letters was dictated by Perchta to a scribe named Henry (she could read but perhaps could not write). These were sent over many years to her father and to her brothers Henry (d. 1457) and John (d. 1472). They represent an eloquent testimony to Perchta's unhappy twenty-year marriage and isolated life in Znojmo. Perchta was apparently neglected and abused by her husband and his family, a situation all too common for medieval and early modern women within arranged marriages. What makes Perchta's letters so unusual for their day is her frankness in discussing the problems in her marriage and her determination to exploit the *ars dictaminis* to publicize her plight.[54]

The consolidation of the Hussites' position in the mid–fifteenth century and their peaceful coexistence with the Catholics following the *Compactata* of Basel (1436) consolidated woman's social position and her monolingualism. Generally speaking, the Protestant vision of the family displaced woman as the carrier of charismatic piety; fathers became the undisputed masters of their households and women's roles became restricted to their function as wives and mothers.[55] This situation was not peculiar to fifteenth- and sixteenth-century Bohemia. In Elizabethan England, where Protestantism finally triumphed over the Catholic faith, Latin learning of any sort was considered to be virtually synonymous with popishness; educated families had their sons and daughters read vernacular translations of works sound in reformed doctrine. Catholic women, however, were free of these monolingual limitations, and the possibility of the convent was still available to them.[56] Among the truly erudite women of the first Jacobean generation were two Catholics who had to leave England: Mary Ward, the founder of the teaching institute of the Blessed Virgin Mary; and Elizabeth Jane Weston (1581–1612), a Latin scholar and poet, who took refuge in Habsburg Bohemia, noted for its tolerance toward Catholics, Utraquists, and Jews.

In September 1583, Joan Cooper Weston and her second husband, the alchemist Edward Kelley, left England for the Continent, accompanied by Kelley's partner in angelic seances, Dr. John Dee. Apparently, Joan's children by her deceased first husband (John Weston)—John and Elizabeth—stayed behind in England, probably until December 1584. A year later, the entire family settled in Bohemia, where the son, John Francis Weston, began to attend the Jesuit Clementine college at Prague. Edward

Kelley was knighted by Emperor Rudolph II in 1589, and moved soon after to the town of Jílov, where he had mining interests given him by his patron Peter Vok of Rožmberk. It was here that his stepdaughter Elizabeth learned to read from one John Saršan Vodňanský. When Kelley was imprisoned in 1591, Elizabeth and her mother moved to the town of Most, where she continued her schooling with another English immigrant, an Oxford graduate named John Hammond. In this manner Elizabeth became fluent in the composition of Latin verse by the age of fourteen. A girl of the same age in Elizabethan England—whether Catholic or Protestant—would have had little chance of receiving a grammar-school education.[57]

Edward Kelley's profligate mode of living occasioned high debts, and, following his sudden death in 1597, his widow, stepson, and stepdaughter found themselves destitute. Weston and her mother went to Prague in the hope of enlisting the sympathy of Emperor Rudolph II, whose cosmopolitan court was a magnet for gifted poets, painters, and architects. Here Weston excelled by her learning and her Latin poems; was praised for her facility in Greek, Latin, Italian, Czech, and German; and corresponded with many of the leading scholars of her day. She spoke mainly German and always wrote, whether prose or verse, in Latin. Her poems were collected and printed at Frankfurt an der Oder by a Silesian nobleman, Georg Martin von Baldhoven, as *Parthenicon Elisabethae Joannae Westoniae, virginis nobilissimae, poetriae florentissimae, linguarum plurimarum peritissimae*. Editions were printed in 1606 at Prague, in 1609 at Leipzig, in 1712 at Amsterdam, and at Frankfurt in 1723. Many of her poems take the form of addresses to princes, such as James I of England. She also wrote epigrams, epistles to friends, and a Latin poem in praise of typography, and translated some of *Aesop's Fables* into Latin verse. English scholars thought highly of her work, and ranked her with Sir Thomas More and the best Latin poets of her day. Her reputation on the Continent was even higher. Around 1602 she married a lawyer, Johann Leon, agent at the imperial court for the duke of Brunswick and the prince of Anhalt. She had four sons, all of whom predeceased her, and three daughters. She died at Prague in 1612 and was buried there.[58] She has remained one of the outstanding writers—and the only female writer—of humanist Latin verse from Rudolphine Bohemia.

In an age when women's self-expression in writing was highly restricted, the epistle was one of the few forms in which they could articulate their thoughts and excel as stylists. The letters produced by the European elite were frequently intended for public consumption and were appreciated by circles of admirers.[59] Following the loss of Bohemian national independence in 1620, the epistolary form became virtually the only genre in which Czech women were able to express themselves. An important and accomplished Czech female letter writer from this period is the noblewoman Zuzana Černínová of Harasov (1600–1654), who conducted a voluminous correspondence with her family members, especially her son Humprecht John Černín of Chudenice.[60] Zuzana was separated from Humprecht when he was sent to be educated at the Jesuit college in Prague and later in life when he became a courtier in Vienna and an inveterate traveler. In spite of his frequent absence from Bohemia, Zuzana managed to maintain a powerful influence on her ambitious son by writing to him wherever he went. Her voluminous correspondence reveals a perceptive, practical mind and a fluent stylist adept in the Czech language. Like the Jesuit priest and historian Bohuslav Balbín (1621–88), Zuzana perceived herself as first and foremost a Czech and looked with great suspicion on her Italian daughter-in-law and her son's enthusiasm for foreign culture.

Conclusion

As we have seen, women were instrumental in the development of Latin and Czech literature during the medieval and early modern period. But their involvement ebbed and flowed with the political vicissitudes of the kingdom. When Bohemia was a powerful, cosmopolitan society, as in the reign of Emperor Charles IV, royal and noble women enjoyed considerable prestige because of their charismatic piety and their patronage of the arts. But when the nation fell prey to religious strife, as in the fifteenth and seventeenth centuries, women's roles were increasingly restricted to the church pew and the household. For a brief period at the end of the sixteenth and beginning of the seventeenth century, the Prague court of Rudolph II became an international cultural center for European artists, scientists, and poets, including the distinguished English Latinist Elizabeth Jane Weston. But with the removal of the court to Vienna following the death of Emperor Rudolph in 1612 and the subsequent loss of Bohemian independence after the Battle of the White Mountain in 1620, there was little evidence of women's writing in Bohemia and Moravia (apart from a few letter writers) until the National Revival in the nineteenth century.

CHAPTER 3

✣

The War of the Bohemian Maidens
Gender, Ethnicity, and Language in *The Dalimil Chronicle*

Ethnicity and Language

After the Latin legends and the Latin chronicles the next step in the spontaneous development of Czech literature consisted of legends and chronicles written in the vernacular, and the so-called *Dalimil Chronicle* (c. 1308–11) was an important link in this development.[1] Just as the *First Cycle of Legends* followed in the footsteps of Latin vitae, so did *The Dalimil Chronicle* follow the Latin *Chronica Boëmorum* by Cosmas. Like the *Alexandreida, The Dalimil Chronicle* was written by a nobleman, yet its position in the contemporary literary context is somewhat different. Not only is its composition very simple — it could hardly be otherwise in the case of an epic poem narrating events in chronological order — but the whole artistic realization is different. Its language is communicative and not poetic, the syntax is almost primitive, the verse is apparently without any metrical pattern, and the rhymes are mostly grammatical. But a closer study of this curious work reveals that it is a remarkably well constructed literary structure whose components are skillfully brought into the right balance. At the very beginning the author reveals his approach to the task of artistic realization when he comments disparagingly on the various chronicles of his time. He is clearly opposed not only to verbalism but to the use of all poetic language and figures of speech, and he puts the main stress on the communicative and not on the aesthetic function. Yet in amazingly precise terminology — which reveals his knowledge of medieval rhetorical principles — he defines his own method: "As far as I am able, I intend to cut redundant speeches while providing the complete sense so that each man may more willingly learn about and strive for the good of his own people/language" (Prologue, lines 44–47).[2]

The whole chronicle is a persistent attempt to realize this intention; hence the maximum suppression of the aesthetic function to the point that the poem almost ceases to exist as a poem. The question might be asked, Why did the author not write in prose? The answer is that although he deviated from the existing literary structure as much as possible, he could not break away from it completely. At the same time, however, because of his different approach to the historical material, the author

50

was in conflict with the tradition even before it was developed in Bohemia, yet he had to write in verse. The development of literary structure is gradual, and it had not, in his time, reached the stage when a transition was possible from poetry to prose. By writing his chronicle in the manner he did, the author contributed decisively to a change in the structure; indeed, his work is of such a transitional character that the inevitable next step in the direction it took led to prose.

Although the author was aware that his work differed from the conventional norms, he was convinced that these norms would continue to prevail and that it was his work that would have to conform to them. These norms—which he calls very precisely, thus revealing his knowledge of contemporary poetical theories, "beautiful rhyme" (*rým krásný*, 54) and "excellent language" (*hlahol jasný*, 55)—were the main attributes of a literary work with a predominantly aesthetic function, that is, metric pattern including rhyme and symbol. The author thought it necessary to preface his work with an apology. He says in fact: I wrote a patriotic political pamphlet and I found that I could not make it into another *Alexandreida*—you try if you like. And the ironical tone suggests that he knew that it would be impossible and that his own approach was the right one.

The core of the chronicle is in its concluding chapters. In these the author speaks directly to those in power, with the clear intention of influencing their policy. The aim of the whole preceding narration is to condition the reader for the final argument and to provide enough illustrations for the author's thesis. For this reason the chronicle differs from other contemporary chronicles in several respects. The interest in political events pushes religious matters into the background; legends, fables, chivalric stories, and anecdotes are (with a few exceptions) left out; individual figures are not described with concern for their physical characteristics but become the personifications of ideas; the author's own political thoughts are not couched in complicated allegories but are expressed quite bluntly.

The author, speaking from the standpoint of the lower nobility and considering the nobles the decisive political factor in the state, tries to build up a philosophy of Czech history and identity. At the very beginning, he registers with obvious fascination the communist organization of the primitive Czechs. Soon afterward he expresses one of his two main ideas, that of duty toward the community, to which all other interests must be subordinated. This point of view is expressed in the speech of Princess Libuše, the founder of Prague, who speaks with the directness of a political orator.

The author's second idea is, of course, that of Bohemia for the Czechs. This idea is carried through the whole work, presented from different angles, and at the end it is summarized in a practical political program for the state. These ideas are also expressed in the speech of the matriarch Libuše. When telling the story of Duke Ulrich, who had an illegitimate son with Božena, daughter of a petty nobleman, and who had to exert all his power to have the bastard recognized as his successor, the author of the chronicle omits all mention of Ulrich's previous marriage (for obvious moral reasons) and presents his affair with Božena as a considered political action. Ulrich, having decided to marry, gives preference to Božena rather than to the German empress, in order to keep Bohemia Czech. Hence the emphasis in the chronicle on promoting the Czech language and discouraging the exclusive use of German by the Czech rulers. If they ceased to speak Czech, they ceased to be Czech.

Again and again the author warns against the danger menacing the Czechs from the German Empire. They should also beware of cultural influence, which, in the hands of the Germans, is yet another weapon for depriving them of their independence. Duke Soběslav I, whose sons the German emperor offers to educate at his court, proclaims to his barons that it is better to elect a simple plowman as a ruler than the germanized sons of a Czech duke. The author criticizes the colonization policy of the Přemyslids often and openly, on the grounds that the Germans cannot be trusted.

The chronicler ends his work at the year 1311, when John of Luxembourg, the son of the Holy Roman Emperor, was crowned king of Bohemia. It is characteristic of the author that he does not indulge in panegyrics on the new king and that he is loath to express any hope for the future. Instead he offers his opinion, which is more an ultimatum than a piece of advice. His address to the king is abrupt and shows that he was not a partisan of the absolutist idea: the king has only one choice — to trust the lower nobility and to do what they tell him or leave the country. But the cornerstone of the chronicle is the chapter dealing with an important event of the time of the chronicler, the armed revolt of the German town patriciate in 1309 against the Czech nobles, from whom they tried to exert political concessions. This, in the view of the author, was the punishment that the Czech nobles brought upon themselves by their selfishness. The foreigners who were invited by them to the country contributed to enormous prosperity; they filled the treasuries of the barons with silver and taught them a new refined way of life. But this was a subtle ruse; the Czech element was weakened and depraved by luxury and foreign customs and stripped of its former roughness and courage. Finally those who came as servants usurped the power. In looking for the forces that could change this situation, the author of the chronicle, much in advance of his time, is inclined to see the salvation of Bohemia in an independent state governed by the lower nobility allied with the peasants. This is precisely what happened in the Hussite period in the fifteenth century, when the Czech king Sigismund was removed from the throne by an uprising of noblemen and peasants. There is, therefore, much justification in the comment of the German historian Joseph George Meinert, who in 1821 called the chronicle "the bugle of the Hussite Wars." The chronicle was extremely popular in the fifteenth century and again in 1620 on the eve of the national catastrophe, when it was printed with the obvious purpose of strengthening resistance against the German expansion. After the Battle of the White Mountain nearly all the copies of this edition were confiscated and burned, and a new edition was not permitted by the Austrian censorship until 1849.

Gender, Ethnicity, and Language

If questions of ethnicity and language have preoccupied scholars of *The Dalimil Chronicle,* the issue of gender and the role of women in the chronicle have been elided, largely as a consequence of the small-nation habit of subsuming all aspects of political representation under the unitary rubric of national identity. Yet the relationship between gender, ethnicity, and language posed interrelated questions about authority and power for medieval writers. Let us return, for a moment, to the marriage of Ulrich and Božena discussed earlier. This story provides a pretext for the author's belief that it is better for a Czech ruler to marry a Czech peasant than a German princess who would bring up her children to speak German and cultivate German manners and customs. When the nobles object to the morganatic marriage, Ulrich retorts with a lengthy didactic speech that clearly expresses the opinion of the author himself:

> Lords, please listen to me! Noblemen are born from churls and noblemen have churlish sons. Old money creates noblemen and the poverty of the nobility is often ascribed to the peasantry. We all come from one father, yet he whose father had a lot of money considers himself to be a nobleman. If the nobility and the peasantry are mixed up in this way, why shouldn't Božena be my wife? I would rather laugh with a noble-spirited Czech peasant woman than marry a German queen. If every man truly cared for his people, there would be less interest in a German. A German would have a German entourage and would teach my children German. Then the people would become disunited and the land brought to certain ruin. Lords, you ignore your own interests when you reprimand me for my marriage. Where would you find a spokesman standing before a foreign princess? (Chap. 42, lines 12–32)[3]

This highly revealing passage tells us a great deal about the changes in traditional society brought about by the economic situation of the time. In Bohemia, as elsewhere, the fourteenth-century nobility was losing ground to the rising burgher class and even the wealthy peasantry, both social groups encompassed by the Czech term *chlap* (i.e., member of the third estate). Judging from the passage, it appears as though the author of *The Dalimil Chronicle* accepts the inevitability of this process and wishes to build a common sense of Czech identity that would transcend the divisions imposed by gender, class, and ethnicity. Thus Duke Ulrich marries a Czech peasant girl in order to keep the dynasty Czech. But this, I suggest, is more what the author wants us to think of as his political program rather than what it actually means in practice. The epilogue of the chronicle makes it brutally clear that the work was conceived and written to advance the interests of the Czech-speaking gentry vis-à-vis the new king. In the final analysis, ethnicity and gender are firmly subordinated to the interests of the nobility, whose power increased enormously when John of Luxembourg became king. In spite of his all-inclusive definition of Czechness as encompassing women, peasants, and noblemen, the author's patriarchal ideology—I shall now argue—works to exclude women from his Czech *communitas*, while gender complicates—rather than complements—his vision of ethnicity.

An important part of this conflict of interests is played by medieval women's traditional identification with the vernacular. Lacking access to Latin, the language of learning, they usually had recourse only to the vernacular in order to express themselves in speech and writing. The author of *The Dalimil Chronicle* wishes to promote Czech, since this is the language of the nobility on whose behalf he is writing his chronicle. The danger inherent in his advocacy of Czech is that it might encourage women to express themselves in the same tongue. This was already a trend at the royal court in Prague, where, as we have seen, a royal princess like Kunigunde could read works written in Latin and Czech.[4] It is not altogether surprising, therefore, that our author refers scathingly to the ladies of the court, ostensibly for encouraging knights in the practice of jousting and gambling with dice. It is women's access to the vernacular rather than their courtly habits as such that fuels the author's antagonism toward them. In *The Dalimil Chronicle* submissive women like Božena are idealized but denigrated once they aspire to their own discourse, like the mythic maidens whose story is the subject of this chapter.

Czech versus Latin

Like many medieval chronicles, *The Dalimil Chronicle* begins with the myth of Babel, which expressed the universal belief in a prelapsarian language—a pure medium of communication between God and Adam in the Garden of Eden before Eve's transgression. Medieval ecclesiastics and scholars saw the post-Babel linguistic diaspora as the first step in the formation of races or peoples. The great encyclopedist Isidore of Seville saw the medieval view of ethnicity as contingent upon language, claiming that peoples (*gentes*) arise from different languages, not languages from different peoples.[5] This belief can be illustrated with reference to the Old Czech term *jazyk,* which meant both "language" and "people," hardly a surprising conjunction of meanings when we consider that the Czechs' principal neighbors were non-Slavic speakers of German and Hungarian.[6] We might contrast this situation with medieval Scandinavia, where belonging to a social group was defined in terms of "law" rather than "language," a consequence of the fact that medieval Scandinavians spoke closely related languages.

As the language of the liturgy, instruction, and prayer, church Latin fulfilled the role of this originary discourse, and all other (vernacular) languages existed in a secondary and inferior relation to it. But by the twelfth century, the vernacular was beginning to emerge as a viable medium of historical and doctrinal truth. Rhymed chronicles in the vernacular abounded, in particular in France and at the courts of the Anglo-Norman kings. One might mention the *Gestes des Bretons* or the *Gestes des Normands*, both from the twelfth century, the latter the work of a canon named Wace. In England there was the so-called *Chronicle of Robert of Gloucester*, dating from the end of the thirteenth century and written by several authors. In German literature there was the so-called *Kaiserchronik*, and in Austria the *Reimchronik Ottokars*. The acceptance of the vernacular as a worthy medium of communication achieved its most eloquent justification in Dante's *De vulgari eloquentia* (c. 1304–7), where it is praised as that potentially perfect and true language that one imbibes with one's nurse's milk, that is from woman. Dante compares the vernacular favorably with the grammatical languages Latin and Greek: "Now of the two the nobler is the vernacular: first because it is the first language ever spoken by mankind; second because the whole world uses it though in diverse pronunciations and forms; finally because it is natural to us while the other is more the product of art."[7] In this fashion, the vernacular became identified with the female and the natural, while Latin—as the discourse of authority—was gendered as male and artificial.

Similarly, the author of our chronicle, in his prologue, insists on the truthfulness of the vernacular (the language he has chosen to use), while identifying Latin—the language of his source, Cosmas's *Chronica Boëmorum*—with unreliable, mendacious writing. At the same time, he reverses Dante's feminization of the vernacular—the language of truth—by reverting to the patristic tradition of mendacious writing as female. When he states in the prologue that he intends to provide the "whole meaning" (*mysl cělú*, 45) where the Latin sources offer only "empty speeches" (*řěči prázdné*, 44), his allusion to Cosmas's self-conscious love of rhetorical style echoes Saint Augustine's equation of the ornate pagan text with the female, and the truthful Christian text with the male sex.[8] The implication here is that the Czech chronicle may lack rhetorical sophistication, but is more truthful and reliable than Cosmas. In this manner, the Czech author combines the innovatory trend of recommending the use of the vernacular as truthful with the patristic inclination to present truthful language as indubitably male.

The rivalry between Latin and Czech as the medium of truth can be explained with reference to the authors' divergent ideologies. The later chronicler presents Bohemian history from the standpoint of the Czech-speaking lower nobility, the class on whose behalf he is writing his chronicle. He is highly critical of those Czech rulers who were too complicitous with the German minority and neglectful of the nobles' interests. Cosmas, by contrast, was the spokesman of the Přemyslid rulers who—unlike the nobility—did not identify with the Czech language and who, by the thirteenth century, had become thoroughly germanized in language and culture. The later author gets around the problem of having to acknowledge the pro-Přemyslid Cosmas as his *auctor* by pretending that he did not use any Latin chronicles written in Prague. Refusing to identify Cosmas by name, he claims that he was given his source text by a priest outside Prague, a spurious assertion that gives his work the necessary semblance of *auctoritas*. From the combative tone employed in the prologue, it is clear that the author of *The Dalimil Chronicle* is determined to write his own autonomous history of Bohemia from the standpoint of the lower nobility without relying upon Cosmas.

A further means of camouflaging his dependence on Cosmas is to amplify and transform stories derived from his source. In the so-called "War of the Bohemian Maidens"—based on Cosmas's laconic account—the Czech author expands the story into a lively narrative in which he articulates his own curious blend of conservatism and radicalism: Cosmas's mythic account of genderless prehistory is inverted to form an exemplum of the threat posed to an originary patriarchal order by female speech, while the subsequent account of the war of the sexes, in which the men (led by Přemysl the Plowman) are triumphant over women (led by Vlasta), becomes a prehistorical analogue to the Czech nobility's heroic resistance to monarchical control, a parallel made all the more apt by the fact that Přemysl the Plowman was considered the mythic ancestor of the dynasty of Czech kings that ruled Bohemia until its extinction in 1306. In spite of—or rather because of—his skill in presenting two diametrically opposite discourses (which simultaneously heroize and denigrate the maidens) as one seamless narrative, the author finds it necessary to bring his ambiguous narrative to a very unambiguous close. The violent denouement, in which the women are murdered and their bodies dismembered, allows the chronicler to erase the discursive contradiction that the maidens embody as Czech women and the related menace they pose to his own stable sense of identity as a Czech-speaking man.

The War of the Bohemian Maidens: Cosmas

In Book I, chapter 9, of his *Chronica Boëmorum*, Cosmas of Prague relates the story of a war between the sexes. When power passes into the hands of Přemysl the Plowman (the husband of Princess Libuše), the female followers of Libuše refuse to acknowledge his patriarchal authority. Having grown up free in the primordial forest, the maidens are used to carrying their own arms, electing their own female leaders, and fighting in battle. Like the famed Scythian Amazons of ancient times, they are indistinguishable in dress from their male counterparts. Threatened at the very base of their power, the men gather to establish their own fortress at Vyšehrad. Stronger in physique than the men, the maidens vanquish their adversaries by means of physical force. The war is brought to a conclusion not by male military superiority but by a ruse. The men propose a truce and invite the maidens to sup with them at their castle, where they intend to overpower the maidens like rapacious wolves breaking into a sheep-pen. The men seize their opportunity, overpower the weaponless maidens, and rape them. The story ends as the empty rooms of Děvín castle are set on fire. In this manner—the story concludes— women came under the control of men in perpetuity.[9]

In his important study of the written transmission of Bohemian history, Vladimir Karbusicky argues that Cosmas did not rely exclusively on an autochthonous folk tradition, as conventionally claimed by Czech scholars, but drew upon various sources, including classical legends, folk customs, and even contemporary political events. Karbusicky detects the same mode of adaptation in *The Dalimil Chronicle*. Far from preserving an unbroken transmission of Slavic oral tradition, the later author was influenced by written analogues and literary sources. In fact, Karbusicky identifies three distinct narratives in the Czech version of the War of the Bohemian Maidens: the founding of Děvín by the maidens; the episode of Šárka and Ctirad; and the war of the sexes.[10] In distinction to Karbusicky, I will be concerned here less with questions of plot than with discourse and ideology, that is to say, not with *what* story is told but *how* it is told. Let us now turn to the first part of the episode—the founding of Děvín.

The Founding of Děvín

For the author, the founding of Děvín provides a parallel to the building of the Tower of Babel, which resulted in linguistic chaos and the breakdown of univocal authority. The act of building Děvín is thus intimately linked with the dangerous quest for autonomous female speech: "Wishing to employ their own speech, they began to build a castle" (chap. 9, lines 8–9).[11]

The pretext for medieval hostility toward female speech can be found both in the biblical text of Genesis 2 and in the patristic exegetical tradition represented principally by Saint Augustine's *On Christian Doctrine*, in which the dangerous lure of pagan texts is equated with the sexual snares of the female body. Stephen G. Nichols points out that Genesis chapters 2–3, in addition to shaping notions of marriage and the relative status of the sexes, were also perceived as a "drama of discourse and interpretation."[12] The breakdown of communication with God, the consequence of which is that man can only dimly and imperfectly understand what God is saying to him, provides the biblical basis upon which the whole of medieval exegesis and hermeneutics are founded.[13] As the first woman, Eve was perceived as the instigator of a drama that led to the breakdown of a perfect communion between God and man.

In adapting the War of the Maidens, the author of *The Dalimil Chronicle* relates to Cosmas in much the same way that patristic exegetists interpret the Genesis story. Just as the latter choose to ignore the account of the Creation according to which Adam and Eve were made at the same time (the Elohist version) in favor of the one in which Eve was created later (the Jahwist version), so does the Czech author deliberately ignore Cosmas's insistence that the maidens and the men lived without gender difference in the primeval forest prior to the war of the sexes. Instead, he makes the patriarchal order an originary norm from which the maidens deviate by leaving the paternal hearth.

The maidens' treachery against their fathers and brothers corresponds to their aberrant and dangerous "speeches" (*řeči*), an automatic threat to a patriarchal system that perceives women's silence as the ideal social practice.[14] In a symbolic reenactment of the "Jahwist" account of the Creation — whereby Eve obstructs the truthful communication between God and man by introducing the deceit of rhetoric — the maidens' aspiration toward speech is said to provide the instigation for their departure from the paternal hearth and their subsequent establishment of Děvín castle.

Following the foundation of Děvín, the maiden leader Vlasta makes a speech advising rebellion against the indolent, drunken men; it is as a consequence of this speech, the author insists (chap. 9, 20), that many maidens flee to join the leader Vlasta at Děvín. *The Dalimil Chronicle* says that, "like doves fly from the dove-cote, so did the girls steal away from their fathers" (chap. 9, lines 22–23).[15] This departure from the *Chronica Boëmorum*, in which patriarchal power is achieved by force, is a direct contradiction of the source. The author of *The Dalimil Chronicle* creates the impression that the maidens deviate from a patriarchal norm that always existed, while Cosmas makes it clear that the ungendered maidens lived in the forests.

Vlasta divides her followers into three groups: the wise to sit in council, the pretty to lure men, and the strong to fight the men in battle. The beautiful maidens are told to use makeup and to learn "cunning speeches" as a way of seducing the men: "She ordered the loveliest ones to put on makeup and to learn cunning speeches" (chap. 10, lines 17–18).[16] The idea that women's appearance — like their speech — is deceitful comports with the established misogynistic discourse of the time. Medieval preachers of the thirteenth and fourteenth centuries called cosmetics the "devil's soap," since they were used by women to deceive and ensnare the beholder in sin.[17] As such they were following in the tradition established by the early church father Tertullian, who claimed that "women sin against God who anoint their faces with creams, stain their cheeks with rouge, or lengthen their eyebrows with antimony."[18]

In the *Chronica Boëmorum* the maidens' decision to build Děvín is said to be motivated by courage (*audacia*), while the men employ the ruses of cunning to overthrow their female foe. The Czech author inverts these generic attributes by depicting the maidens as cunning. In fact, the author devotes two chapters (12 and 13) to describing the maidens' devious entrapment of their male victims. Failing to heed Přemysl's warning, the men succumb to the female snare and end up forfeiting their lives. The maidens invite the men to banquet with them at Děvín, an inversion of the decidedly male ruse perpetrated in the *Chronica Boëmorum*:

> Having seen that there was great hunger at Vyšehrad, they [the maidens] invited them to their castle for a truce. Here the most beautiful maidens, who knew many cunning speeches, sat down with them. (Chap. 13, lines 3–6)[19]

Typically, the author claims that the men use trickery as a defensive strategy against female cunning, although Cosmas states that it is the men who trick the maidens by inviting them to take part in the festival of food and drink. The later author here performs the very ruses associated with rhetoric and women, a strategy that R. Howard Bloch perceives as a general characteristic of misogynistic writing in the Middle Ages.[20]

Ctirad and Šárka

Following the foundation of Děvín comes the episode of Ctirad and Šárka (chapter 14), an episode completely absent from the *Chronica Boëmorum*, which reinforces the misogynistic tenor of the first episode.[21] The maidens plot to entrap a brave man named Ctirad: they tie up one of their number, the beautiful Šárka, and leave her bound on the highway used by Ctirad and his followers. At the maiden's side are placed a horn and a bottle of mead. When Ctirad arrives with his men, the weeping Šárka implores the men to help her, claiming that she has been set upon by those wicked maidens. Ctirad unties the maiden, sits by her side, drinks the mead, and blows on the horn. Hearing the sound of the horn, the maidens realize that their trap has been successful; they descend upon the men before they can remount and offer resistance. Ctirad is taken back to the maidens' castle and his body broken upon a wheel. Eventually the men learn cunning from the maidens and lure certain of them to Vyšehrad on the pretext of a truce; here they rape the maidens, who are too ashamed to return to Děvín.

The War of the Sexes

We come now to the third episode: the war of the sexes. In *The Dalimil Chronicle*, Libuše dies before the outbreak of war, whereas in Cosmas's version she lives through it. By removing Libuše altogether, the later author dissociates the founder of Prague from Přemysl, who becomes the sole embodiment of tyranny against which the Bohemian Maidens rebel (and, by implication, against the dynasty of kings descended from him). In recasting the Latin fable as an exemplum of ethnic heroism, the author of *The Dalimil Chronicle* owes a great deal to the Czech *Alexandreida*, an original adaptation of Gautier of Châtillon's Latin life of Alexander the Great, the *Alexandreis* (1178/82).[22] The author of the *Alexandreida* reveals an ambivalent attitude to the antic hero. In the early sections of the work, he is heroized as a fighter against tyranny following his father's premature and sudden death. But when he aspires to conquer the world, he begins to exhibit dangerous signs of pride. Even though the ending of the work has not survived, it is likely that the moral of the story was meant to illustrate the sin of *superbia*, the first of the seven deadly sins. In addition to imposing his own moral vision on the story, the anonymous Czech author also draws parallels between ancient Greece and contemporary Bohemia: Alexander's knights are given recognizably Czech names; his coronation recalls the Prague ceremony; the graphic descriptions of battle illustrate the tactics of late medieval warfare. King Darius's speech, delivered on the eve of his defeat, contains allusions to the recent defeat of Přemysl Ottokar II at the Battle of the Moravian Field in 1278, when Bohemia was flooded with marauding Brandenburg troops under the banner of the victorious Rudolph of Habsburg. If the Persians are presented as oppressed victims, the victorious Alexander is by now little better than a tyrant. Darius refers to the Greek troops as "these unworthy guests" (1333), a probable reference to the German presence in Bohemia, particularly following the Battle of the Moravian Field.[23] The Persian cause is implicitly equated with the resistance of the Czech nobility to the ignominious foreign invasion.

The author of *The Dalimil Chronicle* draws upon the *Alexandreida* in the third episode of the War of the Bohemian Maidens. Like Alexander's knights in the *Alexandreida*, the maidens are invested with Czech names. Their leader, Vlasta, is compared with a "fury" (*lítice*, chap. 16, line 1) and a "she-bear" (*nedvědice*, chap. 16, line 2), heroic language reminiscent of the victorious young Alexander before he succumbs to the sin of pride. In her address to the maidens, Vlasta explicitly compares them to the Amazons (chap. 11, line 49) who fought bravely against Alexander the Great and other kings of antiquity (chap. 11, lines 57–58). Vlasta's speech opens with a eulogistic apostrophe in which the key word "noble" (*šlechetný*) occurs four times. Vlasta's address to the maidens consciously recalls King Darius's righteous speech to his army in the

Alexandreida in which he invokes the principle of nobility (*šlechta*) three times in the first eight lines (1299–1306). By echoing Darius's speech, the author of *The Dalimil Chronicle* implicitly compares the cause of the Bohemian maidens to that of the Persians. The implication is that the maidens' foe, Přemysl the Plowman, is akin to the tyrannical, foreign invader Alexander, hardly a surprising equation when we consider that the author regarded many rulers of the Přemyslid dynasty to be too complicitous with the German minority and insufficently sympathetic to the rights of the Czech-speaking nobility.

The conclusion of the story is more violent and realistic than in Cosmas. The maidens' attempts at evoking the men's pity go unheeded:

> Some [maidens] knelt before them; others started licking at them.
> But whatever they did, the men's hearts remained hardened. (Chap.
> 16, lines 41–44)[24]

In spite of their entreaties, the maidens' "lovely little bodies" (*krásná tělce*, chap. 16, line 45) are hacked to pieces and thrown over the castle ramparts. In this final episode, the author of *The Dalimil Chronicle* invokes well-known stories from classical antiquity. The scene of murder and mayhem is evocative of the Amazons' defeat by the Greeks in Guido de Columnis's *History of the Destruction of Troy* (1287), in which Queen Penthesilea suffers a violent fate at the hand of Pyrrhus while defending the besieged Trojans against the Greeks.[25] The Greek warrior severs Penthesilea's hand and then takes his full vengeance by hacking her body to pieces.[26] Guido's text was certainly known in Bohemia at the end of the thirteenth century since it served as a source for the exemplum on Troy in the *Alexandreida*.[27] Later vernacular adaptations of the same scene provide an equally graphic and violent account of the Amazon queen's dismemberment. In *The Laud Book of Troy*, a Middle English adaptation of the story from about 1400, misogynistic and epic discourses dovetail in a scene of grisly finality.[28] These Latin and vernacular analogues provide a general misogynistic backdrop against which to view the Czech author's amplification of his source material.

Conclusion

As a spokesman of a patriarchal social group, the anonymous author of *The Dalimil Chronicle* transforms the Latin fable of the War of the Bohemian Maidens into a partly mysogynistic tale of the danger inherent in women's independent speech. Ironically, his subversion of his Latin source represents a parallel to women's increasing recourse to the vernacular in the later Middle Ages. The author's desire to promote Czech as the language of historical truth thus places him—like medieval women vis-à-vis Latin—in a secondary relationship to an originary authority.

But, as we have seen, the War of the Bohemian Maidens is not simply a drama of patriarchal authority under threat; it is also an allegory of Czech resistance to royal tyranny and foreign aggression. On this level the maidens are not denigrated as seekers after their own speech but heroized as ancestors of the Czech nobility. Here too irony accrues. For in dooming the maidens to a violent fate, the author implicitly identifies with the reactionary forces of Přemysl the Plowman, the embodiment of foreign tyranny in the earlier part of the story. The story involuntarily exposes how gender often complicates, rather than complements, ethnicity. At once Czech-speaking and female, same yet different, the Bohemian maidens frustrate the author's attempt to make their story illustrate his ideology. The dismemberment of their bodies is thus the logical and violent outcome of his need to erase the paradox they represent. But we can go further and interpret this murderous conclusion as an example of what psychoanalysts call "projective inversion:"[29] the male author's greatest fear—the disintegration of his identity faced with the encroachment of independent, alien discourses, whether female, Latin, or German—is projected onto the hapless maidens: his repressed anxiety becomes their fictional fate. It is as if by literally tearing apart the female body, the author can—paradoxically—preserve and guarantee the imaginary integrity of his own constructed identity as a Czech-speaking man.

Such a violent continuum between gender, ethnicity, and language is not unique to the Middle Ages but has been a persistent feature of central and southeastern European history. In the recent war fought between ethnic Croats, Serbians, and Muslims in Bosnia-Herzogovina, the rape and murder of women, "ethnic cleansing," and the close identification with one's native language were all interrelated manifestations of a murderous reality. I hope that my close reading of the little-known legend of the Bohemian maidens has helped to provide deeper insights into the proximity between gender, ethnicity, and language in European history and historical representation.

CHAPTER 4

❖

Alien Bodies

Exclusion, Obscenity, and Social Control in *The Ointment Seller*

The Czech-Latin play known as *Unguentarius* (The ointment seller) (c.1340s), which depicts the Ointment Seller episode from the Easter cycle of mystery plays, has long since intrigued scholars because of its obscene sexual and scatological content. The most extensive, detailed study to date of the two extant fragments of this play (Museum and Schlägel MSS) claims that the farce formed part of the *risus paschalis*, a Central European Easter festival that celebrated the resurrection in the spirit of the Bakhtinian carnival. Jarmila Veltrusky has argued persuasively that the sacred and the farcical elements of the play are not mutually antagonistic, as previously thought, but form integral aspects of Christian worship. She concludes her study by claiming that the farce "tends to indicate that its mockery had a very wide scope and aimed, in true 'carnival' spirit, to deride the whole of the society it addressed itself to."[1]

Since the sexual liberation of the 1960s we have come to regard obscenity as a healthy antidote to the repressive legacy of Victorian attitudes to sex and the body, a means of subverting coercive rules and regulations around social taboos. Mikhail Bakhtin's influential model of the carnivalesque, whereby social hierarchies are seen to be subverted from below by various popular forms of entertainment, reinforced this idealistic point of view, which seems to me to be unduly fallacious in positing a universal impulse in human nature to resist and reverse all manifestations of authority.[2] What a close study of medieval and modern humor actually suggests is how commonly the authorities and the population at large collude in enforcing and perpetuating ideological conformity. This was particularly true of the calamitous fourteenth century, when economic decline, famine, and plague combined to polarize society and drive a wedge between "insiders" and "outsiders."[3]

Veltrusky uses the Bakhtinian model in presenting the function of obscenity in *The Ointment Seller* as a healthy mockery of all elements of society. Such a holistic approach ignores the monolithic rigidity of medieval society. Veltrusky thus overlooks how the farce co-opts and manipulates obscene discourse to distinguish between the insiders and the outsiders. A careful scrutiny of the *dramatis personae* and the social relations among them suggests that the obscene humor is not directed against the whole of society at all, but against specific generic, religious, and ethnic groups: women (the wife of the ointment seller, women in the audience, and even the three Marys), Jews (Abraham, his son Izák, and the anarchic assistant Rubín), and Germans (the ointment seller Severín and his wife). The absence of any characters from the Czech-speaking nobility or peasantry leads us to suppose that these classes constituted the principal audience of the play. There are, to be sure, references to the obscenity of monks, but these are formulaic and are in every instance linked with women (a monk sitting on a nun; a woman locked in a barn with a monk, and Havlicě, the seductress of all the monks in Prague). There is also an obscene reference to the phallic lance used in the chivalric pastime of the joust; it is contained in a fragment of a song sung by Pustrpalk in the Schlägel Fragment:

> A magpie on a magpie flew over a river,
> flesh without bone pierced a girl,
> round about the tourney, ho ho,
> a lot got stuck between the legs.[4]
> (Lines 135–38)

Ostensibly this snippet would appear to mock those lecherous knights who participate in jousts and thus reinforce the Bakhtinian argument that the piece satirizes all levels of society regardless of differences in race, language, and class. Yet here we need to be careful to look at the social context within which the text arose. In the reign of John of Luxembourg, when our play was written, tourneys would have been the cultural preserve of French- and German-speaking knights. Thus the satirical song quoted above is perfectly consistent with my claim that the objects of the play's humor are those who speak a different language and represent a different ethnic group. We find an analogous equation of jousting with *luxuria* in the chivalric romance *Duke Ernest*, where the beak of the crane-headed king is compared with a tilting lance as he attempts to kiss the abducted Indian princess on the lips; and of jousting with foreign mores in the counsel of the Horse from *The New Council*, where the unseated knight in the description of the tourney cries out in German as he lands in the sandpit.

Alien Bodies

Medieval Bohemia was not a nation-state in the modern sense but an uneasy association of diverse ethnic, social, and religious groups: the king and court, the nobility (higher and lower), the church, the Germans, and the Jews. The reign of Charles IV was a time of relative peace and prosperity for Jews throughout his domain. When the emperor founded the New Town of Prague he allowed the Jews to settle there with their families. The *Maiestas Carolina* civil code of 1355 (later rescinded) even allowed Jews to hold villages in fee, handing over taxes to the royal coffers.[5] But Jews in Bohemia had always been vulnerable to social and economic resentment in the population at large. As early as 1161, eighty-six Jews were burned in an alleged plot of Jewish physicians to poison the populace.[6] In 1338, some Jews were apprehended for reputedly misusing a Host, and a large number of their coreligionists were promptly put to death for the crime.[7] Anti-Semitic feeling again came to the surface in 1385 (during the reign of Wenceslas IV), when Jews were ordered to be seized during the night and thrown into jail, while their property was to be sealed at the king's pleasure.[8] When the king was absent from Prague in 1389 a pogrom broke out, said to have been provoked by some Jews throwing stones at a priest carrying the sacrament to a sick man. The mob overran the ghetto, setting fire to houses and murdering whoever tried to escape.[9]

Anti-Semitism is also reflected in medieval Bohemian texts in Old Church Slavonic, Latin, and Czech, especially in connection with Christ's betrayal and crucifixion. The First Old Church Slavonic *Life of Saint Wenceslas* compares Boleslav's plot against his brother Wenceslas with the Jews' alleged treachery against Christ.[10] The twelfth-century Czech *Song of Ostrov* refers in the third stanza, line 4, to Christ being "sold to the Jews."[11] Further evidence of anti-Jewish feeling is manifested in various illuminations from *The Passional of the Abbess Kunigunde,* where Jews, wearing their characteristic horned hats, torment Christ (leaves 6b, 7a), burden him with the cross (7b), and draw lots for his garments at the base of the cross (8a).[12]

As the most affluent and influential minority in the Czech Lands, Germans were especially disliked. Invited by the Czech kings to Bohemia in the twelfth century, first as farmers and then as much-needed miners to excavate the country's rich copper, silver, and gold reserves, they enjoyed royal economic and legal protection and even prestige as poets at the court of Prague.[13] Needless to say, the Germans' status as privileged outsiders aroused the ire of the native Czech nobility, who felt threatened by the influence of these relative newcomers on the kings.

The ambiguous attitude to women was as prevalent in the Bohemian Lands as it was elsewhere in medieval Europe. The cult of the Virgin Mary was highly developed in Bohemia by the fourteenth century, as can be seen in the contemporary panel paintings and statues of the Madonna-and-child motif. But conventional misogyny was equally a fact of life. According to this tradition, women were deceitful, garrulous, weak-willed, and sexually promiscuous. We shall see many instances of this negative vision of old women and prostitutes in particular in *The Ointment Seller.*

As Miri Rubin has argued in her discussion of the cult of the Eucharist, it is possible to observe from the twelfth century on the construction of a systematic and necessary Other to that which was emerging increasingly as the doctrinal norm.[14] To counteract anxiety over the acceptance of the new doctrine of transubstantiation (the conversion of the sacramental bread and wine into the Body and Blood of Christ), it was necessary to attribute Christian doubts about this doctrine to those social groups deemed most vulnerable to error, disbelief, and disrespect toward the sacred, namely, women and Jews. Many apocryphal stories arose about women and Jews stealing, mistreating, and mocking the Host. As women and Jews occupied a similarly marginal position within late medieval Christian society, they tended to be seen in terms of each other. And as the Aristotelian metaphor of society as a body became sacralized as the Body of Christ, so too were women and Jews identified metonymically with those taboo or negative body parts associated with dirt and sex— the anus and the genitalia—both of which occupy an inverted relation to the sacred and positive parts of the head, chest, and feet, the loci of sacramental or sacred rituals.[15] If the Christian male body was deemed potent, old women, prostitutes, and Jews were regarded as sterile prisoners of their own sinful flesh. In this essay we shall find an absolute equivalence between female and Jewish alien bodies, an inevitable consequence of a society that perceived the Christian heterosexual male as the norm from which all other bodies occupy an inferior, defective, and secondary relation.

In medieval Bohemia, ethnic conflict between Czechs and Germans was a complicating factor in the constitution of this doctrinal Other. Just as Christian identity was contingent on the creation of an inverted mirror-image, so was the construction of Czech ethnic identity reliant on the demonization of the Germans. The first clerical writer to voice criticism of the Germans was the twelfth-century chronicler Cosmas (1045–1125), author of the Latin *Chronica Boëmorum*. He was followed by many other literati writing in Latin and Czech. In the early-fourteenth-century fragmentary apocryph *Legend of Judas,* the author (perhaps a later redactor) addresses the Germans as the "treacherous tribe," responsible for the assassination of the last Přemyslid, King Wenceslas III, a biblical topos analogical to that applied to the Jews as the alleged murderers of Christ.[16] The linking of Germans with Jews as traitors is especially significant in the context of late medieval Bohemian society. As servants of the kings on whom they were politically and economically dependent, both these minorities were perceived as enemies of the Czech lower nobility.

In late medieval Bohemia, then, women, Jews, and Germans were frequently conflated as the Other. And as we shall see in our close reading of *The Ointment Seller,* they are metonymically linked in their deeds and speech with the taboo body parts of the anus and genitalia. Whatever they do or say, they reinforce their own difference and incite the laughter of the audience by evoking the nether regions connotative of dirt and sex. When a German character in the Czech farce says something innocuous in his own language and it sounds obscene in Czech, he is underscoring his otherness by equating himself and his speech with the obscenity he has unwittingly articulated.

Women

In *The Ointment Seller*, women are either prostitutes or hags in league with the devil. The German merchant's wife refers to the three Marys, who come to buy ointment to anoint the body of Christ, as "young whores" who have cheated her husband. The merchant's Jewish assistant (of whom we shall hear more later) construes their grief-stricken demeanor at the death of Christ as a sign of exhaustion after a night of riotous sex. These are, of course, misogynistic commonplaces. Only when the three Marys chant their Latin and Czech laments are they exempted from such abuse, and only then do they occupy an inviolable space outside the obscene parameters of the farce. Just as medieval women were regarded as sexually promiscuous, so were they accused of garrulousness. Old women, in particular, tended to be seen as windbags and gossips. Perhaps for this reason their vacuous speech was compared with the obscene sound of breaking wind. As Jan Ziolkowski has pointed out, this association derives from the polysemy of the Latin noun *anus*, meaning "anus" and "old woman, hag," common in mnemonic rhymes of medieval Latin poetry.[17] We find the same parallel in the Museum MS of *The Ointment Seller*:

Master, I was over there, starting to heal people,
when old hags started farting under my nose.[18]
(Lines 82–83)

The recompense for reckless female speech is a beating by their husbands. After the ointment seller's wife has finished berating her spouse, he beats her in a scene reminiscent of the realistic satire *On Cobblers* (c. 1360s), in which a cobbler, having gambled away all the money his wife had saved to buy clothes and food for their children, proceeds to flog her in a drunken rage.[19]

Women and Jews

It is in their alleged association with sorcery and promiscuity that women — above all old women and prostitutes — were equated with Jews. The merchant's assistant is the Jewish clown Rubín, who appears in various western plays as Ruvey, Rupin, Robinet, and Rüfel. He must also be a close relation of the Jew Rewfin in the English Coventry play. Ostensibly, Rubín would appear to be the protagonist of the play's humor rather than its object. After all, it is he who generates much of the obscene mockery in the play. So much is true; yet we should not forget how often in contemporary popular culture, minority figures are at once the instigators and victims of their own humor. An obvious equivalent from contemporary culture is the token closeted gay so popular in the British music-hall tradition of the 1930s and 1940s and more recently on British television. Within such a tradition, it was invariably the British gay minority that was being mocked by the majority, not vice versa. The same principle, I submit, characterizes the figure of the medieval Jew in the perception of the Christian majority. The humor instigated by Rubín and his comic sidekick Pustrpalk allows the author and audience to reinforce the artificial difference between the outsider and themselves. And it is the anxiety that this artificial differentiation engenders that fuels much of the play's obscene humor. For example, when Rubín introduces himself to the merchant Severín as a native "of Venice" (z Benátek), the humor lies in the fact that the Czech term Benátky refers both to the Italian city and to a brothel, since the Mistress of the Adriatic had the reputation as the medieval capital of prostitution.[20] In addition, Benátky was not an uncommon place-name in Bohemia. Thus Rubín is deriding himself as an outsider mascarading as an insider, just as the contemporary gay comedian exposes his sexual deviance in the very act of asserting his normality. And like the contemporary token gay, the medieval Jew had a reputation for promiscuity and sexual aberration, as the association of Judaism with prostitution implied. In medieval Frankfurt, for example, it was thought both economical and witty to place brothels in the *Judengasse,* far from the gentile majority.[21] The origins of the equation between Judaism and prostitution reach back to the patristic writings of the church fathers; as early as the fifth century, the poet Prudentius (348–c. 410) compared sinful Jersualem with "an unclean woman."[22]

Another example of how the anxiously precarious line between the insider and the outsider engenders much of the play's humor comes in the Schlägel Fragment when Pustrpalk addresses Rubín with a comic echo of a well-known couplet from the vernacular verse life of the revered Bohemian saint Procopius:

We know you, of what lineage you are:
surely you are a bumbailiff's son from Český Brod.[23]
(Lines 101–2)

To claim—as does Roman Jakobson—that it is Procopius's hagiography that is being parodied here seems to me to misconceive how the play's obscene humor functions.[24] In recognizing the allusion to the verse *Legend of Saint Procopius,* the audience would have been amused by the absurdity of a despised Jewish rent collector's son being equated with a beloved Bohemian saint. In other words, the couplet's comic function serves to mock the outsider Rubín, not the insider Procopius.

Rubín's disloyal behavior to his employer, the merchant quack, only reinforced the common prejudice that Jews were (like women) innately devious and treacherous. Rubín's most egregious act of mischief is to substitute ointment with human feces. Such disrespect for the anointed bodies of the dead comports with the well-established medieval prejudice that Jews took great pleasure in desecrating the sacramental Body of Christ by mutilating it with knives and sticks in a reenactment of the crucifixion.[25] In one episode, which is found nowhere else in the corpus of medieval mystery plays, Rubín sells a pot of excrement to the Jew Abraham, claiming that it is an ointment with miraculous powers to bring the dead back to life. He and his master smear the muck on the buttocks of the dead son Izák, who is revived, an inversion of the more usual anointing of the head, the hands, and the feet. This analogy is made explicit in the resuscitated Izák's speech of thanks to the ointment seller:

> Other masters, according to their rule, use their ointments to anoint the head; but you, master, have suited me well by pouring ointment all over my backside. (Lines 315–19)[26]

According to medieval exegesis, the Old Testament story of the sacrifice of Isaac and his delivery from death by the intervention of an angel prefigured the sacrifice of Christ on the cross. Its farcical reenactment in *The Ointment Seller* underscores its comic function as an inversion of the Resurrection.

According to popular medieval belief, Jews were frequently associated with dirt and especially with defecation. In the middle of the twelfth century Peter the Venerable, abbot of Cluny, warned King Louis VII of France that Jews would subject sacred vessels that came into their hands to disgusting and unmentionable indignities.[27] In the thirteenth century, Matthew Paris, a monk of Saint Albans in England, relates the tale of Abraham of Berkhamstead, who allegedly used his privy as a place of storage for a statue of the Virgin and child lodged with him as a security:

> This image the Jew set up in his latrine and, what is thoroughly dishonourable and ignominious to mention, as it were in blasphemy of the blessed Virgin, he inflicted a most filthy and unmentionable thing on it, daily and nightly, and ordered his wife to do the same. Noticing this after some days, by reason of her sex, she felt sorry and, going there secretly, washed the dirt from the face of the disgracefully defiled statue. When the Jew her husband found out the truth of this, he impiously and secretly suffocated his wife.[28]

This obscene antiexemplum provides an inverted parallel to the hagiographical topos of the female saint weeping in secret before a holy image.

In a popular Latin vita of Saint Catherine of Alexandria (*Fuit in insula Cypri rex quidam nomine Costus*), the pagan virgin locks herself in her chamber with an icon of the Madonna and child, where she sheds tears as she prays.[29] Catherine excretes the sacred bodily fluid of tears from the head while the Jew Abraham, conversely, releases his obscene bodily fluid from the anus. The identity of Jews and women was thus defined through their bodies.[30] One might speak here of the psychological process of "projective inversion," whereby a positive bodily act (weeping before an icon) is inverted as a negative bodily act (defecating on a religious image) and then projected onto a despised or feared social group.[31]

In *The Ointment Seller*, Abraham's inability to distinguish between the true ointment and its scatological substitute confirmed the medieval belief that Jews stank.[32] This prejudice partly derived from the traditional equation of money with filth or dirt. As instruments of the Czech kings' fiscal policies, Jews became linked with money, the root of all evil. Equally important in Abraham's inability to recognize the excrement is the patristic notion of Jewish blindness. Saint Ambrose (339–97), bishop of Milan and one of the four doctors of the church, personified Judaism as a blind woman: "Juda, along with the blind people, rejects the clear path of truth."[33] Crucial in this connection is the typological representation of *Synogoga*—the negative counterpart to *Ecclesia* (the church)—as a blind woman, incapable of distinguishing between doctrinal truth and falsity.[34] In one interesting image of the crucifixion, the angel directs *Ecclesia* to the Lord on the cross, while the same angel drives away *Synogoga*, represented as an old woman who raises her arms in fright.[35]

If women and Jews were stigmatized with anal and genital imagery, they were not alone; so were Germans and heretics. According to fourteenth-century Latin songs composed by Prague students, the treacherous Germans originated in the anus of Pontius Pilate.[36] Jerome of Prague, a follower of John Hus who was burned at the stake in 1416 at the order of the Council of Constance, was accused—among his many alleged crimes—of defecating upon a crucifix.[37] The metaphorical connection between these groups is not accidental here, since excrement is the refuse of the body, eliminated as detrimental, foul, unneeded, and unwanted. These social groups occupied a similar position in relation to medieval Bohemian society.

A further aspect of the medieval equivalence between Jews and women was the widespread belief that male Jews menstruated.[38] Like feces, a foul-smelling and unneeded bodily waste released from the genital area, menstrual blood has an interesting counterpoint in the image of Christ on the cross from the Gospel of John, a scene in which the soldier's lance pierces the side of Christ, whence flow blood and water, presumably sweet-smelling and pure. The open wound then becomes a token for convincing the doubting Thomas of the reality of the death and Resurrection, as opposed to the vaginal or anal openings, which signify death and putrefaction. Ironically, in many late medieval images of Christ's body on the cross, the wound actually resembles a vagina, as in the statue of the crucifixion from the Carmelite convent at Prague (c. 1350).

The smearing of the feces on Izák's buttocks also identifies the Jews with the sin of sodomy, a sexual counterpart to their perceived doctrinal inversion.[39] In the right-hand console of the portal of the Saint Wenceslas Chapel (1367) in the Cathedral of Saint Vitus in Prague, the Devil has mounted the figure of Judas from the rear and is about to wrench his soul from his mouth as the latter plunges into the everlasting flames of hell. This scene portrays in the most repressed yet flagrant fashion a Christian phantasm: if we invert the body parts and the gestures that accompany them—substituting the anus for the mouth, and the act of incision for the act of excision—we have a sodomitical spectacle in which Judas, the evil prototype of medieval Jewry in the Christian perception, is a central participant.

Circumcision was further evidence to medieval Christians that the male Jewish body was defective, unnatural, and incomplete. In a passage attacking the Jewish custom of circumcision and clearly fearful of the need to assert the normative status of the Christian male body, Saint Ambrose of Milan claims that Jews—again like old women and prostitutes—are synonymous with sterility and genital emasculation: "The Christian people are known by their faces, not by their genitals; by baptism, not by a scar."[40]

A correlative of genital and anal imagery for medieval people was sickness, pollution, and death. Old women, prostitutes, and Jews were all considered unclean. Jews were not allowed to handle Christian food at the marketplace unless they purchased it. This prejudice sheds light on an enigmatic mock Hebrew phrase uttered by a Jewish character in the Schlägel Fragment of *The Ointment Seller*: "Judeus dicat, cantat: 'chyry, chyry, achamary!'" According to Jakobson, these words may be Old Czech for "Diseases, diseases! alas and death!"[41] The doctrinal justification for linking Jews with death was their rejection of the life and resurrection of Christ. The Latin play *Ludus de Antichristo* (before 1160) makes Judaism scorn Christ's promise of life after death:

'Tis strange if he yields to death
Who gives life to others.
Can anyone be saved by him
Who is not able to save himself?[42]

Jews were even thought to have introduced the Black Death into European society by poisoning the water supply.[43] In his entry for the year

1349, one Bohemian chronicler relates that many people were dying of the plague in Bohemia and Moravia and that the Jews were accused of poisoning the wells.[44]

Women, Jews, and Germans

According to Veltrusky, the sacred and the farcical aspects of the play divide along clear-cut, dichotomous linguistic lines: the Latin verses sung by the three Marys articulate the sacred message of the story while the vernacular speeches of the other characters are restricted to profanities. But Veltrusky's distinction between the sacred function of Latin and the secular function of the vernacular is not quite hermetic, since the sacred message of the play is sung in both languages. Underlying the Latin-Czech dyad is a more subtle distinction between the elevated discourse of the faithful (for example, the speech of the three Marys) and the denigrated discourse of the outsiders. Although this denigrated discourse is more often than not articulated in the Czech language, there are also interesting examples of third and fourth language elements in the play (mock Hebrew and German).

Hebrew-sounding incantations were commonplace in the medieval mystery plays of Europe, and were often seen in a more sinister fashion as magical, malevolent incantations. It is important to note here that the three languages of the play discussed so far—Latin, Hebrew, and Czech—have an interesting resonance with the three languages of the Cross (Latin, Hebrew, and Greek). The mock Hebrew incantation parodies through inversion Christ's despairing words on the Cross, "Eli, eli lama sabachtani" ("My God, my God, why hast thou forsaken me?").

Like Hebrew, German functions as a language of mockery and exclusion in the play. When the German merchant Severín is looking for his servant, he speaks in corrupt German (note the Czech vocative form of the name): "Rubíne, vo pistu kvest?" ("Rubín, where have you been?") (Museum MS, line 74). Rubín responds to his master's German question with a shameless Czech rhyme, which sounds like an obscene parody of a liturgical antiphon: "Here, master, [holding] a hairy bitch by the arse." As Robert Pynsent has explained, the South German past participle *kvest* ("been") in the question sounds identical to the Czech verb *kvést* ("to blossom," in transferred sense, "to get a hard-on") while *pistu* resembles Old Czech *pizdu* ("cunt").[45] Pynsent suggests that the whole phrase could mean, in comically faulty Czech, "Got a hard-on 'cause you want a cunt?" When Rubín, in the Schlägel MS, is looking for his co-worker Pustrpalk, he also speaks in German: "Pustrpalku, vo pistu?" (95). This line would have reminded the audience of God's anxious words as he seeks Adam after the latter has eaten of the fruit of knowledge (Genesis 3.9). The low-life German merchant and the Jew Rubín are both cast incongruously in the role of God the Father. Their obscene questions incite promiscuity, a perverse inversion of God's commandment to Adam and Eve to desist from sin. In this and in the earlier example of the mock Hebrew lament, Czech—the language of the majority—is utilized to mock and exclude the Other while reinforcing doctrinal orthodoxy. Like the mock Hebrew incantation cited earlier, however, the humor derives less from an exact Czech meaning that can be attached to the German words than the fact that two high and low registers are simultaneously present in one phrase. The macaronic oscillation between innocuous German and obscene Czech in Severín's question produces an inverted parody of the Latin-Czech sacred chant of the three Marys, thus forming a linguistic parallel to the play's use of obscene mimicry.

A similar strategy of highlighting the obscenity of foreign speech exists in contemporary popular culture. A stand-up comic on American television recently compared the Japanese exclamation "aaaaaah!" with the sound of a man evacuating his bowels. Here foreign speech is funny (to the domestic audience) not only because it sounds strange but because it mimes a disgusting bodily function, which constitutes a secular equivalent to the medieval religious taboos associated with dirt and sex. Perhaps medieval and modern notions of how to (mis)represent the Other are not so very different as we sometimes think.

It is within this process of displacement from theological onto secular taboos that we can offer a definition of *obscenity* that will straddle the past and the present and therefore circumvent the trap of anachronism. What has characterized our analysis of religious, ethnic, and generic forms of alterity is the metaphor of the body. If the deployment of this metaphor has changed across time—suitably desacralized and secularized to reflect our secular culture—what has remained a constant is *the trope of inversion* as a permanently defining principle of obscene behavior. Inversion describes a doctrinal, sexual, and political turning away from (*in-vertere*) the socially accepted norm. Thus obscenity may be defined as the multifarious manifestation of this deviation from a preordained and regulated set of rules.

Conclusion

Veltrusky is surely correct in her premise that *The Ointment Seller* reconciles the farcical with the sacred. The selling of the excrement to Abraham and the obscene resuscitation of Izák are intended to remind the audience of the anointing of Christ's crucified body and his eventual glorious resurrection. Where I differ from Veltrusky is how to understand the relationship between the farcical and the sacred. For Veltrusky, the articulation of the sacred takes the Bakhtinian form of a universal mockery of all categories of society, which provides a necessary lifting of the lid of societal repression. Christian doctrine is not seriously undermined, goes this argument, because it allows itself to be parodied at a specific juncture in the religious year—the so-called *risus paschalis*—when the carnivalesque and the sacred collude in a curious dialectic of mutual tension and affirmation. This model implies, as we have seen, a universal mockery of mankind that I find incompatible with the way power actually functions in the late medieval world. Obscenity functions not to deride mankind as a totality but to draw a distinction between an unmarked, unmocked majority and a ridiculed category of outsiders. For Veltrusky, the episode with the feces serves as a parody of the Resurrection; that is to say, the object of the humor is the resurrection itself. How such a subversive practice is compatible with the interests of orthodoxy seems to me to be problematic. The way the humor reinforces, rather than undermines, orthodoxy is by creating an *inversion* of the Resurrection, a reverse reflection of a sacred event that is possible only with a cast of outsiders. The efficacy of this trope of inversion is contingent on the distinction between insiders and outsiders. As we have seen, the insiders are equated with the sacred parts of the body (the head, shoulders, face), while the outsiders are identified with the lower, shameful regions of the anus and genitalia. As Michael Camille has pointed out in a recent essay on the medieval body, vertical hierarchies of heaven and earth, the cosmic and the social, ruled human physiology in the Middle Ages. If the head, the locus of baptism, sacred anointing, and crowning, was the *prima regio*, the genital area was, by contrast, the fourth and lowest region, "a site of shame, the uncontrollable Augustinian signal of man's Fall."[46] Analogously, the medieval vision of hell was commonly expressed as an anal orifice into which heretics and sodomites were sucked. In Middle High German, the word *Ketzerei* meant both "heresy" and "sodomy," since both forms of deviance involved the inversion of doctrinal and sexual norms.[47]

Within the category of the outsiders we can identify various levels of vertical hierarchy. In medieval Bohemia Jews and women were regarded as lower than Germans, who are correspondingly subjected to less obscene mockery in the play as a whole. In spite of these secondary and tertiary distinctions, the construction of a denigrated Other is fundamental to all formations of a positively marked identity and to the ability of those in power to perpetuate their ideological sway over the majority. As universal and popular entertainment, the sacred drama of the Middle Ages presents a particularly accurate barometer of everyday prejudices about and perceptions of the Other. The fifteenth-century English Croxton *Play of the Sacrament* includes the interpolated comic episode of the quack who performs parodic miraculous healings. Here the money-grabbing physician in question is a Fleming who lives in a tollhouse. This ethnic detail reflects English economic resentment against Flemish incursions into the lucrative East Anglian wool trade.[48]

Although Christian theology has itself become increasingly liminal since the Enlightenment, marginalized by the secular and scientific be-

lief in Man, the Christian practice of using the perfect body to distinguish between insiders and outsiders has continued to play a vestigial,
yet still effective, ideological role in the exercise of power in modern
culture. Consider, for example, the preoccupation with hygiene and bodily
functions demonstrated by commercials on American television. These
tend to prey upon our anxiety about bodily decay, a secular displacement from the Christian yearning for immortality and corporeal integrity at the Resurrection: if modern bodies cannot be physically resurrected at the end of time, they can at least be preserved and cleansed in
a perpetually hygienic present by any number of sprays, unguents, and
creams.

If there is indeed a displacement from the medieval Christian sancti-
fication of Christ's body onto the modern fethishization of the hygienic,
healthy body, what is the modern referent of the inverted body parts of
the anus and the vagina that Christianity equated with Jews, prostitutes, and old women? Has this negative equivalent withered away as a
useless appendage of a bigoted past? I think not. The urge to vilify the
Other by means of the inverted body persists in the late twentieth century. To be sure, obscene inversion has lost its theological valency. Instead
of the doctrinal outsider—the Jew and the fallen woman—the trope of
inversion is deployed to vilify the ethnic, economic, or political outsider.
During the Persian Gulf War, an American T-shirt depicted a camel with
its rear end facing the viewer, an image of Saddam Hussein's face super-
imposed on the anal cavity. The accompanying slogan punned: "America will not be Saddam-ized."[49] Here the Iraqi dictator is equated both
with sodomy and with excrement to be flushed out as so much waste.
But, as in the Middle Ages, the most effective medium for the authorities
to exercise power and enjoin the support of the population at large is
popular culture. Obscene imagery of lower body parts (especially the anus)
is frequently deployed to demonize outsiders in Hollywood cinema, the
closest modern equivalent to medieval street drama. In the film *Brave-
heart* (1995), the English oppressors of Scotland are mocked as sodomites
when the wild Scots, lined up for battle, bare their backsides in a defiant
taunt to the invaders. In *Independence Day* (1996), the body of a captured alien invader of earth emits a foul stench akin to excrement when
it is operated upon by the scientists. Throughout this film, the aliens
are equated with the anus and, by extension, with sodomy; hence the
inclusion of a remark like "kicking E.T.'s butt"; the scene of alien space-
craft pursuing a human pilot through narrow, anal-like rock crevices;
and the inverted phantasm of the aircraft entering the alien spaceship
through a narrow, anal-like fissure in the final sequence of the film. The
relationship between exclusion, obscenity, and social control, therefore,
is very real and its consequences frequently dangerous,[50] and to represent the enemy through the trope of inversion is the surest way to guarantee his radical, inexorable vilification. Inversion implies obscenity,

which calls for cleansing or purgation. In the Middle Ages this purgation tended to take the crude form of burning bodies; for modern man, the results are the same even if the technological apparatus is more sophisticated. In the imaginary world of movies, this yearning is disguised by inverting and then projecting it onto the Other. Perceived in this light, the alien genocide of earth in *Independence Day* can be seen as a projection of America's fantasy of world dominion. Instead of bonfires to burn heretics, Jews, witches, and sodomites,[51] our century has made use of guns, gas ovens, and bombs to eradicate the obscenity of alien bodies.

CHAPTER 5

✛

A Bohemian *Imitatio Christi*
The Legend of Saint Procopius

To strengthen his dynastic links with the kingdom of Bohemia, Charles IV revived almost everything associated with its history and its church, including the Old Church Slavonic liturgy. In 1347 he founded the Slavonic Monastery (Monasterium Slavorum) and invited Benedictine monks from Croatia to practice the Slavonic liturgy in Prague. On March 29, 1372, the archbishop of Prague, John Očko of Vlašim, consecrated the monastery and dedicated it to the Virgin Mary and the Slavonic patrons Jerome, Cyril, Methodius, Adalbert, and Procopius. The ceremony was attended by the emperor, his son Wenceslas, many of his Luxembourg relations, and the whole court.[1] The foundation and consecration of the Slavonic Monastery was part of the emperor's grand plan to make Bohemia the spiritual and temporal heart of his vast empire. Practiced at the Sázava Monastery until its dissolution at the end of the eleventh century, the Slavonic liturgy embodied Bohemia's providential role at the spiritual crossroads of eastern and western Christendom.

A central figure in this revival was the founder of the original Sázava Monastery, the Benedictine abbot Procopius, whose cult became particularly popular around the middle of the fourteenth century. In fact, we might more accurately speak of several cults, since, as we shall see in the course of this chapter, the life of Saint Procopius meant different things to different people. The diversity of opinion about what a Christlike life should entail tended to divide along dichotomous reformist versus orthodox lines. For those who supported the Bohemian reform movement, the significance of Procopius's life — as in any Christological typology — lay in his dedication to preaching and his espousal of poverty; for the Dominican friars at the university and within court circles, his principal importance derived from his activity as a lay preacher and as a sacerdotal dispenser of absolution; for the radical Hussites in the fifteenth century, the emphasis was placed on his anti-German role in driving out the foreign monks from the Sázava Monastery.

The three extant Czech versions of Procopius's life — two in prose and one in verse — exemplify these differing perspectives on Procopius's life and ministry. Informing all three, however, is an attempt to reconcile the historical with the transcendental and the social with the theological aspects of the legend. For the Hussites and for their fourteenth-century forebears, Procopius was at once a local Bohemian saint and a universal exemplar of Christlike perfection. As David Aers has put it in connection with the *imitatio Christi* in Langland's *Piers Plowman*, "The model and imitation of Christ contributes forcefully to the poet's refusal to separate the spiritual from the social, the individual pursuit of the virtuous life, of salvation, from the pursuit of justice in communities where what might count as justice seem far from clear."[2] This social *and* religious vision of Procopius's life has been occluded by Czech Marxist criticism, which emphasizes the secular and teleological aspect of the verse legend's ideological message. I have argued elsewhere that this anachronistic perspective distorts the medieval understanding of human existence as a quest toward the perfect Christlike life.[3] The principal aim of this chapter, then, is to explore with close reference to the verse *Legend of Saint Procopius* the manner in which it combines religious and social ideals to create a localized form of piety — a specifically Bohemian *imitatio Christi* — within the larger community of the Church universal.[4] This aspiration has been defined by the prominent English historian John Bossy as the modest goal of the Hussite reformers of the fifteenth century.[5]

The Three Czech Versions and Their Latin Sources

The oldest extant Latin version of his legend (dating from the eleventh to the twelfth centuries) is the so-called *Vita s. Procopii antiqua,* allegedly based on a lost Old Church Slavonic redaction (1061–67), the official language of the liturgy at the Sázava Monastery.[6] The *Vita antiqua* was the source of the *Vita s. Procopii minor* on which all the subsequent Latin and Czech adaptations of the story are based. These vitae of Saint Procopius are extant in at least fifty manuscripts and reflect the growth and popularity of his cult in the mid–fourteenth century.[7] The most important Czech version of the saint's life is the verse *Legend of Saint Procopius* (c. 1350s). At 1,084 lines, it is by far the longest of the three vernacular versions and presents a dynamic, lively account of the saint's life based closely on the mid-fourteenth-century *Vita s. Procopii maior.* The story, according to the *Vita maior* and its Czech adaptation, which coincide in most particulars, is as follows:

Procopius is a poor Czech peasant from Český Brod who does not play with other children and devotes himself to the affairs of the church. As a young man he becomes a canon at Vyšehrad but, following a conversation with an elderly Benedictine monk, receives the habit of the order. Consistent with the Benedictines' avowal of poverty, Procopius goes to a desolate site in his native region where, two leagues from Kouřím, he finds a cave by the Sázava River. Having banished the devils that inhabit the cave, Procopius builds a cottage and a chapel dedicated to the Virgin Mary. Procopius remains there for some time undisturbed by the outside world, until, one day, Duke Ulrich, having lost his retinue during the hunt, sees a deer with a cross mounted between its antlers, which leads him to the place where Procopius is cutting wood. The monk hears the duke's confession. The duke then asks Procopius for a cup of water to drink. Procopius draws the water from the Sázava River and gives a cup to Ulrich, who drinks delicious wine instead of water. Recognizing in Procopius a saintly man who has performed a miracle, Ulrich decides to found a monastery on the spot and insists on appointing the reluctant Procopius as its first abbot. Procopius proves to be an excellent abbot. He also performs many miracles, such as causing a boat to ferry a pilgrim named Menno of its own accord. Procopius also exorcises an evil spirit from a tormented man. Later Procopius drives a group of devils out of a cave. There follows the miracle of sight restored to a blind woman. One day a leper comes to the monastery and after a week's stay, intends to return home. Procopius is sad that he has nothing to give the leper as a farewell gift. But God has told him that he will die on the third day, so Procopius persuades the visitor to wait so that he will receive his habit after his death. Procopius prophesies that after the death of Břetislav (Duke Ulrich's successor) and under the rule of the ill-counseled Spitihněv, the Slavonic monks will be expelled from the Sázava Monastery and replaced by German monks devoted to the Latin rite of the Roman Catholic Church. He also foretells that one day the Slavonic monks will return to the monastery and the Slavonic rite will be reintroduced. After the death of the abbot, his habit is given to the leper, who puts it on and is immediately cured of his disease. Spitihněv drives out the Slavonic monks and introduces their Roman Catholic counterparts. The saint's ghost comes to the German monks and tells them to leave or they will be punished by God. This visit is repeated twice more; on the third day Procopius uses his stick to drive out the monks by force. Spitihněv dies as a punishment for failing to heed the German monks' warning, and is succeeded by Vratislav, who brings back the Slavonic monks from their exile in Hungary and reinstates them in the Sázava Monastery. The story concludes with the fulfillment of Procopius's prophecy.

In addition to the verse legend, two Czech prose versions of the legend survive, *The Older Czech Prose Legend*, based on the *Vita s. Procopii minor*, and *The Younger Czech Prose Legend*, based loosely on the *Vita s. Procopii maior*. The former is the accomplished work of an anonymous Dominican friar writing for a court audience at the command of Charles IV. Forming part of the Czech prose *Passional* (dated to the third quarter of the fourteenth century), it amplifies two Dominican concerns:

the importance of preaching to the laity and the sacramental rite of penitence: "His [Procopius's] pronouncements the Holy Spirit made sweet for sinners, and so many heard him gladly, sighing with regret for their sins and repenting with tears as they made their way back home."[8] Although it tells the same story as the version in verse, *The Older Czech Prose Legend* differs in one crucial respect. It does not present the expulsion of the Slavonic monks from Sázava in terms of contemporary Czech-German ethnic relations and as the consequence of an avowedly anti-Czech or ethnically driven policy—as the verse version does—but as the evil deed of the German abbot. Thus when the ghost of Procopius returns to the monastery to confront the enemy, it is this individual and not the Germans as an ethnic group whom he castigates and finally expels by violent means. Writing for a court audience, the Dominican author of *The Older Czech Prose Legend* is not concerned with stirring up ethnic strife but with affirming orthodox values, in particular, the sacraments of marriage and confession. Consequently, all references to Procopius's marriage and to his son are glossed over.

Perhaps the most interesting feature of *The Older Czech Prose Legend* from the social point of view is the moral it draws about the envy of inferiors within hierarchies. The harmonious relationship between Procopius and Duke Ulrich in the legend serves as a paradigm for the intimate rapport between churchmen and the king of Bohemia. But Charles's early support for reforming preachers like Konrad Waldhauser, who attacked the mendicant orders for their corruption, and Milíč, the ex-Dominican and chancellery official turned charismatic preacher, must have been a source of considerable anxiety to Charles's clerical counselors. Particularly significant, in this regard, is the following aside addressed to those in power:

> Observe, you kings and princes, how much evil envy works in brotherhoods. The sin of envy does not suffer truth, and whatever it cannot have for itself, it seeks through evil words to obtain from all. If an abbot or superior wishes to instill veneration and piety into his brotherhood, he must suffer many lying speeches against himself from his inferiors. Therefore it is not always appropriate to believe all speeches.[9]

The last line is particularly significant as an admonition to the ruler to be wary of his enthusiasm for dangerously idiosyncratic preachers. Given that the author of the legend was a high-ranking Dominican within court circles, the reference to "inferiors" within the brotherhood may be an allusion to the former Dominican Milíč.

The Younger Czech Prose Legend leaves us in no doubt as to the author's political agenda.[10] More avowedly xenophobic and more extreme in its pronouncements than the verse legend, this version has been attributed on the basis of its anti-German sentiments to an anonymous Hussite of the early fifteenth century. Here the universal conflict between good and evil that characterizes the older versions of the story becomes a localized and polarized struggle between Czechs and Germans for the political control of Bohemia:

> Let us request him [Procopius] to defend us, drive our enemies from the land, and afford us peace and quiet, for he is our defense and the patron of the Czech land. Close to the German lands, Bohemia would have perished long ago if Saints Procopius and Wenceslas had not protected it.[11]

The Verse Legend of Saint Procopius

Recent research into medieval hagiography suggests that Latin and vernacular versions of saints' lives were intended for different audiences: prose works in Latin were conceived as edifying reading and listening for clerics or monks and were delivered either at the lectionary (as part of sermons) or in the refectory. Vernacular saints' lives, conversely, were frequently written in verse for the oral entertainment of a larger, more heterogeneous audience of laypeople.[12] While the monks were a captive audience at prayer or at meals, the layperson could come and go at will, requiring the adaptor to make the story as lively as possible in order to maintain the listener's attention.[13] Authorial interjections, appeals to the audience, and the use of frequent dialogue helped to entertain as well as to edify. Verse was a versatile medium, since it allowed the performer to extemporize and expand or contract the story as he went along. If the audience seemed distracted, for example, he could easily include a formulaic apostrophe to attract its attention or cut out an episode that was beginning to pall. *The Verse Legend of Saint Procopius* includes several such formulae typical of oral recitation style, as the opening apostrophe illustrates: "Listen, old ones and children, to what I wish to tell you about our Slavonic inheritance, and about Saint Procopius, who was born in Bohemia" (lines 1–3).[14]

The *Verse Legend* survives in a unique copy in the early-fifteenth-century *Hradec Králové Codex*, which is now housed in the university library in Prague.[15] The legend is written on leaves 1a to 29a, with the second leaf missing.[16] The fact that only one copy of the text has survived further supports the claim that it was recited to large group of people rather than read privately.[17]

The manuscript contains several works of related devotional and homiletic interest, such as *The Lament of Mary Magdalen* (leaves 29a–51b), *The Lament of the Virgin* (leaves 51b–61b), *The Nine Joys of the Virgin Mary* (leaves 61b–74b), *The Lord's Passion* (leaves 75a–94a), *The Decalogue* (leaves 94a–120b), *Hail Mary* (leaves 120b–123a), *Saint John the*

Evangelist (leaves 123b–124b), *The Satires of the Artisans* (leaves 125a–130a, 132a–138b), *The Fable of the Fox and the Jug* (leaves 131a–131b), and *The Composition about the Rich Man* (leaves 138b–146b).[18] These works were considered worthy of preservation because of their shared religious themes: *The Lament of Mary Magdalen* is based on a well-known Latin homily traditionally ascribed to Origen,[19] *The Decalogue* illustrates the Ten Commandments with reference to contemporary social issues, and *The Satires of the Artisans* present the sins of perfidy and pride in terms of dishonest tradesmen and corrupt legal officials. Even the seemingly slight *Fable of the Jug and the Fox* is based on a Latin sermon exemplum on the need for repentance.[20]

That the manuscript was probably compiled for the provincial Czech-speaking gentry—perhaps by a poor member of the Benedictine rule—is borne out by the antiurban and anti-German bias of both *The Satires of the Artisans* and *The Verse Legend*. Until the second half of the fourteenth century, when Czech speakers began to settle in what is now the New Town of Prague, there was a clear ethnic division between the German towns and the Czech countryside: Germans dominated the Old Town and the Small Side of the capital. But these localized elements have to be seen within the overall religious context of the time. William Langland's *Piers Plowman* contains opprobrious references to the moral corruption of bakers, butchers, and other artisans. In the same way, the sinners castigated in the Czech *Decalogue* and the artisans censured in the *Satires* were intended as a mirror of mankind's failings.[21] By contrast, Saint Procopius provides a virtuous model of the Christlike life. Thus several of the works in the codex present a unity of intention. The artisans and legal officers singled out in the satires personify the vices of self-indulgence and pride, whereas the peasant Procopius embodies Christlike asceticism and humility. The artisans cheat their customers and the judges subvert the law, while Procopius performs pious deeds for the benefit of the poor and sick. Thus the works in the *Hradec Králové Codex* contrast virtue with vice, humility with pride, and asceticism with greed. Within these dichotomies we can also detect an opposition between virtuous Czech peasants and wicked German artisans and officials.

It is not difficult to conclude that the author of the verse legend speaks for the Czech-speaking gentry in his antagonism toward the German burghers and German clerics who dominated the Bohemian church. Ethnicity and class coincide in the legend, since the Germans in Bohemia tended to be merchants or clerics. Of great significance in this respect is the author's admonition to those "outsiders" who refuse to dispense charity to the poor: "Listen, you foreign merchants and all you traveling singers who wander through the world and cheat people, who steal others' goods, beware of your soul's damnation from which there is no redemption, only eternal torment" (lines 619–26).[22] Typical of local saints' lives is this kind of parochial, insular suspicion of "outsiders"—

those who speak another language, do a different kind of work, or come from a different region from that of the initiated audience. As Donald Weinstein and Rudolph Bell state, "Christian practise has always been inclined to accommodate the human need to create structures of identity—to separate 'us' from 'them.' "[23]

In its concentration on Procopius's Christlike poverty and care for the needs of the poor, the legend is typical of the spirit of the Benedictine rule. But its attack on the corruption of the rich and its violent apocalyptic ending (the driving out of the German monks from the monastery) are also redolent of the Caroline reform movement. In the 1360s and 1370s, the preachers Waldhauser and Milíč were clamoring for radical religious reform in the church and in society in general. These preachers were influenced by pervasive notions of the approaching end of the world and the Second Coming of Christ. Driven by such chiliastic ideas, Milíč even went so far as to identify Emperor Charles with the Antichrist, the personification of evil in the medieval mind.[24] *The Verse Legend of Saint Procopius* combines these religious and social concerns, just as, in contemporary England, "religious understanding went hand in hand with evaluations of social evil that were seen as incommensurate with social and religious ideals."[25]

While the historical Procopius was of noble birth, the saintly hero of the verse legend is of humble origins. In hagiographic legends peasant birth is often regarded as a qualification for the kind of miraculous powers possessed by the adult saint.[26] In the detailed description of Procopius's physical appearance (lines 875–96), the author stresses his subject's masculine features—broad shoulders, wide black beard, and penetrating look—in thoroughly conventionalized male terms. Even as abbot, Procopius shuns the trappings of prestige, preferring to retain the clothes and footwear of the poorest member of the Benedictine order.

Both in terms of word and image, medieval hagiographers present the consistent repetition of conventional motifs that minimize—in the words of Magdaleno Carrasco—"the unique spatiotemporal details of historical experience, stressing instead the collective identity of all the saints in fulfilling a divinely ordained pattern originally established by Christ."[27] It was in the context of twelfth-century monasticism that the problem of male monastic identity was discussed and resolved as a collective ideal dedicated to emulating Christ's earthly existence. The life of Procopius exemplifies this stereotypical ideal. As a child, he typifies the Benedictine love of diligent study and shuns the company of frivolous children. We are told in the *Vita maior* that the young Procopius did not play with other children but spent all his time in church.[28] Similarly, the verse legend states that this *venerabilis puer* likes only to sing religious music: "He was never seen to laugh and play with other children; he just sang the *horae* or the *pater noster*, sometimes privately and sometimes in a choir" (lines 55–58).[29] The model of the saintly diligent child is the young Jesus of the New Testament. For example, when Procopius's knowledge of the Scriptures evokes the amazement of his teachers (lines 41–43), it recalls the impact of the young Christ's learning and wisdom on those in the temple (Luke 2.47): "And all that heard him were astonished at his understanding and answers."[30]

Procopius's years of study are spent at Vyšehrad, where he becomes a canon (line 68).[31] Here he conforms to the conventional virtues of Christlike *humilitas*: he is said to be humble (line 65), eschews worldly wealth and power (line 73), and refuses to wear expensive clothes or consume luxurious food and drink (lines 79–80). Procopius's rejection of rich food and drink in favor of a forest diet of wild apples, acorns, and water (lines 156–58) would have been seen as particularly meritorious in the eyes of the medieval audience.[32] In the first of the Ten Commandments enumerated in the Czech *Decalogue*, special opprobrium is attached to the drunkard and to gluttons who hold their own bellies more important than God (line 81).

Following the example of Christ, who abandons his earthly family for the life of the spirit and spends forty days and forty nights in the desert, where he is tempted by Satan (Luke 4.1–3), the young canon turns his back on his family and friends and enters the wilderness, where he—like Jesus—confronts devils (lines 131–34). This parallel with Christ's early mission is explicit only in the *Vita maior* and in the Czech adaptation (lines 131–36).[33] The Czech narrator goes on to tell us that God did not intend the young man's gifts to be hidden under a bushel for long (lines 173–74), for it is in the wilderness that the first miracle associated with him takes place: the turning of water into wine (lines 241–46). This event parallels Christ's first miracle at the marriage at Cana in Galilee.

Following the foundation of the monastery at Sázava and the appointment of Procopius as its first abbot, the author reinforces the identification of the saint with Christ and his monks with the apostles. Like Christ, Procopius witnesses to God's commandments so that his word is heard near and far (lines 292–95). An important feature of biblical parallelism is the simile of the mother hen who gathers her chickens under her wing.[34] Although the simile occurs in the Latin prose model, it originates in the New Testament, where it is closely identified with Christ's pastoral care for his flock. In the Gospel according to Matthew 23.37, Christ likens his role of pastor to the people of Israel to that of a mother hen gathering her chickens under her wing: "O Jerusalem, Jerusalem, thou that killest the prophets and stonest them which are sent unto thee, how often would I have gathered thy children together, even as a hen gathereth her chickens under her wings, and ye would not!"[35] The *Vita maior* introduces the simile twice to evoke the abbot's affective concern for his flock, while the Czech verse legend includes the same simile at three crucial moments in the story to emphasize this relationship even more: "The poor things huddled up to him just like chickens

to their mother hen" (lines 300–301);[36] "I have reared you from the beginning as a mother hen rears her chickens" (lines 745–46);[37] "We poor
ones have been orphaned by you, as chickens by their mother hen" (lines
821–22).[38]

This example of trichotomy is consistent with similar devices of parallelism in other works of Czech literature, for example, in *The Decalogue*, where the definition of each commandment is followed by three
concrete examples of transgression.[39] The Czech chivalric romances *Lavrin*
and *Tandariáš a Floribella* also contain examples of triple parallelism.[40]
In *Saint Procopius*, trichotomy clearly serves both a religious and a struc-
tural function by reminding the listener of key moments in Christ's life,
for example, Peter's three denials of his master after he has been arrested
and the risen Christ's three appearances to the disciples (John 21.14).

Fundamental to the application of the mother hen simile to evoke
Procopius's care for his monks is his gender status. The widespread application of maternal imagery from the twelfth century on to describe
male monastic piety reflects an uncertainty about appropriate gender,
especially the authority of the abbot as head of his monastic flock. In
their writings, twelfth-century Cistercians like Bernard of Clairvaux and
Aelfred of Rievaulx represent Jesus as a mother and abbots as mothers to
temper the severity of traditional masculine roles in monastic society.
According to Caroline Walker Bynum, this anxiety about male authority was related to the need for a new *imago Christi* as loving, nurturing,
and caring to replace the older and decidedly male figure of a remote
and punitive God.[41] We find a particularly good example of Procopius's
gentle qualities in his dealings with the blind woman to whom he re-
stores the gift of sight. As he makes the sign of the cross and blesses her,
he is explicitly compared to Christ, who restored the sight of the blind
(lines 500–501).

But Procopius's words and deeds do not always express maternal gen-
tleness. When appropriate, he can be paternally harsh, even violent, like
Jesus in the New Testament. When he rebukes the devils and drives
them from a cave with a scourge (line 446) his words — "You cursed seed, /
you are of the serpent's line" (lines 449–50)[42] — consciously evoke Jesus'
anger at the corrupt Pharisees in Matthew 23.33: "Ye serpents, ye generation of vipers, how can ye escape the damnation of hell?"[43] Thus even
in anger, Procopius's story forms an exemplary *imitatio Christi*.

At the beginning of the scene with the devils, the author emphasizes
his virtue as a Czech peasant. The devils refer to Procopius as "Czech"
(line 434), implying that they themselves are foreigners. As in many vernacular saints' lives, *Saint Procopius* presents Christian piety in a familiar, accessible form. In the late Middle Ages, saints were seen increasingly
as friends and fellow countrymen.[44] Important in this connection are the
manifold references to local place-names and topographical details in
Saint Procopius. The dates of events and the lineage of Bohemian dukes are

also carefully recorded to reinforce the sense of a local identity. To quote from an authority on medieval English saints' lives, the vernacular legend "anchors the narratives in reality and lends them, to a certain degree, the character of historical narrative, if not historical documentation."[45]

Like Christ in the Gospels, Procopius foresees his own death and prophesies that his followers will be dispersed and eventually reunited. Procopius predicts that the Sázava Monastery will one day be returned to the Slavonic monks. As Weinstein and Bell state, "The most common hagiographic prophecy attributed to holy people was the prediction of their own death, a foreknowledge that stressed the saint's acceptance of mortality and joyful anticipation of impending reunion with God."[46] Not only does the author attach greater prominence to the fulfillment of the prophecy than does the *Vita maior*, he also omits the list of posthumous miracles present in the Latin model. By focusing on the saint's earthly deeds rather than on his supernatural power as a representative of the holy dead, the legend is anticipating the Hussites' aversion for miracles and their preference for Christ's earthly mission.

In accentuating the fulfillment of the prophecy, the legend presents the triumph of the Slavonic rite—and by implication the Czech language—as the culmination of his story. This was a topical theme in the middle of the fourteenth century. By reviving the Slavonic liturgy after its abolition 250 years earlier (in 1096–97), Charles IV intended to strengthen his dynastic links with the past and to reinforce the alliance between the church and the kingdom of Bohemia. In effect, the Czech reformers waylaid the emperor's political plans in order to promote their own ideological agenda. Whereas Charles envisaged the Czech language as one of several equal languages within Bohemia and the empire, the author of the verse legend presents the victory of the Slavonic rite over its Latin counterpart as equivalent to—even an allegory for—the triumph of the Czech language over its German rival. Hence, when Procopius dies, he is eulogized by the narrator as "the glory of the Czech land" (line 832),[47] and when he returns from the dead to warn the German monks to leave the monastery, they are castigated several times as "rivals": "O you unfaithful rivals, / you are the devil's messengers!" (lines 959–60).[48]

In spite of his pro-Czech agenda, the author always presents the struggle between Procopius and his enemies in terms of the religious battle between good and evil. He achieves this by the skillful narrative device of parallelism. When the German monks are confronted by the ghost of Procopius, they are implicitly equated with the devils who took refuge in the cave in the wilderness. The scene of the German monks' violent expulsion from the monastery also parallels the earlier scene of exorcism, when Procopius drives the evil spirits from the cave: "He held his staff with which he mercilessly beat the Germans. The Germans did not have any response, just ran one before the other; they did not bother to ask the way, just jumped along like goats" (lines 1037–42).[49] This scene also recalls Christ's righteous act of driving the moneylenders from the temple in the New Testament. In the Hussite period, this biblical episode came to exemplify the reformers' desire to reform the concupiscence of the church. In the famous *Jena Codex*, for example, the Jewish moneylenders are dressed as corrupt Catholic clerics. Procopius's expulsion of the German monks and his restoration of the exiled Slavonic monks to their rightful inheritance equally suggest the popular medieval episode of the Harrowing of Hell, in which Christ crushes the devil underfoot and leads the Just, the Patriarchs, and Adam and Eve into the light. In the midst of these universal, Christological parallels, however, the author does not forget to mention that the monks were driven "back to Prague" (line 1036), since that city was still equated with the German-speaking patriciate. In art and life, Prague connoted for the rural audience the supreme sin of pride. When, in 1420, Czech peasants came from the countryside to defend Prague from the anti-Hussite league, they stripped the rich clothing from the German burghers, since they regarded their fine array as sinful manifestations of pride.[50]

Procopius's final deed in expelling the German monks and returning the Slavonic brothers to their true inheritance also suggests the millenarianism of the Bohemian reform movement in paralleling Christ's restoration of justice to the earth at his Second Coming. Although the conflict between the Slavonic and Latinist monks narrated in the verse legend mirrors the localized ethnic and political rivalry between Czechs and Germans in fourteenth-century Bohemia,[51] it would also have been perceived as a metaphor for the apocalyptic struggle between God and the devil, in which local historical events were seen *sub specie aeternitatis* as part of the universal presence ordained by God.[52]

CHAPTER 6

The Radiant Rose

Female Sanctity and Dominican Piety in the Czech *Life of Saint Catherine*

The affective sensibility exhibited in the relationship between Christ and female saints in late medieval vernacular hagiographies looks back to the tradition of twelfth-century spirituality, where we first see evidence of a new emphasis on Christ's humanity. The valorization of Christ's flesh inevitably came to encompass and elevate the maternal body that had borne him. This more favorable view of womanhood helps to explain the coexistence of intellectual *and* bodily female ideals in that most cerebral and somatic of saints, Saint Catherine of Alexandria. It has become de rigeur of late to specify the saint's gender as a way of explaining the corporeal emphasis of late medieval female sanctity. Caroline Bynum, for example, argues that gender is overlooked in traditional discussions of eucharistic piety among lay and religious women from the thirteenth century on.[1] In this chapter I shall argue, with close reference to the Czech *Life of Saint Catherine,* that one ought to consider the monastic denomination of the author, the gender of his audience, and that of his chosen saint as a syncretic unity. Just as in late medieval art the male figure of Christ often merges mystically with his mother Mary, so is there frequently a deeply affective bond between a male author, his chosen subject, and the female audience for whom he writes his vita. Such an affective bond is particularly strong in the case of male religious who served women as confessors.

In this chapter, I shall maintain that the probable author of the Czech *Life of Saint Catherine* was a Dominican friar, university professor, courtier, and confessor to Emperor Charles IV and his family. Although there is little extrinsic evidence to support this claim, a great deal of textual authority points to Dominican authorship. I shall argue that the author's status as a member of the Dominican order is as significant to our understanding of the text as the audience for whom it was intended. I detect an important connection between the author's secular and religious concerns as a courtier-priest and the ideals of virginity and maternity propagated in the course of the legend. As we shall see, these ideals tell us a great deal about how the author perceived female sanctity and the religious and social role of his (partly) female audience.

Saint Catherine of Alexandria

Catherine of Alexandria was one of the most popular saints of the Middle Ages, beloved in the eastern and western churches alike. According to legend, she was martyred in A.D. 307. In the eighth century her body was discovered by Egyptian Christians and translated by them to the monastery on Mount Sinai. This monastery was founded by Saint Helen (c. A.D. 250–330), the mother of the emperor Constantine, and was embellished by the emperor Justinian I and renamed in Catherine's honor in A.D. 527. Here her bones were said to exude the heavenly oil with which her wounds were miraculously healed.[2]

The earliest versions of the legend were written in Greek, but from the eleventh century on we find Latin adaptations of the Greek sources. All of these stories deal exclusively with the martyrdom and the debate with the pagan scholars. At a later point, two other episodes (Catherine's conversion through the agency of a hermit and her mystical marriage to Christ) were added to the core story of the debate and martyrdom.[3] The cult of Saint Catherine was one of the most popular in medieval Europe. Numerous images and literary representations of her life and martyrdom survive, most of them based on the immensely popular *Golden Legend* by Jacobus de Voragine.[4] The presence of her relics at the Abbey of Sainte-Trinité-du-Montin Rouen in the first half of the eleventh century probably inspired several of the Latin versions of her life. In fact it was the Abbey of Sainte-Trinité in Rouen that was largely responsible for disseminating the cult of Saint Catherine in northern Europe.[5] Her renown as a teacher and protector increased, the former aided no doubt by the spread of schools, such as the Sorbonne, of which she became the patron saint. Her cult was also important in England, where her legend was one of the most frequently represented subjects in late medieval churches.[6] Several versions of her life are extant in English, ranging from a twelfth-century text in prose for anchoresses to a fifteenth-century verse adaptation by an Augustinian canon from Suffolk.[7]

Saint Catherine owed much of her popularity in fourteenth-century Bohemia and Moravia to Emperor Charles IV, the founder of the University of Prague (1348), who venerated her as a philosopher and teacher. She had also become his personal protector since the Battle of San Felice, fought on Saint Catherine's feast day, November 25, in 1332, when the emperor's army had relieved the fortress besieged by the armies of the Italian League.[8] A passionate collector of relics and a mystic typical of the age in which he lived, the emperor built a church in Catherine's honor in the so-called New Town of Prague (1356) and dedicated a special chapel to her in his castle at Karlstein (after 1347).

On a lintel of the chapel, which served as the imperial oratory, we find a double portrait of the emperor and Empress Anne of Schweidnitz.

Both figures face each other in profile and touch the Holy Cross, which cuts the painting into two distinct halves. This portrait recalls the Byzantine iconographic type of "Constantine and Helen raising the Cross," developed in Constantinople before the ninth century and widely known in Orthodox churches in the Balkan peninsula. It was also found in Byzantine cameos and coins, through which it might have reached Charles's court.[9] According to tradition, Constantine's mother, Saint Helen, discovered the three crosses of the crucifixion, along with the nails, when she went on a pilgrimage to Jerusalem. There she founded a monastery, which was later named for Saint Catherine and which became the resting place of the virgin-martyr's bones. The connection between Saints Helen and Catherine explains why the double portrait of the emperor and the empress was placed in the chapel of Saint Catherine. This chapel provided an architectonic mirror image of the monastery of Saint Catherine on Mount Sinai, thus complementing the Chapel of the Holy Cross as a reflection of the celestial Jerusalem (see Figure 5). The layout of the chapels at Karlstein illustrates the emperor's apocalyptic vision and also his sacral vision of kingship and his desire to unite western and eastern Christianity under his personal rule. The emperor's devotion to Saint

Figure 5. The Chapel of the Holy Cross, Karlstein Castle, Karlstein, Czech Republic.

Catherine was so great that he instructed the archbishop of Prague, Ernest of Pardubice, to set aside November 25 as her holy day.

The Author and His Audience

The anonymous author of *The Life of Saint Catherine* was most probably a member of the emperor's household. Whoever he was, he must have been highly educated, almost certainly a cleric and perhaps attached to the university in some capacity. A figure who fits this profile very well is John Moravec, a Dominican theologian and a professor at the new University of Prague who had studied at Paris and Oxford. John was part of the emperor's inner circle of courtiers, and was entrusted by him with an important diplomatic mission to the papal court of Avignon.[10] He belonged to a preaching order known for using the vernacular in order to spread the word of God to a wide audience of lay men and women. In Germany and in the Low Countries they were especially involved in the Inquisition and in the fostering of female piety.[11] The Dominicans were the spearhead of the emperor's strategy to impose religious unity and orthodoxy on his divided realm. Their presence in Bohemia dates from 1226, when they founded a monastery in the Prague Old Town. In the course of the thirteenth century, nineteen Dominican monasteries were established in Bohemia and Moravia, all of which belonged to the Polish province of the order. Only in 1301 did the Bohemian branch of the Dominicans manage to establish their own independent province. But because of internal discord, in 1307 they were placed under the control of the Saxon provincial master, the mystic Meister Eckhart.[12] The Dominicans in Bohemia and Moravia were theological writers, representatives of German mysticism and instruments of the papal Inquisition. They were especially important to the conservative emperor as enforcers of orthodoxy, both in their capacity as inquisitors and as writers in the vernacular, communicating the tenets of the faith to lay men and women.

The Dominicans had played an influential role at the court of Prague since the reign of Přemysl Ottokar II, who gave special support to the order.[13] His wife, Kunigunde, is known to have lent financial support to the so-called *sorores Rotharinne*, a group of Dominican female religious at Nuremberg.[14] Her daughter, the abbess Kunigunde, had close links with the Bohemian Dominicans Domaslav and Kolda of Koldice. The Czech *Prayer of Lady Kunigunde* (c.1290), with its Thomist devotion to the Eucharist, was most likely written by a Dominican friar.[15]

The emperor Charles invited the Alsatian Dominican theologian John of Dambach (1288–1372) to become the first professor in theology at the University of Prague. John was a pupil of Meister Eckhart and had taught previously at the universities of Paris and Bologna.[16] Like his Alsatian namesake and fellow Dominican, John Moravec was also active as a professor at the University of Prague. In 1348 he was granted the title master of theology by the pope. Like Domaslav and Kolda of Koldice before him, he was active as a writer in the Czech language, and may have had a hand in the first Czech translation of the Vulgate, consistent with the mendicant orders' concern to make God's word available in the vernacular to lay men and women. The mid-fourteenth-century Czech prose *Life of Christ* has also been attributed to a Dominican.[17] In MS University Library (Prague) XVII A 9 of this work, the author informs the reader that he is a member of the Dominican order of preachers, and in MS University Library XVII H 19, leaf 172, he mentions that the work was composed at the instigation of Emperor Charles himself.[18] According to Vilikovský, the Czech prose *Passional* was also composed by a Dominican.[19] In fact, Vilikovský claimed that the *Passional* and *The Life of Christ* were probably the work of the same author.[20] The affective tone of both texts is similar to the language of *Saint Catherine*. Even more revealing are the high-style rhetorical correspondences between the legend and *The Life of Christ*, in particular the use of anaphora in lines 1564–69, 1756–59, 1846–73, and 3298–303. Added to the Dominican preference for affective language that characterizes all three texts, such rhetorical features suggest a single authorship for all three texts.

It is reasonable to assume that the legend was written for the spiritual edification of men and women within court circles, since Catherine provides an example both to knights, because of her courage and faith, and to women, because of her physical *imitatio Christi*. Moreover, virginity and maternity, emphasized in the legend, are the two ideals to which late medieval noble women were expected to aspire, either as nuns or as bearers of healthy male offspring. Although the work was probably commissioned by the emperor, there is a strong possibility that his third wife, Anne of Schweidnitz, was the primary audience, just as Anne of Bohemia was the real-life surrogate for the literary figure of Alceste in Chaucer's *Legend of Good Women*. Significantly, there is a reference to Saint Anne (the mother of the Virgin Mary) in the Czech version of the legend, where there is none in the Latin source. And we should not forget that Empress Anne was praised for her maternal, as well as her intellectual, potential as the mother of the future Holy Roman Emperor by Petrarch in his *De laudibus feminarum*. It is precisely this kind of emphasis that, I suggest, characterizes the Czech legend in its celebration of female intellect and fecundity. The legend was written at about the same time Petrarch penned his *De laudibus feminarum*. The empress was newly delivered of a baby girl, and the illustrious Italian humanist was at pains to reassure the empress that she would soon give birth to a much-needed son and heir to her husband as emperor and king of Bohemia. Such concern with the virtues of motherhood would certainly help to explain the inclusion of maternal bodily imagery in the Czech legend (for instance, a lactating angel in the prison scenes), as well as the more conventional focus on Catherine's virginity and superior intellect.

Sources and the Manuscript

There are seventeen extant Latin manuscripts of the Catherine legend in Prague. These can be divided into three groups: those that (1) relate the conversion and passion (five), (2) confine themselves to the conversion (four), and (3) deal with the passion alone (eight). The Czech author seems to have used two sources, one belonging to the first category and known by its opening words as *Tradunt annales historiae* (which tells the whole story but concentrates on Catherine's dispute with the fifty pagan scholars), the other belonging to the second category (the conversion) and known by its opening words as *Fuit in insula Cypri rex quidam, nomine Costus*, which tells only of Catherine's conversion and her mystical marriage to Christ.[21] The Czech author includes all the episodes found in the two sources (the conversion, the mystical marriage, the debate, and the passion) but reduces the debate with the pagan scholars while amplifying the scourging scene.

The verse legend, written in the standard trochaic meter and octosyllabic line of medieval Czech poetry, is 3,519 lines long and contains certain East Moravian dialect features. According to George Cummins, the extant redaction was one of many Moravian versions copied between 1350 and 1400 and based on an original of Bohemian provenance.[22] If our theory of authorship is correct (John Moravec, as his name indicates, was Moravian), the Moravian linguistic features would also have been present in the original Bohemian redaction. The manuscript is preserved in a paper codex (129 leaves) (Moravian Provincial Library, Brno, III F 6) dated to the beginning of the fifteenth century and is first recorded in a catalog entry by the scribe Wenceslas Březan, dated 1602–8, in the library of Peter Vok of Rožmberk, the last of his illustrious line. Consisting of eleven thousand volumes, Peter's library was the largest in humanist Europe. Until the nineteenth century, the manuscript was a treasure of the Royal Library of Sweden, where it was taken in 1647 as booty of the Thirty Years' War. It was returned to the Bohemian Lands in 1878, along with other manuscripts from the Rožmberk library, and is now in the State Archive in Brno, capital of Moravia. The same codex contains four other titles in Czech, all of a devotional nature: an exposition on the *pater noster*, a prose version of the Passion, a treatise on the battle against sins, and a Good Friday sermon.

The question remains how the manuscript found its way into the Rožmberk library. The Rožmberks were one of the most important and powerful noble families in Bohemia from the thirteenth to the seventeenth century, when the line died out with the death of Peter Vok in 1611. Peter I and his son Peter II were both art lovers and were closely associated with the court of Charles IV. Since the text survives in a unique manuscript dating from the beginning of the fifteenth century, it is likely that it was already in the family library by this time. This hypothesis is supported by the fact that Ulrich of Rožmberk (1403–62) was one of the few Bohemian magnates to remain a Catholic during the Hussite Wars. It was probably during his lifetime that all the other copies of the legend were lost or destroyed. That it survives—miraculously—in one small manuscript may attest to the fact that the Rožmberks would have constituted a suitable audience for such a high Catholic work. Significantly, three female members of the Rožmberk family at this period were named Catherine: Ulrich's first wife, Catherine of Vartenberk (d.1429), his sister (d.1405), and one of his daughters. It is plausible, therefore, that the text was copied and preserved in a family codex to honor the holy namesake of one or all of these Rožmberk women.

The Conversion

The legend tells of how Catherine's father, Costus, king of Cyprus, was banished to Alexandria by the emperor because of a slander of treachery leveled against him by his rivals at the court. In devoting much more space to this episode than the Latin source does (lines 37–71), the author wishes to enliven the rather dry, matter-of-fact tone of his model. Costus is presented in hyperbolic terms as the most trustworthy adviser at the court (lines 37–45), who is maligned like Roland and Ernest (the hero of *Duke Ernest*). Costus is forced into exile by evildoers at the imperial court. The language at this point (lines 51–52) recalls the prologue of the Czech epic *Alexandreida*, which distinguishes between the positive and negative members of his audience and condemns the two-faced men who harbor enmity in their hearts. The plight of Costus also recalls the early episode in *Duke Ernest* in which the eponymous son-in-law of Emperor Otto is slandered by rivals at the court and is forced to undertake the Other-World Voyage to expiate for sins he never committed (lines 820–47). The most striking parallel to our legend, however, is an aside in *The Older Prose Legend of Saint Procopius* in which the Dominican author criticizes the envy of inferiors within the order (see chapter 5).[23] Common to all these parallels is the expression of feudal distrust toward social and class inferiors, whether at the court or the monastery. In the case of *Saint Catherine* and *The Older Prose Legend of Saint Procopius*, it indicates that the author enjoyed a high social status at court and at the university and regarded the reformist elements in Bohemia to be motivated by envy.

Like her father, Catherine is also described in a hyperbolic fashion redolent of chivalric romance: she is said to have received the best education in the world, and these intellectual gifts—added to her striking physical beauty—make her contemptuous of any living suitor. Here, too, Catherine resembles the proud knight of the secular epic. Just as the young Alexander in the *Alexandreida* refuses to lead a subjugated life, so does Catherine reject subordination to any earthly spouse (lines 138–40). The wording in the *Alexandreida* and in *Saint Catherine* is strikingly similar in both passages:

> When he ceased to be a child, he well understood that it is wrong to be subject to someone else.[24]
>
> (Lines 161–63)
>
> For she well understood that it is wrong to live in subjugation, and did not wish to marry.[25]
>
> (Lines 138–40)

The phrasing in lines 163 and 139 respectively is so similar that it is most likely that the author of *Saint Catherine* deliberately echoed the story of the young Alexander in the *Alexandreida* to make his story more congenial to a courtly audience familiar with the narrative conventions of secular epic and chivalric romance. We find the same tendency in thirteenth-century France, when hagiographic writers incorporated lively romance features into their accounts in order to make their rather dry hagiographic subject matter more palatable to a public enamored of the romances of Chrétien de Troyes.[26]

When the wicked emperor Maxentius seeks out her hand in marriage for his son, Catherine refuses. Her disappointed mother solicits the advice of a hermit, who meets the girl and tells her that there is an ideal spouse whose name is Jesus. Catherine desires to see this spouse, and so the hermit takes out a diptych representing Christ and his mother, gives it a vigorous wipe with his sleeve (line 649), and hands it to the girl. Before leaving the hermit's lair, Catherine receives the hermit's absolution (line 669), a detail absent from the source, which illustrates the author's concern with penance (also a Dominican concern). Catherine makes her way home, concealing the diptych under her expansive sleeve (lines 650–51). When night falls, when the residents of the castle are asleep and the lights have been extinguished, Catherine goes into her chamber, locks the door, and opens the diptych. These realistic elements (the hermit dusting the diptych; Catherine hiding it under her sleeve and locking the door behind her) are notably absent from the Latin source[27] and point to the probable influence of contemporary panel painting and especially the art of book illumination.

Significant also is the connection between Catherine's physical gestures and the late medieval belief in the corporeality of female sanctity. Here, too, we find parallels between the word and the image. In contemporary Bohemian art, female tears and imagery of blood often mingle, as in the Deposition scene from the Vyšší Brod Altarpiece. In the legend,

Catherine's longing for her celestial spouse is so intense that her face becomes stained with tears and her eyes become bloodshot: "Tears rolled down her white little face and her eyes became murky and bloodshot from great longing" (698–70).[28] This description is more concrete and physical than the Latin equivalent, where before and after the first vision, Catherine's emotions are denoted simply with the formulaic phrases *cum lacrimis* and *multis lacrimis*. The amplification illustrates the Czech author's view of female sanctity as somatic, a belief influenced by Aristotelian theories of the physiological differences between the sexes: women in their humors were thought to be colder and wetter than men, and humidity the cause of their desire.[29] Catherine's corporeal yearning for her celestial spouse both reflects male beliefs about the physical nature of women's spirituality and defines the audience's response to the story in similarly affective terms.

After fervent prayer, Catherine falls asleep from exhaustion. She dreams that she is in a *locus amoenus* more beautiful than any clearing or meadow she has ever seen (lines 706–20). The familiar European landscape gleams with fresh summer grass, which contrasts with the immutable imagery of the jeweled hall in the second vision. Catherine beholds Christ and Mary seated on a throne. The mother and child are described in considerable detail (lines 721–39). Since she has not yet been baptized, Catherine cannot see Christ's face, only his lovely lily-white neck and golden curly locks, which are compared with rings made from pure imagination, an allusion to the impending mystical marriage with Catherine (lines 736–39). There is also an interesting reference to the Virgin's mother, Saint Anne, in the Czech version, while in the Latin there is none, and only the briefest description of Jesus himself.[30] The Czech text contains a much longer description, couched in the affective language of courtly love and caught in a subtle tension between the physical and the spiritual realms:

> Mary, the blossoming maiden, whose mother is Saint Anne, holds her only one, Christ, her beloved little son, loving him most fervently. Above his dear little shoulders his white neck shines and glistens like a pure-white lily gleaming from the most radiant love. And his desirable, immaculate hair gleams just as precious pure gold glints more precious than other gold. In his hair above his shoulders his curls curve like golden rings wrought beyond belief. (Lines 723–39)[31]

The reference to Christ's grandmother here is significant in the context of the late medieval cult of Saint Anne, which coincided with the phenomenon of the Immaculate Conception, the belief that the Virgin Mary was born without taint from an earthly mother just as Christ emerged sinless from the womb. Chiefly because of the influence of *The Golden*

Legend, Saint Anne's prominence as *mater materis dei* stresses Jesus' matrilineal descent, rather than the patrilineal descent of the Gospels and Jesus' membership in a human family.[32] Saint Anne's prominence in the Holy Kinship and related devotional objects such as the popular statues of Mary and Jesus seated on Anne's lap (known as the *Anna Selbdritt*) also came, increasingly in the fourteenth and fifteenth centuries, to reflect and sanctify women's domestic and biological experience.[33] As the patron saint of midwives, Anne represented the central importance of the family to the gentry and aristocracy mindful of the need to produce healthy offspring.[34] Associated closely with childbearing, she was revered by noble families.[35] Her domestic role as grandmother provides a maternal, nurturing model with whom medieval women could identify more readily than the lofty and idealized Virgin Mary.[36]

Significantly, two of Charles IV's wives and one of his daughters were named after Jesus' grandmother: Anne of the Palatinate (1329–53), Anne of Schweidnitz (1339–62), and Anne of Bohemia. Even beyond the court, the cult of Saint Anne was growing in the Bohemian Lands in the fourteenth century, signaling a growing recognition of women's positive role in the religious life of the society as a whole. Many Bohemian and Moravian churches and chapels were devoted to Saint Anne, one of which was the Dominican convent at Prague, with its adjacent church dedicated to Mary's mother.[37] Anne's growing cult is also attested in the vernacular writings of the time. Thomas of Štítné lists "the widow Anne" along with other positive women (Judith, Esther, and the Sibyls) in the preface to his translation of *The Visions of Saint Bridget of Sweden,* a work intended for his daughter Agnes.[38] Saint Anne was also the patron saint of miners because of the precious jewel (Mary) she carried in her womb. In this capacity she was venerated in the Bohemian mining towns of Kutná Hora and Jáchymov (Joachimsthal) in the Ore Mountains.[39]

There can be little doubt that the affective description of Catherine's first vision of the Virgin and Child owes a great deal to the emotional realism of contemporary religious art. A possible model for the first vision were the panel paintings of the Virgin and Child with Man of Sorrows and the Virgin and Child with Saints Wenceslas and Dalmatio by Tommaso da Modena (c. 1325–79), the latter given pride of place in the Chapel of the Holy Cross at Karlstein, where our author (as a cleric) may have seen them.[40] In the two paintings by Tommaso extant in Bohemia, Christ's golden curly hair reminds us of the description of Jesus in the legend. In both the paintings and in the legend, an emphasis is placed on the profoundly affective relationship between mother and child, which comports with the Dominican preference for a human Christ whom medieval women could love as a son and as a spiritual lover. A good example of this double role are the indeterminate child-adult features of the doll of the Christ child owned by the thirteenth-century German Dominican mystic Margaretha von Ebner.[41]

The simile of the pure white lily (line 730) incorporated into the description of Jesus in the first vision combines several possible functions: the purely religious function, since it symbolizes the purity of Christ and Mary (the lily is the symbol of the Annunciation);[42] the heraldic function, since the Capetian fleur-de-lis was inherited by Charles IV from his first wife, Blanche of Valois (1316–48);[43] and the denominational function, since the lily is the principal attribute of Saint Dominic. This third factor is also important in the representation of the Virgin in the first vision. Here Mary is identified in *circumlocutio* as the "radiant rose" (*svetlá ruože,* line 827) where there is no reference to her at all in the Latin source.[44] The image of the rose is amplified considerably in the Czech version of the legend with reference to Catherine's beauty and Mary's purity. The rose is also important within Dominican piety since it was Saint Dominic who traditionally introduced the use of the rosary as a widespread devotional practice.

Mary's amplified role as mediatrix between Christ and Catherine comports with the widespread medieval belief that the perfection of God incarnate could be represented to human eyes only through the female image of his mother, the most perfect creature known to man after Jesus. For this doctrinal reason, Catherine's oblique exposure to the feminized features of her lover is mediated through the symbolic attributes of Mary (the lily and the flowers in Christ's hair). It is thanks to the intercession of the Virgin and the mediation of Saint Dominic that Dante is granted the vision of the Trinity in canto 32 of *Paradiso.* According to his guide, Saint Bernard of Clairvaux, it is only by regarding the brightness of her face that Dante will be able to look at Christ's face (canto 32, lines 85–87).[45]

Following the first vision, Catherine is pale from love-longing. She rises at the crack of dawn, puts on her cloak, hurries to the hermit's lair, and knocks on his little window (lines 866–73), once again concrete details peculiar to the Czech version and typical of its attention to somatic detail. The perceptive hermit asks the maiden why she has come so early and what has caused her pallor (line 879). The hermit now instructs Catherine in the Christian faith and baptizes her. Catherine returns home and locks herself in her chamber at nightfall to pray once more before her diptych. After more weeping, she falls asleep. In a second vision she sees Mary and Christ seated in glory and holding scepters at the end of a jeweled hall. No longer veiled from view, Christ welcomes Catherine in the sweet words of a wooing lover and sings an epithalamium to her, details all peculiar to the Czech version.

The courtly iconography of the first and second visions reveals the contamination between devotional and romance secular texts, a characteristic of western literature since the twelfth and thirteenth centuries.[46] The theme of Christ the Lover was introduced in the twelfth-century sermons of Saint Bernard but can be traced as far back as Origen (A.D. 185–254), whose allegorical commentary on the Song of Songs interprets the heroine, the Shulamite bride, as the soul and the hero as Christ.[47] Bernard built on this allegorical foundation in his influential sermons on the Song of Songs delivered between 1135 and 1153.[48] His originality lay in the introduction of the themes from the love poetry of the troubadours and the secular romances of the twelfth century. Bernard's Christ is not only a lover; he is also a knight who saves his beloved lady — the soul — from damnation. The earliest attestation of the theme of Christ as Lover-Knight in the Bohemian Lands is found in the Dominican Kolda's parable *De strenuo milite*, which we encountered in chapter 2.[49] Kolda's Christ is not strictly allegorical, as he would be for a male audience, but a real lover anxious for the welfare of his lady and courageous on her behalf. Similarly, in the second vision of *The Life of Saint Catherine*, Christ has become a fully human, loving bridegroom who makes himself radiant and beautiful for his bride (lines 1037–39) and sings an epithalamium to her in a "dear, sweet, precious voice" (*drahým, sladkým hlasem*, line 1064). His bridal song is more intimate and affective than the formalized restraint of the Latin model,[50] as deemed appropriate for a female audience:

Welcome, my most precious one.
Welcome, my beautiful spouse.
Come here to me, my darling chosen cheeks,
my dear little dove.[51]
(Lines 1067–70)

The epithet "dear little dove" originates in the erotic diction of the Song of Songs 5.2. The same sobriquet is also found in Oriental literature and is current in both the folk and literary styles of the Slavic languages, having equal currency in secular and religious verse. In the Czech verse romance *Duke Ernest*, it is applied as a term of erotic endearment by the emperor Otto to the eponymous hero's beloved mother; and by the jilted lover to his girlfriend in the parodic context of *The Weaver*.[52]

In her nuptial response to Christ, Catherine states that she has need of no other mirror than the one provided by her beloved spouse (lines 1086–87). The specular motif to designate maidenhood can be traced to the writings of the early eastern church father Gregory of Nyssa (c. A.D. 339–394), a Platonist of the Origen School.[53] Writing about Saint Gregory, Peter Brown states:

The virgin body was an exquisitely appropriate mirror, in which human beings could catch a glimpse of the immense purity of the *image of God*. The woman's untouched flesh was both a mirror of the purity of her soul and a physical image of the virgin earth of the garden of Eden.[54]

According to Gregory's Platonic view of virginity, the translucent body of the virgin is like a mirror in which the image of God is reflected. In the Czech legend, Christ's face has become the mirror where the virgin Catherine sees her own ideal reflection. Woman is thus no longer a mirror wherein Christ sees His own perfection but an autonomous image. This inversion illustrates the great prominence accorded to the sanctity of the female body in the later Middle Ages.

The setting of the mystic marriage is a beautiful jeweled hall with hard glittering surfaces (lines 962–1009), its immutable imagery of eternity contrasting with the ephemerality of the eartly setting of the first vision.[55] The transition from a familiar earthly landscape to an unfamiliar interior glistening with bright colors symbolizes the saint's progress from the world of the senses to the transcendental realm of mystical experience. On the ceiling of the hall the sun, moon, and stars shine as they move in their orbits, measuring every moment of time (lines 984–89). It is clear from the wording of the passage that we are dealing here with a simulacrum (*podobenstvím*, line 986) of the celestial spheres rather than the planets per se, suggesting the influence of trompe l'oeil in contemporary Italian painting on the murals at Karlstein (see Figure 1) and perhaps also an interest in the art of astrology. Long ago Franz Spina maintained that the author had seen the Chapel of Saint Catherine and Chapel of the Holy Cross at Karlstein and possibly also the Chapel of Saint Wenceslas in the Cathedral of Saint Vitus.[56] This hypothesis was later refuted by Jan Vilikovský, who argued that the author drew rather upon the description of the heavenly Jerusalem in Revelation 21.18–23.[57] But this argument supposes a false opposition between the medieval understanding of image and the word: it was perfectly possible for the author to have been familiar both with the Karlstein chapels and the biblical text of Revelation. The presence of scenes from the Apocalypse in the Chapel of the Virgin Mary at Karlstein further underscores the likelihood that court writers and artists were influenced by Saint John's vision of the celestial kingdom. Like the jeweled hall of the second vision, the Chapel of the Holy Cross and the Chapel of Saint Catherine (the imperial oratory) on the third and second floors, respectively, of Karlstein Castle are embellished with semiprecious stones.[58] In the Chapel of Saint Catherine, there is a painting of Mary and the Christ child seated on a throne and receiving the fealty of the emperor Charles and the empress Anne. Since only the emperor and his closest advisers (invariably clerics like John Moravec) were allowed access to the imperial oratory, it is possible that the author of our legend had actually seen this painting and was influenced by it.

If the Chapel of Saint Catherine provides an architectonic analogue to the first vision, the Chapel of the Holy Cross surely corresponds to the jeweled hall of the second vision. The Chapel of Saint Catherine is on a smaller scale and on a lower level than the Chapel of the Holy Cross. Moreover, the former leads up to the latter, just as the first vision is followed by the spiritually more elevated second vision. Like the jeweled hall of the second vision, the Chapel of the Holy Cross was perceived and designed as an evocation of the New Jerusalem, where the resurrected bodies of the holy reside in eternity. Thus in the hall of the second vision, the symbol of jewels conflates the celestial city of the New Jerusalem with the pure bodies of the virgins who reside there. The New Jerusalem is also linked with the cosmic Woman, who is described as "clothed with the sun, and the moon was under her feet, and upon her head a crown of twelve stars" (Revelation 12.1). One of the most popular apocalyptic agents, the *mulier amicta sole* is a dominant image in medieval literature and art, identified both with *Ecclesia* (the Church) and the Virgin Mary.[59] At Karlstein there is a symbolic identification between the Apocalyptic Woman and Empress Anne, for whose edification, I have already suggested, our legend may have been conceived.[60] Like the Woman of Saint John's vision, Anne gave birth to a son, Wenceslas; this was an important event for the Luxembourg dynasty, since the emperor had no surviving male heir until this birth in February 1361. The importance of the event is stressed in the opening words of the emperor's own autobiography, addressed to those who would follow him and sit on the two thrones of Bohemia and the Holy Roman Empire.[61] And the dynasty, whose posterity had been assured in real life, is traced backward in art along the walls of the palace portion of Karlstein. Religious-mystical and dynastic-social concerns dovetail here, as they so often do in late medieval society.

Absent from the Latin source, the twelve precious gems that adorn the walls of the hall correspond to those enumerated in Ezekiel 28.13 and to the description of the New Jerusalem in chapter 21 of the Revelation of Saint John. This amplification can be explained in connection with the ideal of virginity and the resurrected body in late medieval piety. The gems in the Book of Ezekiel clothe the body in paradise,[62] while the city and the gems that adorn it in the New Jerusalem are closely identified with the virginal Bride of Christ. In Revelation 21.9–10, the Bride of the Lamb is conflated with the holy city, just as in the Middle English poem *Pearl* the Pearl-Maiden is fused with the heavenly landscape.[63] In medieval literature, the Lamb at the center of the Revelation is associated with martyrs and virgins, especially with dead children, probably because Revelation 14 is read at the Feast of the Holy Innocents. The marriage imagery associated with the Lamb could be appropriated as well by the mystic visionary (such as Saint Catherine), who thus becomes synonymous with the Bride of the Lamb.[64] The typological link between Catherine's mystic marriage and Saint John's vision is widely attested in late medieval art, most notably in Hans Memling's beautiful altarpiece *The Mystic Marriage of Saint Catherine* in the Sint-Jans Hospital at Bruges.[65]

The religious symbolism of the gems that encrust the walls of the hall was familiar to a medieval audience through the availability of lapidaries in upper-class houses and castles. In the later Middle Ages, precious gems came to denote specifically female virginity: Aldhelm in his *De Virginitate* describes holy maidens as *Christi margaritae, paradisi gemmae*;[66] the Bohemian monk Christian, author of the tenth-century Latin legend of the lives of the martyrs Saints Wenceslas and Ludmilla, *Vita et passio sancti Wenceslai et sancte Ludmile avie eius*, speaks of Ludmilla "adorned with the jewels of virtue" (*virtutum gemmis ornans*),[67] and in the Middle English *Seinte Margarete* the eponymous saint refers to her own virginity as a "precious jewel" (*deore gimstan*).[68] In Dante's *Paradiso* the purity of the Virgin Mary is compared to a blue sapphire, the color of Mary and the azure sky traditionally associated with her: "the fair sapphire by which the sky is so brightly ensapphired" (canto 23, lines 101–2).[69]

The Passion

The wicked emperor Maxentius has begun a campaign to persecute Christians. The newly baptized Catherine begins to spread the Gospel among her subjects and goes to the emperor. They argue and Catherine is put in prison. To coerce her into relinquishing the new faith and marrying his son, the emperor invites fifty pagan scholars to dispute with the virgin. Fortified, however, by the Archangel in her dungeon, Catherine succeeds in converting the pagan scholars to the true faith, whereupon the furious emperor has them all thrown into a fiery furnace and Catherine scourged. Her snow-white naked body is beaten with horsehair whips with three lashes ending in lead knots in which steel hooks are fixed. This scene of torment culminates in a comparison between Christ and Catherine and Tristan and Isolde: the love potion is Catherine's faith, strengthened by her suffering on Christ's behalf. Catherine is returned to a deep, dark dungeon, which, when the empress and her captain of the guard, Porphirius, visit her there, is found to be fragrant and suffused with light, for now Catherine is kept company by an angel who anoints her wounds with heavenly oils and unguents. The empress and Porphirius are converted and subsequently martyred in a grisly fashion, along with two hundred heathen knights. The emperor orders Catherine to be brought from her cell and is amazed to find that she is even more beautiful than before the scourging. Intent on maiming her lovely body, the emperor orders a torture machine to be constructed that consists of four-bladed wheels, the blades resembling the hoe used to rake the soil in the field (a rural simile perhaps indicative of preaching style). But an angel shatters the wheels, and the splinters that fly from them kill four thousand heathen onlookers. Unable to persuade Catherine to abandon her faith, the emperor orders her to be decapitated. Just before she dies, Catherine hears Christ speaking to her as his true bride. Her head is severed, and milk instead of blood flows from her neck. She dies at the sixth hour like Christ on the cross, and her body is translated by angels to Mount Sinai, where her miraculous relics are still preserved.

Catherine's debate with the pagan sages is largely in direct speech, compared with the predominance of indirect speech in the Latin model. Altogether 52 percent of the Czech text is in direct speech.[70] Importance was attached to demonstrating doctrinal points in dramatic form to make the theological abstractions more palatable to a secular audience untrained in the niceties of ecclesiastical dogma.[71] This mode of adaptation is certainly consistent with the sermon techniques of a preacher concerned to present events in vivid, dramatic terms. Also important in the debate is the amplification of the term *blud* ("doctrinal error"), which occurs three times (lines 1131, 2190, 3119), and the adjectival form *bludný* ("erroneous"), which qualifies six different nouns (lines 1445, 1212, 2616, 3128, 2756, 1217). One of Catherine's many functions in the Middle Ages was her role as theologian and teacher, a role with which the Dominicans closely identified in their zeal to seek out and persecute heresy. It was on account of her status as a theologian that she was venerated as the patron saint of the Sorbonne at Paris. Hence her primary function in the debate is to represent Catholic orthodoxy and to convert the pagans to the true faith. It is in this role as teacher that Catherine rebukes the emperor Maxentius for his stubborn refusal to embrace Christianity: "Catherine boldly went to the place where the emperor was standing and said to him: 'What is the use of your misguided power, evil Emperor? You know I am right, so why do you dare to persist in your error?'" (lines 1214–20).[72] It is instructive at this point to compare Catherine's embodiment of the truth with the similar role of the martyrs in the Old Czech *Passional*. In *The Life of Saint Eustace*, Christ appears in a vision and congratulates Eustace for having crushed the Devil through the true faith.[73] Occasionally, the author of *The Passional* allows the pagans to claim the truth as their own, as, for example, in *The Life of Saint George* when the evil emperor tells his wife (who wishes to become a Christian) that she is deviating from the true faith.[74] The point of this curious appropriation of truth by a pagan is to demonstrate just how insidious and dangerous is the discourse of the heretic.

The second theme of Catherine's speech is the Incarnation, exemplified by her own passion. The debate is conducted in a civil and courteous fashion; these are no philistine pagans but eager seekers after truth, a further indication of a refined, courtly audience. It is Catherine's role to witness this truth and to embody the Church, first through the literal word of the Gospels and the teachings of the Church (the debate) and later through the Word made flesh (the Passion). As we have seen, the Czech author enhances the affective bond between Catherine and Christ through vivid, concrete description and courtly language in the scenes of the conversion and the mystic marriage based on the first Latin source. Similarly, in those scenes based on the second source, he cuts the debate and expands the flagellation and Passion. This change of emphasis tells us that the author regarded female sanctity as essentially somatic, a male-centered assumption with which medieval women were expected to identify. For the author there was no contradiction between Catherine's intellectual role as a theologian and her physical role as a martyr; on the contrary, he perceived a seamless unity between the verbal truth she represents as a teacher and the higher, mystical truth she embodies as a martyr. Yet the greater emphasis placed on Catherine's physical imitation of Christ, and the corresponding diminution of her intellectual prowess, tells us a great deal about his conservative vision of religious practice and the perceived role of women within it. In an age when heresy among women was greatly feared and severely punished, it is not surprising that a text associated with the orthodox emperor's family and household should be highly traditional in its theological and social outlook.

The scourging scene provides a direct parallel to the flagellation of Christ before the crucifixion and incorporates courtly love symbolism to reinforce the theme of the *sponsa Christi*. With its special code of meanings, the color symbolism introduced in the flagellation scene appears to have been devised for a noble audience of initiates. Color symbolism is attested both in secular and in religious writings of the later Middle Ages. One possible source for the color coding in the flagellation scene of our legend is the French *Château d'Amour* by the English Dominican Robert Grosseteste, bishop of Lincoln, whose works were known in medieval Bohemia. The *Château d'Amour* is a religious allegory written in a courtly manner for a noble audience in England. The castle of the title symbolizes the pure body of the Virgin Mary; it is painted in three colors—green, blue, and red. The green foundation of the castle signifies faith, blue symbolizes hope, and red, love.[75]

In Czech medieval literature, color symbolism is attested in the prose romance *Štilfríd*, in certain parodic elements in *The Weaver*, and in the Czech love lyric known as *De amore mundi cancio de coloribus*. Vilikovský has also found references to color symbolism in a Latin treatise entitled *De confessione* in a manuscript in the library of the chapter house of Olomouc Cathedral.[76] This treatise is concerned with the confessional preparation for the taking of Communion and distinguishes between the secular and spiritual connotations of the colors green, black, gray, red, white, azure, brown, violet, and yellow. These spiritual connotations correspond closely to those enumerated in the legend, although they sometimes differ from the verses of the lyric *De amore* cited by the author of the treatise.

Catherine's skin changes color under each cruel blow of the whip: the green covering the face from shame denotes dawning love. As in the treatise, green here has a positive spiritual meaning where it is negative in the lyric ("et signat spiritualiter deum incipere amare, quod fit per timorem"). In German *Minnesang* poetry, green also denotes incipient love.[77] In the mystical writings of the German Dominican Elsbeth von Oye, whose imitation of Christ was especially physical, the color green is associated with the continual blossoming of the sharpened crucifix with which she mortifies her own flesh.[78] The white of the body signifies hope, as in the treatise *De confessione* and in the secular courtly context of the German love lyric *Von den farben* (lines 65–69). The red of the blood denotes the fervor of spiritual love, as in the *Château d'Amour* and in the treatise *De confessione*, as well as in the secular context of courtly poetry (*Von den farben*, lines 29–32). The black of the wounds, from which the flesh has been torn away, is the symbol of grief or sadness, in religious terms for Christ in his humiliation and in secular terms because of sadness at the lover's neglect (*Di siben varben*, lines 3–5). The color blue, in traces left by the whip, denotes constancy and perseverance both to God and to the lover (*Von den farben*, lines 51–53).

The gold of Catherine's loosened hair is the symbol of the fulfillment of all desires and the gratification of love in her mystical union with Christ (lines 2301–80). Gold (or yellow) also connoted love and marriage in classical times; Hymen, the male god of marriage, is usually dressed in saffron robes.[79] The color gold is also associated from the time of the early church with the malleable perfection attained by bodies in future ages.[80] Thus Catherine's virginal body takes on the hue of heavenly perfection. Indeed, her celestial destination is anticipated from the beginning of the legend by her golden hair, which resembles Christ's in the two visions (in the Latin model it is brown). This color correspondence further underscores her distinctly female, literal imitation of Christ.

Where the Catherine legend differs most remarkably from any known source or parallel is the extraordinary tension between corporeal and spiritual description. The key to this polarity is surely the contradictory vision of woman as fallen woman and as virgin, defined through her physical and idealized body. The description of the flagellation — complete with metal hooks attached to the end of the scourge — reflects actual medieval religious practice. In 1349, large groups of flagellants from various cities in Belgium congregated in Tournai; one group from Liège was accompanied by a Dominican friar who preached a sermon in which he extolled the sacrifice of these so-called "Red Knights of Christ."[81] Self-chastisement was also an aspect of Dominican female piety. The nun Elsbeth von Oye frequently whipped herself with a barbed scourge and wore a sharpened crucifix so close to her waist that it cut into her skin. The Czech author was clearly concerned to attenuate such an extreme imitation of Christ to suit the courtly sensibility of his noble audience.

At the moment the color red is introduced the bloody wound in the broken skin becomes aestheticized as a rose. On the realistic level, this image connotes the corrupt female body (the wound-associated vagina was a particular source of horror to the male imagination); on the spiritual level, it symbolizes the Passion and Mary's compassion for her crucified son. The Virgin's affinity with her son's suffering developed from the eleventh century onward, linking the Incarnation and the Passion in a unified vision of the Christian faith.[82] As Miri Rubin puts it, "In vernacular literature a strong bond was created between the eucharistic body and the original body born from a virgin womb, to produce a powerful image linked both to crucifixion and to nativity in the Virgin Mary."[83]

The connection between the flagellation and confession followed by Communion is important for an understanding of the legend's religious function. The correspondence discussed earlier between the treatise *De confessione* and our legend suggests that the flagellation scene can be interpreted in liturgical terms as the penitence and confession that precede Holy Communion. Significantly, the elaborate emphasis on confession points to Dominican influence, since one of their main functions was to assist the bishops with their increased pastoral workload by preaching, the hearing of confessions, and the provision of spiritual advice.[84]

Following the flagellation is the courtly comparison of Christ and Catherine with the lovers Tristan and Isolde (lines 2385–90). The author assumes that his female audience would be familiar with the courtly love code and would understand the connection between the secular conceit and its eucharistic associations. The "precious drink of Isolde" (*drahé Izaldy napitie*, line 2385), for instance, is the faith she receives after her mystic marriage to Christ, which fortifies her in the midst of pain and suffering. The Czech author introduces the secular *matière* of the Celtic lovers to convey to his lay audience the love bond between Christ and Catherine; conversely, the German poet Gottfried von Strassburg, in the prologue to his romance *Tristan*, incorporates the image of the eucharistic bread to describe the salvific effect of his story on his intimate audience of "noble hearts." Both poets combine religious and courtly elements, and their common source of influence was, without doubt, Saint Bernard's popular sermons on the Song of Songs.[85] Dominican authorship would explain the coexistence of courtly language and eucharistic symbolism at this point, since the Dominicans and the women to whom they preached were especially noted for their eucharistic piety.[86]

Catherine's flagellated body is cast into a deep dungeon. But angelic light suffuses the cell and illuminates the darkness. The virgin is comforted by angels who anoint her tortured flesh with heavenly and fragrant ointments. Here the Czech text is quite faithful to the Latin source. But the Czech version amplifies the somatic nature of Catherine's experience and the maternal tenderness Christ feels for her: "They [the angels] rub the blows and wounds with heavenly balms; thus with his angelic physicians Christ comforted his bride" (lines 2563–66).[87] As well as "to comfort" or "to console," the Old Czech verb *kojieše* (line 2566) also means "to breast-feed." Thus Christ's body incorporates the maternal function of lactation. We see a parallel feminization of Christ's body in the Nativity panel of the Vyšší Brod Altarpiece, where Mary's right hand, poised below Christ's breast, displays the characteristic pinching gesture of lactation (see Figure 2). His eyes turned toward the viewer, the Christ child appears to offer his own breast to the faithful supplicant, thus combining male and female bodily attributes. From the twelfth century on, writers frequently saw Jesus as a mother and nurse, as well as a lover, brother, and father (and sometimes all of these things at once). Saint Bernard associates Christ the bridegroom with nursing,[88] and Guerric of Igny (died c. 1157) envisages Christ as a feeding mother and a nurse because of his loving care, as well as a father in his qualities of strength and authority.[89]

In the Latin model, Christ sends a white dove from heaven to give Catherine spiritual sustenance, just as he fed Daniel for seven days in the den of lions. In the Czech version the dove is replaced by an angel who nurtures Catherine back to health. This detail is characteristic of the Czech author's concern to make Christ's love for Catherine more corporeal and human than does the author of the Latin model. This emphasis on the love between Christ and his spouse also characterizes Catherine's defiant speech to the stupified emperor as she emerges, unscathed, from her dungeon:

> Know that I received bodily food from no one but only from the angel who sated Daniel when he was imprisoned by the Babylonian king in the den of lions. *He generously fed me, gave me milk and healed me from his breast and glorified me with his love.* (Lines 2679–87; my italics)[90]

The fifteen-verse description of the torture machine devised by the wicked emperor introduces a comparable simile drawn from the everyday world of experience: the blades of the machine are likened to a harrow, the spikes of which break up the clumps of soil in the rye field (lines 2769–77).[91] Although it may seem odd to find such a homely detail in a high-style context, it does perhaps tell us something about the author's training as a preacher used to introducing vivid rural images drawn from the world of everyday life.

The destruction of the infernal machine—its blades as sharp and deadly as the swords of the heathen Tartars and Saracens (line 2777)—guarantees the maiden's invulnerability to physical pain and her triumph over death through faith.[92] Almost out of his mind, the emperor orders Catherine to be decapitated with a sword, hence the two iconographic attributes of the wheel and the sword in visual images of the saint.[93] In her final prayer before execution, Catherine beseeches God to bless and protect from fire and storm those faithful people whose walls or books are adorned with images of her passion (lines 3365–80); she prays that children born and unborn should not suffer deformity but grow up to be fair and comely (lines 3375–80); and she intercedes for the salvation of the dead (lines 3381–87). We find a similar set of formulae in *The Legend of the 10,000 Knights,* where the author mentions that scenes from this legend, besides being hewn in stone, cut in wood, and drawn in books, were painted in black and white on the walls of the rooms of private houses.[94] Vilikovský claims that in this passage the author is promoting artists and their workshops.[95] In fact, such words of protection occur in other hagiographic legends, for example, in the fifteenth-century English lives of Saints Dorothy, Margaret, and Catherine by the Suffolk Augustinian canon Osbern Bokenham. In a passage strikingly similar to the one in the Czech legend, Saint Dorothy asks God to care for those mothers in childbed who remember her passion and to protect from lightning those houses that depict the events of her passion:

And yf wummen wyth chyld of hyr had mende,
That he tham hastly wold socour sende;
And that noon hous where were hyr passyonarye
Wyth feer ner lyhtnyng shuld neuyr myskarye.[96]
(Lines 4908–10)

In all these cults of the Roman virgin-martyrs, one of their principal functions ever since the early church has been to protect people and intercede for them with God.[97] In paintings of Catherine, the artists also stress her protective powers. In the miniature book of hours known as the *Heures du Maréchal de Boucicaut* (1410–15) by an unknown Flemish-Franconian artist, the marshal kneels before the saint, his hands lifted in supplication. The inscription surrounding the smiling virgin articulates her response: *Ce que vous voudres* ("Whatever you want"), a promise of aid and acceptance.[98] Marshal de Boucicaut belonged to the nobility, that privileged group that expressed its devotion to her more fervently and consistently than any other class of society. What they admired above all was her courage and dignity in the face of suffering, virtues expected of brave knights and warriors. Knights made pilgrimages not only to Jerusalem, but also to Catherine's shrine on Mount Sinai, in the hope of being accepted into the elite ranks of a "Knight of Jerusalem." If accepted, the knight would be allowed to wear the emblem of the saint: the wheel penetrated by a sword.[99]

Moments before death, Catherine casts a bold look at the executioner and pulls back her golden hair to spare it from the blade before lowering her neck (lines 3435–37). These concrete, physical details are peculiar to the Czech version, and combine the corporeality of female sanctity with the general doctrinal importance of bodily integrity as a prerequisite for resurrection.[100] Catherine's slender neck is pure white (line 3437), recalling Christ's lily-white neck in the first vision and underlining her literal *imitatio Christi*. Her head is severed at one stroke and, instead of blood, milk pours from her neck as a token of virginal purity (lines 3451–55). The adverb used here is *ščedře* ("generously," "copiously"), the same word used to describe the lactating angel in the dungeon (line 2685). Important here is the maternal, nurturing function of the female body. The posthumous miracles of milk gushing from the saint's severed neck and the curative oil that oozes from her bones (lines 3495–3501) illustrate the Aristotelian equation of the female body with moisture and bodily fluids.

In addition to its symbolic significance as a sign of virginal purity, milk denotes the salvific blood of the Eucharist, the visible proof of the doctrinal truth of the word made flesh to which Catherine witnesses before the heathen scholars. In late medieval religious practice we find numerous instances of the association of milk with blood. According to the physiological theories of the time, the mother's milk was believed to be produced from her blood.[101] This equation explains the presence of maternal, feeding imagery in *The Prayer of Lady Kunigunde*. The speaker addresses Christ as present in the bread and wine and requests that he feed his children with his body and blood: "Deign to feed us today, fill us with living food, strengthen us with its strength and pour its delight into our soul."[102]

Conclusion

How do we explain the curious intrusion of maternal bodily imagery (the lactating angel, tears of blood) into a vernacular saint's life written in praise of a learned virgin and bride of Christ? The answer, I have proposed, lies within the complex late medieval image of woman as teacher, virgin, *and* mother. In his *De laudibus feminarum*, a letter addressed to the empress Anne, Petrarch stresses the neo-Platonic importance of female intellect as well as the traditional significance attached to her bodily function as a mother. The author of our legend similarly associates woman with all three virtues—intellect, motherhood, and virginity. Like the courtier-poet Petrarch, he is responding to the pragmatic needs of dynastic continuity and to his own ideals as a humanist intellectual. The most likely addressee of the legend was the empress Anne, who was yet to give birth to a son and heir to her husband's kingdom. I have also maintained that the most likely author of our legend was the Dominican John Moravec, whose complex profile as courtier and cleric goes some way to explaining the text's secular and doctrinal concerns and its successful fusion of courtly love discourse with the intricacies of theological debate.

CHAPTER 7

Bohemian Knights

Reflections of Social Reality in the
Czech Epic and Verse Romances

Like the saints' lives examined in the previous two chapters, the secular chivalric romance is a difficult genre to place into a social context since, by its very nature, it is concerned to evoke the Other World rather than this one. To discern the "real" within such genres one must take an oblique, lopsided look at what is being represented. Just as the hagiographic legend presents reality through the filter of religious values, so does the romance refract the social through an idealized world of chivalric ideals. In his pioneering study *Mimesis: Dargestellte Wirklichkeit in der abendländischen Literatur* (1948), Erich Auerbach pointed out that, unlike the medieval epic, which accurately reproduces the world of social reality, the otherworldly space of the chivalric romance provides no direct mimetic link to the real.[1] Since Auerbach's seminal definition of the romance genre first appeared nearly half a century ago, studies of the medieval romance have begun to suggest how this gap between ideal and reality might be bridged. Scholars have increasingly discerned in medieval romances not so much an absence of the real as a complex refraction of it through the distorting lens of chivalric ideology.[2]

Ideology does not correspond directly to reality but exists in an intermediate position between culture and the actual material conditions that bring it into being. Borrowing the term "acculturation" from the language of contemporary anthropology, Jane Taylor attempts to define this off-centered relationship between text and its social context as "a process whereby the socio-culturally unfamiliar is recast in familiar terms, so that the reader can understand systems and phenomena in a source text as corresponding to his own ideologies, preconceptions and behavior patterns."[3] Taylor goes on to argue that this ideological familiarization often functions in an unconscious fashion, manifesting itself through microcosmic detail rather than through the wholesale transformation of the original text. Thus the common assumption that epigonic adaptations are slavish, uninspired, and mechanical reproductions of their high courtly models is frequently based on a misconception of the adaptation and its author's intentions. In this chapter, I shall examine the fourteenth-century Czech chivalric romances in precisely such terms of "acculturation" by placing less emphasis on the alleged aesthetic superiority of the German models and more on the relationship between the adaptation and the social context that produced it.

Alexandreida

Interest in the world of epic and romance in the Bohemian Lands can be dated to the second half of the thirteenth century, when the Czech kings, by then thoroughly germanized in language and culture, were beginning to emulate the chivalric and courtly tastes of the princes of the empire. Wenceslas I and his son Přemysl Ottokar II invited German poets to their court at Prague, the most celebrated of whom was Ulrich von Etzenbach, the author of a voluminous romance about Alexander the Great (in 28,000 verses!) that flatteringly compares Přemysl Ottokar with the Greek hero. This work was conceived and written in conformity with the fashionable chivalric ethos of the day. Alexander does not simply become a proto-Christian crusader; he also takes part in tournaments, seeks the favor of ladies, and undertakes *aventiures* in distant lands.

The anonymous author of the Czech *Alexandreida* (c. 1290–1300) rejects this secular model of knighthood, preferring the prechivalric ideal of the *miles Dei*, the crusader who fights on God's behalf. Probably written by a cleric attached to the household of a regional nobleman or perhaps by an educated nobleman himself, the *Alexandreida* arose in a provincial, noncourtly milieu. Its weltanschauung is quite distinct from—and even antipathetic to—Ulrich's tale of exotic travels, jousts, and ladies' favors. Its vision of Greece is not a fairy-tale world but recognizably the author's own society: the landscape resembles that of medieval central Europe, Alexander's knights are given Czech names, his military tactics are characteristically medieval, and even his coronation is modeled on that of the Prague ceremony. Above all, Alexander himself is an idealized Czech warrior-king who always keeps his nobles in his counsel and shuns the trappings of worldliness.

The only description of a tournament in the *Alexandreida* is scathingly laconic: while describing the entertainments laid on for Alexander by the citizens of Babylon, the author states that these chivalric amusements lasted a long time (*dlúhé chvíle*, B, 178), thus punning sardonically on the Czech word *kratochvíle* ("pastime," B, 177), and affirms that Alexander curtailed them with a wave of his hand. This passage, and the subsequent description of the opulent gifts presented by the Babylonians to the king, allude to the nouveaux riches of the royal court at Prague and the growing power of the German urban patriciate.

Analogously, the attitude to women in the *Alexandreida* is a far cry from the chivalric ethos of Ulrich's romance.[4] In fact, there are only three separate references to women in the whole work: to Alexander's mother Olympias (lines 73–81), Helen in the interpolated story of Troy (lines 807–28), and the widow and the mother of the vanquished Darius, to whom Alexander shows magnanimity (lines 1874–921). There are no courtly descriptions of women in the work, although Olympias's beauty is remarked upon in passing (lines 73–74). We find, rather, an emphasis on companionship between the partners in marriage in the spirit of Saint Augustine's *De bono coniugali*. Olympia is above all a virtuous and honorable wife to Philip of Macedonia, a gift from God to man (lines 75–76).[5] Such sobriety recalls Ulrich von Etzenbach's courtly hagiography *Wilhelm von Wenden*, with its attempt to reconcile secular practices with religious ideals.[6] The importance of an honorable wife is the subject of a special gnomic tercet: "A tired man reaches for a drink; moisture comes timely to drought-ridden meadows; an honorable woman is most precious to a man" (lines 78–81).[7] In this tercet woman is strictly ancillary to her partner, his dutiful helpmate and solace. There is no hint whatsoever here or elsewhere of the courtly veneration of the lady that had become part of the stock-in-trade of French and German courtly romance. Line 79, quoted above, is clearly based on a universal image of woman as a source of refreshment to man, as in Proverbs 5.15.[8] Also important is the conventional medieval equation of women with water and the female sex with dampness.[9]

So far the text has revealed a neutral or even slightly positive image of woman. At the conclusion of the interpolated story of Troy, however, it hints at the traditional negative picture of woman as the source of shame: "The following rarely receive praise: a dry meadow without grass, and a beautiful woman without shame" (lines 820–22).[10] The word *příslovie* is polysemic, meaning "shame," "fault," or "slander," so that line 822 can read "a woman rarely remains without slander." Although the word may possibly be an allusion to the slanderer of the courtly love code, it would seem doubtful, considering the text's aversion to courtliness in general. It is more likely that here we have an oblique allusion to Eve's shameful role as temptress of Adam in the Garden of Eden.

Ironically, most references to sex in the *Alexandreida* are characterized by restraint bordering on moral prudishness. In the Judgment of Paris from the Troy episode, the poet fails to mention that the three goddesses undress before the shepherd-prince Paris, unlike the account in the probable Latin source.[11] In the scene of pillage following the defeat of the Persians by Alexander's army, the Latin source refers explicitly to the rape of the Persian noblewomen. The Czech poet restricts his remark to the following euphemistic couplet: "Many a gracious woman was unworthily stripped naked" (lines 1880–81).[12] Later the author condemns the vices of Babylon, alluding to the mothers' practice of selling their daughters into prostitution for a small sum of money (B, 271–72). The attitude to women in the *Alexandreida*, therefore, combines two opposite traditions that the Middle Ages inherited: she is the virtuous partner to man (as in

Augustine's *De bono coniugali*) and the temptress who brought about man's fall from grace.[13]

The religious ideal of knighthood corresponds to the ideal of womanhood in the *Alexandreida*. If the young Alexander begins as a paradigm of Czech kingship, the conquering Alexander exemplifies what he should avoid becoming—a self-serving tyrant. As a representative of the nobility, the author applauds Alexander as long as he is perceived to be defending his birthright and asserting his feudal privileges, but as soon as he becomes an aggressor, he begins to conform to the feared image of tyrant and usurper of the time-honored rights and priviliges of the nobility. Whereas the Alexander of the Greek model by Gautier of Châtillon *Alexandreis*, is consistently extolled as the fear of all the kings on earth (VI, lines 1–27), his Czech counterpart is criticized for succumbing to worldly sin (B, 273–74). As he approaches India, he reduces all before him to fire and ruin (Š, 42–56, corresponding to Gautier IX, lines 336–40). The poet's earlier sympathy for his hero now changes to outright condemnation as Alexander veers toward self-destruction like a furious storm (Š, 49–51). In contrast to Alexander's moral decline, his defeated opponent, Darius of Persia, is treated in a sympathetic manner. His moving speech to his army on the eve of battle is couched in terms of *dignitas humanae naturae* and Christian *humilitas*. With its reference to "unworthy guests" (*hostie nehodní*) and its emphasis on freedom and subordination, it evokes the recent historical events in Bohemia that led to the defeat of Přemysl Ottokar's army at the Battle of the Moravian Field in 1278 and the humiliating occupation of the kingdom by the troops of Rudolph of Habsburg: "Remember that you are free and these unworthy guests are already subject to you" (lines 1322–34).[14] These events led to a period of political uncertainty and instability that did not come to an end until Count John of Luxembourg assumed the Bohemian throne in 1310. It is this climate of social uncertainty and moral breakdown that is reflected in the powerful evocation of social reality in the *Alexandreida*.

The moral censure of Alexander does not happen suddenly but is carefully and gradually built up through the powerful descriptions of warfare and the appalling deeds of plunder that succeed them. The evocation of the bloody battlefield must rank as one of the most powerful and devastating witnesses of the horrors of war in the whole of medieval European literature: men are crushed by horses; the dying dig their teeth into the soil, while some are slain by mallets; others vomit blood and drag their entrails behind them as they die (lines 1747–58). In the scenes of pillaging, which follow the battle, men stop at nothing to further their own material gain, stuffing booty into their jerkins when every available sack is full (lines 1855–56). Throughout the account, the author treats the weakness of human beings in a realistic fashion: silly squires snore or are tormented by their dreams (an effective psychological touch); others ignore their lord's call by crawling between the wheels of a cart to sleep a little longer (lines 2441–46).

Man's perversity in war is contrasted with his natural role as the cultivator of the land. The description of the abandoned farms whose owners have been conscripted into the Persian army is both a realistic evocation of medieval rural life and an elegiac tribute to the practices of peacetime: the fences lies unmeshed; the beet is left in the soil; the scythe lies unused; the ox gives a weary grunt, for there was no one, the narrator informs us, to harness the beasts for plowing or to break the clods of earth (lines 224–58). The whole passage echoes the woe and despair expressed in the *Chronicon aulae regiae,* in which the author describes the effect of the famine, which afflicted the populace of Bohemia with the greatest force between 1281 and 1282 during the minority of Wenceslas II.[15]

Duke Ernest

John of Luxembourg brought to his new kingdom an appetite for chivalry and courtliness. One of the first things he did when he arrived in Prague was to inaugurate a Round Table, to which he invited the nobles of the realm. But, as the author of the *Chronicon aulae regiae* informs us, no one came to these festivities, and the entire project came to naught. The lack of interest in Arthurian culture can be explained partly by the Czechs' ignorance of the chivalric romance and partly by that ideological animosity to secular chivalry we have seen at work in the *Alexandreida.* By resisting John's model of chivalry, the nobility was implicitly expressing its distrust toward a centralized western European monarchy. Having extracted even more power from the new ruler than ever before — a price John had to pay for the Bohemian crown — they were disinclined to indulge his foreign tastes in chivalric culture.

Charles IV persisted with his father's centralizing policy, but his tactics were different and certainly more subtle. He was shrewd enough to see that promoting western-style tournaments and Round Tables was not the most effective way to enjoin the support of the Bohemian nobility. Instrumental in promoting his vision was the fostering of cultural paradigms that encouraged peace and conciliation rather than war and conquest. The idealized courtly mode of the hagiographic and chivalric romances conformed more readily than the realistic martial mode of the epic to this vision. Many of the literary and plastic artworks commissioned by the emperor — like the vernacular *Life of Saint Catherine* or the lovely statue of Saint Wenceslas as a knight by Henry Parler — reflect the Caroline vision of a Court of Peace at the intersection of the earthly and heavenly realms. Notably absent from this vision is the glorification of secular chivalry: if Catherine of Alexandria is a doughty "knight," it is to Christ she is devoted, not her own glory; and if Wenceslas is the patron of the Bohemian Lands, his shield betokens his status as *miles Dei* rather than the conquest associated with secular chivalry.

Charles's essentially spiritual understanding of chivalry is important for our appreciation of the sole chivalric romance to date from his reign— *Duke Ernest* (c. 1350s). Extant in *The Codex of Count Baworowský* (1472), this work reflects the blend of courtliness, mysticism, and exoticism that characterized the life and times of Charles IV.[16] In harmony with this zeitgeist, *Duke Ernest* betrays more devotional, religious features than its German model, *Herzog Ernst* (version D) by Ulrich von Etzenbach. Mediating between the demands of tradition and the expectations of change, *Duke Ernest* combines stylistic echoes of the epic *Alexandreida*—such as the gnomic verses so integral to the older work—with a new enthusiasm for the strange, mystic, and exotic. There is, moreover, less sobriety and greater exuberance, and there are fewer descriptions of warfare and more scenes of courtly love, in *Duke Ernest.*

To be sure, such love is not of the erotic and physical variety but spiritual and platonic, like the bond that exists between Saint Catherine and Christ. In the homosocial world of the romance, Duke Ernest's emotions are invested in two other characters, his mother, Adlička (Adelheit), and his companion-in arms, Vecl (Wetzel), the counterpart to Roland's friend Oliver.[17] The relationship between mother and son is more pronounced than in the German version and is colored by many of the affective features of contemporary Marian poetry.[18]

The Czech adaptation shares with its German source almost the same plot and very similar stylistic features, including a prologue whose sharpening of emotional extremes is symptomatic of the lyric poetry that describes the lover's alternation between hope and despair, desire and frustration.[19] As in the source, love is introduced as the central theme, although the Czech adaptor removes the German personifications of Lady Fortune (*Vrau Selde*) and Lady Love (*Vrau Mynne*) and places a moral emphasis on the wrongdoings of the slanderer who seeks to destroy the true love of the couple. This emphasis on the evil outsider capitalizes on the exclusionist mentality that we have witnessed in so many works of medieval Czech literature, from the chronicle and the drama to the hagiographic and chivalric romances.

What all the narratives in the Czech romances seem to have in common is the desire to provide a contrast between maligned noblemen and oppressive, arbitrary rulers, a reflection of how the audience of the romances perceived iself in relation to the figure of the king. In *Duke Ernest,* the widowed emperor Otto seeks the hand of the Bavarian princess Adlička, mother of Duke Ernst (Arnošt). Otto sends a love letter to Adlička to woo her into accepting his marriage proposal. When the princess accepts, her son is maligned by the emperor's nephew Henry.

To expiate for a sin he never committed, Ernest embarks with his companion Vecl on a voyage to the Holy Land. Most of the story is concerned with the duke's marvelous experiences during his Other-World Voyage. One such fabulous encounter takes place in the land of Grippia, where Ernest and his men discover a deserted castle filled with food and the semblance of hospitality. But soon the scene turns into a murderous nightmare. While Ernest and his companions watch from behind curtains, a beautiful princess is brought to the castle by crane-headed men who have abducted the princess from her home in India, having murdered her father and mother. When the crane-headed men discover that Ernest and Vecl are hiding and poised to rescue the girl, they stab her to death with their beaks. The two men barely escape from Grippia with their lives. Finally, after many subsequent adventures and encounters with fabulous creatures in strange lands, Ernest returns to Germany, where he is forgiven by the emperor and is reunited once more with his beloved mother Adlička.

As in the *Alexandreida*, there is little love interest in this epic saga of sin and expiation. The only strong emotional bonds are those that Otto and Ernest have with Adlička. At these junctures in the story, the language is colored by the courtly love lyric. When Otto sends the marriage proposal to Adlička, he adopts the role of faithful servant to the lady and desperate petitioner for her favor; the lover's heart is placed in the hands of the beloved—formulae reminiscent of the Czech love lyric, especially line 103 of *The Song of Záviš*. There is also an interesting variety of diminutive forms in Otto's love letter not present in the later love lyric; for example, the sobriquet *zvieřinička* (line 376) derives from *zvieřinicě* (Venus or morning star), itself derived from the word for zodiac (modern Czech *zvířetník*).

When Ernest embarks for the Holy Land, he and his men sing the old Czech hymn *Hospodine, pomiluj ny!* (lines 2274–75), a detail that, like the *Alexandreida*, locates the story in a familiar setting. The narrator reminds his audience of the special relationship between the hero and his mother by introducing features of the devotional language shared with religious works of the time, such as *The Life of Saint Catherine*. Adlička's cry to her long-lost son is also reminiscent of the Virgin's lament to the dead Christ in *The Lament of Mary*. The theme of maternal love means so much to the adaptor that he returns to it later in the story when the ship is stranded on the Magnetic Mountain. Here the source refers only to the grief of the soldiers' wives as the men begin to die of starvation (lines 1933–37). The Czech narrator skillfully weaves into this passage the affective bond between mother and son, thus situating the special relationship between Ernest and Adlička in a universal context: "A mother would have wept if she had seen her son..." (lines 2285–86).[20] Consistent with his amplification of the mother theme, the adaptor incorporates Marian formulae in Adlička's prayer to the Virgin that her son be returned safely to her (lines 5608–11), which reflect the importance of the cult of the Virgin Mary in Bohemia, in particular, and the pious tendency of medieval Czech literature in general. The Czech prayer has been criticized on the grounds of verbosity by the editor of the text, who misunderstands the adaptor's intention to intensify the affective bond between mother and son at this crucial and poignant point in the story.[21]

Adlička's eventual reunion with Ernest on Christmas Eve (line 5759) is described in a manner characteristic of erotic mysticism. Her heart "dances" (line 5769) as she hurries to the chapel to greet the newly returned hero. In *The Life of Saint Catherine*, Catherine's mystical marriage to Christ is depicted in a similar fashion: her heart plays in her body as she feels the radiant light streaming from his face (lines 1036–41), in accordance with Saint Augustine's first category of vision—the bodily vision—in which religious experience is received directly through the natural senses. The Indian princess, too, is described by means of the courtly code: the most original simile in the whole poem and one of the most unusual images in medieval Czech poetry is the conceit of the moon borrowing its light from the sun: "She was like the moon when it reaches the greatest light and dresses itself in the sun" (lines 3108–10).[22] This image is a topos of Marian poetry: the Virgin's beauty is a reflection of the light of grace that descends from God. Poets and exegetists derive the image from the Song of Songs 6.9: "pulchra ut luna, electa ut sol."[23] The beautiful line "a v slunečnost sě odievá" (3056) originates in yet another Marian formula, the *mulier amicta sole* of Revelation 12.1. The motif of the lady clothed in the rays of the sun was also popular in the contemporary visual arts. In the fresco cycle of the prophetess Sybil by the Austrian painter Nicholas Wurmser in the Prague monastery Na Slovanech (founded in 1360), Mary is depicted as the Queen of Heaven, but in a more human, affective form than had previously been fashionable: she stares lovingly at the playful Christ child and is surrounded by the radiant light of the sun.[24]

The description of the king of the crane-headed men, who tries unsuccessfully to woo the beautiful Indian princess, is accorded the dignity of the courtly love code, as befits a sovereign ruler. But the adaptor accentuates the king's ungainly deformity in a more graphic fashion than the German model does: he is flat-footed (line 3131), smiles like a suitor, and crows through his beak (lines 3131–34). When the princess is forced to sit with the king at the dining table, he behaves in a more extreme fashion than his counterpart in the German model; his beak tilts to and fro as he pays court to the girl, jabbing her on the cheek in an obscene mime of lovemaking: "He courted her, tilting his nose here and there before her" (lines 3145–46).[25] The whole of this passage suggests the aversion to secular courtliness that we also find in the *Alexandreida*. When the king's beak "tilts," the author is alluding to the joust in the same sardonic terms as the author of the *Alexandreida*. We may also interpret it as a sexual innuendo in connection with the phallic image of the beak. Furthermore, the beak is compared to a two-pronged pitchfork (*vidle*), a lowly image that reminds us of the torture scene in *Saint Catherine,* where the spiked wheel is likened to a harrow that drags clumps of soil in the field (lines 2769–72). The whole scene casts the figure of the king in an unfavorable light, equating secular courtly rituals with promiscuity and perverse behavior.

Lavrin or *About Dietrich of Verona*

The direction taken by Czech romance after the death of Charles IV in 1378 reflected the very different tastes and temperament of his son and successor, Wenceslas IV. Where Charles favored the mystical and the otherworldly, Wenceslas had a predilection for the realistic and the down-to-earth aspects of humanity. Even his pious reading reflected his secular tastes, as witnessed by his personal German Bible—the so-called Wenceslas Bible—which is illuminated with marginal portraits of himself and female bath attendants in various states of undress.

Not only did Wenceslas diverge from his father's taste in matters of culture; he also departed from his policy of including high noblemen and churchmen in his inner court circle. Wenceslas alienated both the higher nobility and the church hierarchy and allied himself with the lower nobility and the middle class.[26] The resulting social mobility, and the changing perception of the royal court that this involved, may explain the popularity of noncourtly verse romances in the last two decades of the fourteenth century, in which the traditional values of the gentry and nascent patriciate were dressed in the borrowed garb of chivalry. What this marriage of opposites produced, as we shall see, was a realistic ethos stripped of courtly values and tinged with the piety that, as we have seen, typified the *Alexandreida* and medieval Czech literature as a whole.

Typical of this new romance is *Lavrin* or *About Dietrich of Verona* (c. 1380),[27] modeled on the German *Laurin,* a twelfth-century Tyrolean epic.[28] It tells the story of the dwarf king Lavrin, who abducts the sister, Krinhulta (Künhilt), of Dětleb (Dietleib), one of the companions of the hero Jetřich Berúnský (Dietrich of Verona), a well-known actor in the vast, sprawling drama of the Nibelungen Cycle. The story tells of an expedition undertaken by Dětleb and his companions to Lavrin's rose garden to rescue the lovely Krinhulta. When they arrive, the knights break the silk thread that surrounds the garden, trample the roses, and proceed to make their bed in them, comportment hardly compatible with courtly etiquette. After a great deal of fighting between Lavrin and his opponents, the dwarf king is finally defeated, Krinhulta is liberated, and all ends happily—except, that is, for the hapless Lavrin, who is taken prisoner by Jetřich.

The most obvious feature of the Czech adaptation is its earthy realism (for example, making a bed in the roses) and the inclusion of a prologue and an epilogue that serve as a moral frame for the story. The prologue consists of various formulaic expressions of conventional piety familiar from the verse *Legend of Saint Procopius*; they are included to establish the moral theme of the story as the adaptor envisages it. But one is left with the distinct impression that they serve a merely perfunctory role, as if the adaptor were responding mechanically to the moral animus of Czech literature without restructuring the whole work to reflect it. The epilogue draws a similar moral conclusion by accusing Lavrin of the sin of pride (*pýcha*) and the crime of trespassing (*pych*) (lines 2075–78), thus conflating the ethical and the social dimensions of the dwarf king's transgression.[29] All this is in the spirit of the contemporary sermon tradition and reveals the pervasive extent of the national mood of reform.

More characteristic of the Czech story as a whole, however, is a light-hearted, playful treatment of the chivalric material: the knights behave in a rather comic fashion, and their battle against Lavrin is mock-heroic rather than true to the spirit of epic combat. This burlesque style is reminiscent of the *drôleries* of contemporary Bohemian manuscript illumination, and the epigonic narrative mode provides a literary parallel to the mannerist spirit of late-fourteenth-century Czech visual arts.

Tandariáš and Floribella

Tandariáš and Floribella (c. 1380), based on *Tandareis und Flordibel* by the Austrian writer Der Pleier, who worked perhaps in Salzburg between 1240 and 1270, ranks as the best-crafted, most expertly structured, and liveliest of the surviving Czech romances. The poem is preserved in three manuscripts, dated 1463, 1472 (the *Codex of the Count Boworowský*), and 1483. Internal linguistic evidence (morphology and rhymes) suggests that it was composed around 1380. One-tenth the size of the source, it is redolent of the English tail-rhyme romances of the period. The emphasis is placed on a dynamic plot, which is punctuated by lively realistic dialogue in order to make Der Pleier's amorphous tale of love, loss, and reconciliation more accessible to the Czech audience. It tells of the love between two characters, Floribella, an Indian princess who arrives at the court of King Arthur to seek protection as an orphan, and the king's nephew, Tandariáš. In the German model, Pleier provides the basis of the story when he announces that his theme is to be a tale of two young people ("Ich vil iu sagen wie zwei kint / liebe alrest begunden," lines 172–73). From henceforth it follows the basic tripartite structure of the model, which, as Peter Kern has indicated in his detailed study of the German model, adheres closely to the structure of Greek romance: two lovers meet, are forced to part, and are finally reunited.[30]

But here the similarity between the two works ends, for the Czech version is conceived in a very different spirit from its source, lacking the complex background of French and German classical romance to which Pleier is indebted.[31] *Tandariáš* has many of the formulaic trappings of the courtly romance but little of its ethos.[32] The courtly values that the German work enshrines were irrelevant to the Czech audience brought up on pious saints' lives (*The Legend of Saint Procopius*), epic tales of bravery (the *Alexandreida*), and vivid, realistic satires. Although this conservative audience required a conventionally moral mode of presentation, they could not tolerate an alien courtly ethic. In *Tandariáš*, the generic distinction between romance, lyric, epic, and satire blurs into a lively, moral tale of true love and fidelity triumphing over adversity.[33]

In the prologue to the romance, the Czech author speaks of the bond of service between the lover and his lady, which clearly owes something to the influence of the love lyric (lines 107–11). In general, however, the relationship is free of formality and restraint. There is none of the rigid hierarchy and ritualized conventions of Pleier's Arthurian court. Instead, the Czech author universalizes the lovers' experience, placing it on a par with the world of everyday life (lines 328–31). The first scene with Tandariáš and Floribella sets the tone for the rest of the work. Tandariáš tries to outwit the other gentlemen of the bedchamber by arriving at an increasingly early hour to serve Princess Floribella (lines 119–33). He does not behave according to the rules of courtly etiquette — as in the source — but follows his own impulses. Floribella behaves in the same way. She gets up earlier every day to test Tandariáš's dedication, the test being a typical occasion for irony in the romance.

The Czech author shows certain psychological insights as well as narrative skills by refraining from disclosing his characters' feelings too early in the story. Pleier, on the other hand, is unconcerned with the gradual unfolding of the love affair, allowing Tandareis to reflect for 130 lines (775–905) with an apostrophe addressed to *Vrow Minne*, while Flordibel articulates her feelings for 19 lines (924–43). The Czech author's more abbreviated approach is well illustrated by the scene in which Tandariáš accidentally cuts himself with a knife while staring at Floribella (also in Pleier's original and in the French romance *Jehan et Blonde* by Philippe de Rémi).[34] In contrast to Pleier, the Czech author evokes the love affair through direct description shorn of conventionalized gestures such as blushing. The characters respond realistically to the situation: Floribella tells Tandariáš to be careful while he does not even notice that he has cut himself.

A similar emotional directness characterizes the tryst by the window, which is better motivated in the Czech version of the story: Tandariáš's accident gives Floribella the excuse to take her squire to one side and speak to him alone (lines 143–48).[35] In the German model, Tandareis is visibly awkward and nervous; he jumps up when Flordibel approaches and hesitates before accepting the invitation to sit with her by the window. Tandariáš is more impulsive: he kneels devotedly at his lady's feet, only rising at Floribella's kind request. When she inquires as to the cause of the accident, her attitude is more familiar than Flordibel's so that her language is more direct and vigorous (lines 151–56). Tandariáš's admission of love is more effective than in the model because it takes place only at Floribella's repeated insistence (lines 167–75). The princess understands her squire's feelings but wishes to be certain. She urges him to speak openly, pausing to reflect on the implication of his words (lines 157–67). In the German version, Tandareis has a lengthy monologue that tends to weaken the dramatic quality of the encounter (lines 1178–207). Flordibel's speeches are more diffuse: when she asks Tandareis whether she has caused him pain, the question takes up thirteen lines (1209–21).

As Karel Brušák points out, the lovers are given greater prominence in the Czech version at the expense of the minor characters. Floribella defends herself at the trial, revealing her forceful and independent nature. Tandariáš does not send his prisoners directly to Arthur as in the model, but to Floribella, who intercedes for them to the king.[36] The exclusion of the king from the feudal triangle (Arthur-Tandareis-Flordibel) at this point may well reflect the diminishing power of the monarch and the growing influence of the nobility in the last two decades of the fourteenth century. It is not just Floribella who takes a more active role in the story; the queen and her maidens, rescued by the hero from the clutches of the dragon, run to catch sight of their deliverer (lines 994–95). In the scene where the wounded hero is healed in a steam bath by a maiden princess, the girl is more playfully erotic than in the model. At first she is intent on revenge, for Tandariáš almost killed her brother in combat. But her anger turns to affection so that she beats him lightly with a straw to feign punishment. The adaptor adds that the maiden pretends to scold Tandariáš (lines 1440–43). This game provokes the hero's laughter (lines 1446–69). This scene in general perhaps alludes to the fashion of taking hot baths (established by the king), while specifically line 1444 may also suggest some contamination with the antifeminist satires, in particular, *On Irate Women*, a mock counsel to husbands on how to placate their irate wives.[37] The ironic tone of the bathing scene is similar to that of the satire, in which the woman is more forceful and domineering than the man (lines 15–18).

The courtly conventions of Pleier's world are consistently discarded in favor of the kind of medial-style realism characteristic of the satires and *The Legend of Saint Procopius*. The heroine is more forceful, spontaneous, and independent-minded than her German prototype. When Tandariáš departs on his first adventure in the early stages of the story, Floribella turns to books for comfort and to forget her misery (lines 1418–19), whereas Flordibel retreats to her chapel to pray in the manner of conventional heroines of epic and romance.[38] A further example of Floribella's direct intervention in the story is the tournament scene toward the end of the romance. When Tandariáš returns incognito to enter the lists, Floribella casts aside all courtly pretensions as she catches sight of her beloved entering the lists and cries out in distress, thus earning the rebuke of the queen, who sits by her side (lines 1575–78). A masterly touch by the Czech adaptor is Floribella's sudden nosebleed when she sees Tandariáš leave the field (lines 1607–10). Brušák considers this incident to be an example of psychosomatic parallelism.[39] But nosebleeds are found in other medieval romances (for example in the Middle English *Athelston*) to denote a female character's psychological distress in extreme circumstances.[40] The medieval identification of women with their bodily functions is surely crucial here, as it is to so many similar realistic scenes in *The Life of Saint Catherine*. Women may be active, but the consequences of such behavior, one should infer from the nosebleed, are frequently comic and absurd.

Tandariáš has been described as the only "pure" courtly romance in medieval Czech literature, a judgment that is mistaken since it confuses the intention of the author of the German model with the intention of the Czech adaptor. A close attention to detail shows that *Tandariáš* was written with a different conception from its German courtly source and for a different kind of audience. By introducing down-to-earth features, the adaptor was able to remove the restraints and restrictions of courtly etiquette and present his characters in sharper, more vivid outline. In social terms, he skillfully makes both the experience of the characters and their situation more accessible and relevant to the values of his audience.

Tristram and Izalda

The realistic and popularizing trend we have witnessed so far in our analysis of the Czech verse romances reaches its furthest point of development in *Tristram and Izalda*, dated to the end of the fourteenth century. The work of an anonymous jobbing poet, *Tristram* is a skillful conflation of three German sources: Eilhart von Oberg's *Tristrant* (twelfth century), Gottfried von Strassburg's courtly version, and Heinrich von Freiberg's continuation of Gottfried's unfinished masterpiece. Its nine thousand lines make it the longest narrative poem in medieval Czech literature. The text, preserved in two manuscripts, the Strahov MS (A), dated 1449, located in the Strahov Monastery, Prague, and the Brno MS (B), dated 1483, located in the Moravian Provincial Library, is of particular interest because it offers a complete version of the Tristan story.

The poem has received scant attention from scholars. An early critic, Václav Nebeský, argued that the Czech poem is in a spirit very different from Gottfried von Strassburg's courtly conception of *hohe minne*.[41] It has in fact more in common with the epic spirit of Eilhart von Oberg's precourtly *Tristrant* (twelfth century), yet little of Eilhart's complex artistry and symbolism.[42] Although *Tristram* contains some love lyric formulae of the time, it has little in common with the world of courtly poetry and much more in common with the unvarnished simplicity of *Tandariáš* and the burlesque exuberance of the mystery plays. When the adaptor introduces lyrical language, it is usually to create a convenient rhyme. When Tristram offers to fight the giant Morholt (in an episode based on Eilhart), his motive is not knightly renown and honor (as in the source) but the idealistic desire to gain his lady's favor (lines 387–88), expressed in a formulaic couplet quite out of place in the context of the feudal relations that exist between King Mark, his nephew, and his bride-to-be. (Here again, as in *Tandariáš and Floribella*, the figure of the king recedes in relation to the two protagonists). The point is that the story provides the Czech adaptor with the excuse to reproduce the conventions of the popular romance genre when and where he pleases.[43]

As in *Tandariáš*, the author of *Tristram* simplifies the courtly or pre-courtly symbolism of the German sources to produce an idealized, unvarnished tale of two individuals who fall in love as a consequence of accidentally consuming a love potion intended for Mark and his bride Izalda. He deliberately cuts out all courtly conventions, such as the long-winded soliloquies addressed to *Frauwe Amur*, and focuses instead on the emotional bond between the two protagonists. The love potion scene, which takes place during the voyage from Ireland to Cornwall, is a good example of the adaptor's skill in portraying human emotions. When the protagonists have drunk the potion, the Czech author suggests that each is afraid the other may already be in love with someone else (lines 1914–17). The German Isolde's soliloquy, addressed to *Frauwe Amur* (lines 2440–550) is omitted, as are the long meditations on love by Flordibel. The Czech adaptors prefer to explore human relationships with the use of dialogue rather than with private reflection and monologue.[44] What emerges is a sense of the true love of the players in this drama. Like anyone deeply in love, Tristram is impulsive, touchy, prone to paranoia. When he sees Izalda, he is so overjoyed that he forgets to greet her and ask after her health as befits a courtier (lines 2094–99). In both the German and the Czech versions, Izalda invites her interlocutor to approach and sit by her. In Eilhart, the effect of the potion on Tristrant is symbolic: as if stricken by a mysterious illness, he advances slowly and with great difficulty (lines 2706–8). In the Czech version, on the other hand, Tristram betrays no trace of illness; he runs impulsively to his beloved (lines 2118–21). (Tandariáš behaves in a similarly spontaneous fashion, even to the point of throwing his companions over his shoulder in sheer joy at the prospect of being reunited with Floribella.) The author of *Tristram and Izalda* is much more idealistic about love and prudish about sex than is Eilhart, who specifies that the protagonists sleep together after drinking the potion. This detail is suppressed in the Czech version, reflecting the sober, moral outlook of the noncourtly Czech audience. In distinction to such idealism, we find several negative comments about women. At one point, the narrator introduces a Czech idiom: "Women have long hair but short reason" (lines 7125–26). Sometimes he makes Izalda behave like the wife in *The Ointment Seller* and the women in the antifeminist satire *On Irate Women*. When Izalda and Izalda of the White Hands meet at Tristram's funeral, for example, the former pushes her rival aside with a vicious thump in the flank and the following reproach: "You are like a wolf that steals sheep, and you do not know how to weep for your husband. I know better how to mourn for him" (lines 8643–45).[45]

Conclusion

This chapter has explored the Czech epic and verse romances as reflections of social reality. Whereas the *Alexandreida* reproduces reality in an overt, direct fashion, the chivalric romances do so obliquely. In addition to being adapted from one language into another (German into Czech), they are all conditioned by the preconceptions and assumptions of their audience. I have argued that the best way to discern these ideological preconceptions is to focus one's critical attention on the Czech adaptations rather than on their German models. Here, social reality is manifested in small yet significant additions, of which the authors themselves were unconscious, since they were responding mechanically to the cultural expectations of the target culture. The fact that the protagonists in *Tandariáš and Floribella* and *Tristram and Izalda* enjoy a prominent position at the expense of the heroic figures King Arthur and King Mark suggests a great deal about the relation of ruler to ruled in the last quarter of the fourteenth century in Bohemia, when royal power was on the wane and the influence of the gentry and urban patriciate—the social groups that, I have argued, occupy the subject position within the romances—was in the ascendancy.

The fact that there was interest in these epigonic tales of love and adventure suggests that times were changing by the reign of Wenceslas IV, when the last three romances considered in this chapter were written; moreover, their unique presence in manuscripts from the second half of the fifteenth century suggests that they survived the destruction of the Hussite Wars and continued to function as literature of entertainment for several years afterward. By the last two decades of the fourteenth century, then, the moral sobriety and the noncourtly ethos of the *Alexandreida* had been attenuated by the downward movement of courtly culture and the upward mobility of its audience.[46] We might see this process as *gesunkenes Kulturgut*, whereby elements of high, exclusive art are adopted by a lower social class to reflect their ideological vision of the world.

✛

CHAPTER 8

From Courtier to Rebel
Ideological Ambivalence in Smil Flaška's *The New Council*

*T*he *New Council* is one of the few works of medieval Czech literature whose author is known to us by name: Smil Flaška of Pardubice (1340s to 1403), nephew to Ernest of Pardubice, archbishop
of Prague.[1] Around 1357 Smil took a baccalaureate degree at Prague University, where he was exposed to the most advanced literary and theological trends of the day. After his father's death (1389/90), he inherited vast
estates, which he eventually lost or sold. In the 1390s he was propelled
into political affairs and military action against Wenceslas IV (1361–1419).
Smil joined a series of baronial leagues aimed to prevent the king's encroachment on the ancient rights of the nobility. Between 1394 and his
death in 1403, he occupied a key position in the administration of the
noble opposition, the Lords' Union (Panská jednota), as the chief notary
of the land court. In 1402 the king was captured, and during his captivity,
negotiations proceeded for the renewal of orderly government in the kingdom. But the royal towns, which consisted mainly of German settlers,
refused to recognize the new hegemony of the nobility and remained loyal
to the Crown. The royal city of Kutná Hora was besieged by the nobles,
and it was here, on August 13, 1403, that Smil was mortally wounded.[2]

Smil is generally considered to be the author of *The New Council* and
the earlier *A Father's Advice to His Son* (c. 1380s), a treatise on the role
of the ideal courtier intended, ostensibly, for the author's son but more
likely for an audience of noblemen.[3] *The New Council* (c. 1394) was also
intended to offer advice, this time to a prince or ruler in the manner of
the *speculum principis*, one of the most valued and popular forms of
late medieval literature.[4] Although *The New Council* is the first beast
allegory of its kind in medieval Czech literature, there are many examples of the genre in Latin and in other European languages. Medieval
beast poems can be divided into three broad categories: the religious fable of the schools represented by the *Physiologus* and the later bestiaries,
in which animals express or embody spiritual and moral truths;[5] the
satirical epic; and the "trickster" stories, such as those about Reynard
the Fox.[6] Generally speaking, the first category is limited to the early
Middle Ages, while the second and third categories became popular in
the later medieval period. But the distinction between all three is not
watertight; occasionally there is leakage from one to the other.

A good example of a late medieval beast fable that is more difficult to define is Geoffrey Chaucer's *The Parliament of Fowls* (c. 1380).[7] This poem, which assumes the form of a courtly dream vision in the manner of Dante and Guillaume de Machaut, describes how three tercel eagles compete for the hand of a formel eagle and are counseled in their wooing by a congregation of birds ("fowls"). The work alludes to the three principal suitors for the hand of Anne of Bohemia, sister of Wenceslas IV: a minor German prince, Frederick of Meissen, to whom she had been engaged for six years; the Dauphin of France (the future Charles VI), and Richard II of England.[8] Written at the time of the marriage negotiations in 1380 or at the time of the marriage of Anne and Richard in 1381, *The Parliament of Fowls* is principally a celebration of courtly love, but it also provides a humorous political commentary on the intricacies of international diplomatic negotiations.

A good example of the second category of beast fable—the satirical epic—is *Le Roman de Fauvel* (c. 1310) by Gervais du Bus, a French satire aimed at the government of Philippe IV (1268–1314) in which the corruption of the state and the church is allegorized as a shabby dun-colored horse named Fauvel.[9] This text presents several interesting points of similarity with *The New Council*. Both were inspired by monarchical policies of centralization: just as the Capetian kings strove to reduce the power of the French nobility from the twelfth century onward, so too were the Luxembourg rulers of Bohemia engaged in a long-term policy of bringing the realm under royal control. Both works were expanded over a period of time. *Le Roman de Fauvel* consists of two parts, the first more satirical, the second more entertaining in response to popular demand. *The New Council* is a conflation of two redactions. Both allegorize the debased ideal of knighthood as a horse. The Fauvel of the French work embodies all that is corrupt in the state of Philippe IV, while the Horse in *The New Council* articulates the vices of the Luxembourg court.

In this chapter I shall argue that *The New Council* occupies a state of ideological transition from a courtly *speculum principis* in the manner of *The Parliament of Fowls* to a satirical poem in the mold of *Le Roman de Fauvel*. In doing so, I shall be departing from the received scholarly opinion that *The New Council* is a work of conscious irony.[10] I shall propose that the ironic tension evinced in the work between courtly and satirical elements is the consequence of the author's changing social identity from courtier to rebel rather than the effect of a conscious artistic strategy. Admittedly, the presence of irony in the text may also owe something to the ambiguity of animal symbolism in the Middle Ages. Joyce E. Salisbury attributes the ambiguity of beast poems to the complex relationship between humans and animals in the Christian worldview: "Christianity was defining people as different from animals, yet it inherited morally uplifting texts that depended upon seeing parallels between people and animals."[11] But to take animal symbolism as the sole explanation for the text's shifting voices places too much emphasis on Smil's indebtedness to his Latin sources and not enough on his changing social position and the complex reception of his work.[12] To make sense of the text's mediation between a benevolent courtly poem like *The Parliament of Fowls* and a political satire like *Le Roman de Fauvel*, we need to pay more attention to the social context by tracing Smil's fluctuating political fortunes from courtier to rebel, and the concomitant narrowing of his audience from a general courtly public to a small but specific group of confederate rebels.

The New Council

Animal fables for the purpose of moral edification were popular in the fourteenth century, a tradition well represented in medieval Bohemia by the Latin *Quadripartitus* by Gregory of Uherský Brod, which deals with the moral attributes of quadrupeds,[13] and the encyclopedia of Bartholomew Claretus of Chlumec, which includes a list of bird fables known as the *Physiologiarius*.[14] *The New Council* consists of forty-four counsels of birds and quadrupeds convened to advise the Lion King, an allegorical allusion to the double-tailed lion of Bohemia. Clearly, therefore, the Lion King represents Wenceslas IV.

The other counsels can be divided into three groups: those which offer positive advice, those which are negative, and those which are ambiguous. The extant version, now known as *The New Council* to distinguish it from the earlier redaction (presumably known simply as *The Council*), dates from 1394–95, when Smil was briefly reconciled with the king after a long period of conflict. The extant work is not only bigger in scale than the earlier version; it also mirrors the author's modified attitude toward Wenceslas after fifteen years of alleged misrule. Here negative, ironic counsels alternate with positive ones, the former reflecting the presence of foreigners and upstarts in the king's council. Many of these satirical speeches express the author's aversion to royal policy and the king's alleged personal peccadilloes: indolence, fondness for alcohol, love of public baths. Although some of these complaints are commonplace and can be found in other examples of the *speculum principis* genre, others are undoubtedly grounded in historical reality and reflect an accurate awareness of the king's personality and his policies.

Like his brother-in-law, Richard II of England, Wenceslas was of a temperamental disposition.[15] But unlike Richard, who had an extremely elevated sense of his own royal dignity, Wenceslas liked to mingle among the ordinary people and enjoyed the pleasures of everyday life (as can be readily seen from the margins of his personal German Bible).[16] More seriously, this demotic streak translated into disastrous political policies: as we have seen in chapter 7, Wenceslas turned his back on the church hierarchy and alienated the most powerful magnates in the land, preferring to ally himself with the gentry and the middle classes. To be fair, international events beyond his immediate control exacerbated his policies at home. In 1378 (the same year he came to the throne), the Great Schism divided the church into the Roman and Avignonese parties. Wenceslas initially supported the Roman pope but, under pressure from the king of France, assumed a neutral posture. This change in policy brought Wenceslas into conflict with his pro-Roman archbishop, John of Jenštejn. In the course of the ensuing bitter struggle between Wenceslas and his archbishop, the king had the latter's vicar general, John of Pomuk, arrested, tortured, and murdered (1393). The body was thrown from the Charles Bridge into the Vltava River, where, according to Catholic legend, signs of martyrdom were manifested. John of Pomuk was later canonized (1729) and—suitably metamorphosed into Saint John of Pomuk—became the Catholic counterpart to the Protestant martyr John Hus and one of the most popular saints in Counter-Reformation Europe.

Archbishop John of Jenštejn was forced into exile and died, a broken man, in Rome. With his ruin, the close relationship between church and state so carefully constructed by Charles IV came to an end. The instability caused by this major rift and the power vacuum it created encouraged the nobility to reassert their ancient rights and privileges at the expense of the weakened monarchy.[17] The king's policy of excluding the higher nobility from the great offices of state—positions they had traditionally occupied during Charles IV's reign—and replacing them with members of the lower gentry and the rising middle classes only made things worse.[18]

The sense of resentment that Wenceslas's policies aroused among the higher nobility are accurately reflected in *The New Council*, in which Smil introduces three complaints against the king: Wenceslas had opened up his council to outsiders, had permitted men to buy positions in the land court (zemský soud), and, like a feudal landlord, claimed his right of reversion, requisitioning property when its owners apparently died without heirs. As for acting like a feudal landlord, Wenceslas was following the example of his predecessor, John of Luxembourg, who had introduced into Bohemia the foreign practice of feudal tenure as a means of reducing the lands of the nobles.[19] Feudal tenure was a device used by King John to raise cash by granting royal land to be held from him as a fee. Wenceslas resumed the efforts of his grandfather but his tactics were different. Using governmental machinery when possible and force when necessary, Wenceslas on several occasions deprived baronial families of their property. The nobles, threatened at the base of their existence with the loss of their estates, formed several armed leagues in an effort to put a stop to what they regarded as the king's abrogation of their customary practices.

Smil's own family had been the alleged victim of one such case of escheatage. In 1384–85, Smil's paternal uncle, Smil the Elder, died without male issue. The property passed to the husband of Smil the Elder's daughter, upon whose death in 1384 the king proclaimed his right to the family estate of Pardubice in eastern Bohemia. Smil the Younger and his father William contested the case but without success. According to a document of the land court dated February 25, 1390, Wenceslas IV was declared the rightful owner of Pardubice. As a result of this ruling, Smil and his father lost their property there. The satirical counsel of the Wolf (lines 699–742) alludes to this case. Here, and in the counsel of the Scavenger, later interpolations allege that the records had been falsified to favor the king's act of escheatage.

Framing the animal counsels are the speeches of the Eagle and the Swan. Josef Tříška treats these birds as eschatological symbols of life and death, respectively,[20] overlooking the heraldic significance of the eagle as the emblem of the empire and the swan's Christological identification with the Church. Thus the Eagle and the Swan symbolize the king's temporal *and* spiritual authority as king of the Romans. Wenceslas had been elected king of the Romans after his father's death in 1378, a position he retained until his deposition by the electors in 1400.

The Eagle articulates Smil's initial benevolence toward the king and his hopes for a harmonious relationship with him.[21] As the first of the counselors, he also represents the king's younger brother, Jošt of Luxembourg, margrave of Moravia (whose heraldic device was an eagle) and the leader of the first baronial rebellion against Wenceslas in 1394. If the audience of the first redaction might have understood the Eagle's counsel in terms of Wenceslas's imperial responsibilities, the rebels for whom the second redaction was intended would have interpreted this bird's prominence at the head of the council, and the Lion King's laconic acquiescence, as an accurate mirror of Wenceslas's decline and their own rising fortunes. The speech, then, had a different meaning at different times for different people. We cannot really assume a univocal textual authority or monolithic meaning but rather a set of meanings contingent on the changing historical situation.

The Horse's counsel is another example of the text's resistance to one monolithic interpretation. At first the Horse encourages the king to adorn himself in splendid apparel (echoing the counsel of the preceding speaker, the Peacock). For the earlier courtly audience this would have been understood in a benevolent sense, especially since Wenceslas quickly established a reputation as a shabby dresser at a time when Bohemian couture was at the height of European fashion:

You ought to dress, king, bright and bold
and deck yourself in purest gold.

To make your court a joyous place
is surely not a king's disgrace:
dancing, jousting, tournaments,
and ladies swathed in ornaments;
let all these sights your heart elate.[22]
(Lines 863–69)

Yet as the counsel progresses, the satirical elements grow as the courtly benevolence diminishes:

And now the joust begins, behold!
So many skillful in this feat
end up falling from their seat,
in the sandpit, shocked and dirtied.
But be not, therefore, disconcerted
when—lances lowered, visor down—
they strike each other on the crown.
"O rette, rette!" comes the sound
of knights prostrated on the ground,
unhorsed by their most vicious foe,
quite toothless now and full of woe.
At such a brave chivalrous tilt
much precious, noble blood is spilt.[23]
(Lines 874–86)

The ironic description of the tournament, in particular, recalls *Quadri-partitus,* book II, chapter 5, which condemns the recklessness (*audacia*) of the horse and—metonymically—the knight who rides it.[24] Smil's satirical treatment of the joust is also indebted to the antitournament opprobrium of the medieval sermon tradition dating from its first condemnation by Pope Innocent II in the twelfth century.[25] His biting wit, especially the satirical description of the knight unseated by his foe, recalls the sardonic scene of jousting in the Babylon episode of the *Alexandreida* and the caustic remarks of the author of *The Dalimil Chronicle,* where gambling and jousting for ladies' favors are castigated as degenerate activities. We see something of the late Luxembourg court in the jousting scene from the early-fifteenth-century Bohemian illuminated manuscript of *The Travels of Sir John Mandeville* (now in the British Museum).[26] This *de luxe* courtly manuscript illustrates the decadence of the late Luxembourg court in the 1390s, with its love of outlandish costumes and unrestrained coiffure. While the knights and their accoutrements are represented as at the height of European fashion, one cannot fail to notice the inclusion of certain discordant details. At bottom left a hideously devilish retainer urges a horse into the fray, while an attendant knight at bottom right sports a shield emblazoned with a malevolent face. For the artist there was, one cannot help feeling, something rather immoral about this kind of secular splendor.

Ambivalence toward jousting in medieval Bohemia was particularly pronounced because of the influence of the church on Czech knights, who were encouraged to be fighters on God's behalf.[27] Inevitably, this religious ideal of the *miles Dei* clashed with the secular model of knighthood introduced by King John. One reason for the enduring appeal of the ideal of the *miles Dei* in Bohemia throughout the fourteenth century was the strong contrast it provided with the secular model of courtier-knight fashionable at the Luxembourg court, helping to define the Bohemian nobles' difference from the courtly norm and reinforcing their sense of class identity and solidarity.

Another ambiguous counselor is the Wolf, whose speech would have been present in the first redaction, although the autobiographical reference to forged legal documents was added to the later version.[28] Hooded in grey, the Wolf may have been initially intended as a wolf-monk, the *lupus monachus* of traditional beast fables.[29] As such, the Wolf's counsel was probably meant to highlight the greed of the ecclesiastical authorities rather than the king. By the second redaction, however, the Wolf is associated with the king's "new men," who were being recruited into the governmental machinery and who were instrumental in the royal policy of requisitioning noble property. Such men caused enormous resentment among the nobility and would have been involved in the case of escheatage against Smil's family.

Analogously, the counsel of the Peacock (lines 836–60) can be read in both positive and negative, benevolent and critical, terms. Admittedly, such ambivalence may owe something to the ambiguous significance of animal symbolism in the medieval bestiaries. Within this tradition, the Peacock connoted the vanity of physical beauty, as in *Quadripartitus*, book II, chapter 25. In his encyclopedia, Claretus states that the Peacock is proud and has the light tread of a thief (*sicut fur*),[30] perhaps a sardonic dig at the king's forcible annexation of Smil's property. Yet the Peacock's encouragement to Wenceslas to dress like a king may also be interpreted as a benevolent advice to a man noted for his shabby attire.

The Beaver's counsel (lines 1633–65) is similarly ambiguous. According to the bestiary tradition, this animal, which was devoted to physical hygiene, symbolized the virtue of inner spiritual purity, as in *The New Council* (lines 1641–42). In addition, this dam-contructing creature is probably offering benevolent encouragement to the king to emulate his father's (Charles IV's) great reputation as a builder. By contrast, the rhyme *hlúpé/kúpe* ("silly"/"bathes") of the opening couplet can also be read in negative terms as a satirical reference to Wenceslas's well-known habit of taking frequent hot baths, an unusual practice that spread to the English court of Richard II.[31]

The Nightingale's counsel (lines 1683–1722) can also be understood in benevolent and negative senses. His recommendation that the king maintain good spirits by surrounding himself with singers and musicians comports with the positive connotation of the bird in *Claretus*.[32] It is also applied as a positive simile to Chancellor John of Středa in a laudatory letter written by the Italian humanist Cola di Rienzo from Roudnice in 1351.[33] But in *Quadripartitus*, book II, chapter 26, the Nightingale connotes the pride and vanity of the human voice and of musical instruments, corresponding to *The New Council*, where the bird praises the polyphonic art of singing and playing. With its allusions to the joy of youth and springtime, the speech also reads like a witty parody of the contemporary courtly love lyric.

Finally, the speech of the Swan, albeit probably derived from the first redaction of the text, places the emphasis on the king's vices rather than on his positive qualities. In distinction to the Eagle, the Christological Swan rejects the ways of the world completely and insists on the urgent need for penance and reconciliation. The whole speech is overshadowed by the later Smil's preoccupation with the failings of a king who appears to have lost not only his political integrity as a temporal ruler but also his moral right to command the allegiance of his subjects.

Conclusion

Like all medieval writers, Smil inherited a moral understanding of beast poetry from the *Physiologus* and the bestiaries. But medieval animal symbolism does not fully explain the ambiguous speeches of the beasts in *The New Council*, nor does the argument that the author was consciously manipulating the counsels for ironic effect. If the first point of view suggests that the author had no control of his material, the second implies that he had absolute control, an assertion that is patently untrue, since Smil did not overhaul the first redaction entirely but merely modified and amplified it. The truth, I think, lies somewhere between these polarities. As a work of transition, the text as we have it represents the views of an individual whose initial allegiance to the king and status as a courtly insider was being modified by the resentment of a nobleman excluded from the influential courtly circles to which he formerly belonged. If the earlier redaction of *The New Council* reflects the author's benevolent attitude to the young Wenceslas, the later redaction expresses the growing antagonism of a rebel. Commensurate with this modified role is a narrowing of the text's reception from a broad courtly public to a (relatively) small group of disaffected fellow noblemen familiar with the king's personal and professional failings.

Such a blend of loyalty and political self-interest lies at the heart of what Morton W. Bloomfield describes as the late medieval conflict between "conscience" and "fame."[34] Not all medieval writers, however, were vulnerable to this conflict of interests. Neither the satirical French author of *Le Fauvel* nor the English author of *The Parliament of Fowls* seems to have had any difficulty disengaging himself from loyalty to the Crown when political events dictated. In the words of Paul Strohm, Chaucer was "neither bound by oath nor secured by land tenure"[35] to the king, a situation that allowed him to transfer his allegiance from the discredited Richard II to the usurper Henry of Derby (later Henry IV). Chaucer's marginality and sense of not belonging to any social group engendered a subjectivity and range of artistic irony unavailable to most medieval writers.[36]

By dint of his noble status, Smil was never on the margins of society like Chaucer. Yet, like the author of the *Alexandreida*, whose gnomic wisdom is echoed in *The New Council*, Smil presents an ambiguous mirror of kingship. In the *Alexandreida* Alexander is initially a positive ruler acting in God's interests and keeping his nobles in his counsel, but later he foolishly strives to conquer the whole world, a probable allusion to Přemysl Ottokar's II's encroachment on the rights of the nobility. The author of *The Dalimil Chronicle* similarly lauds Přemysl in lyrical language as a rose placed by God in the meadow and praises his campaigning zeal against the pagans of Prussia, yet, elsewhere in the work, castigates the same ruler for stealing land and villages from the nobility and giving them to the German settlers.[37] More than a century later, the same kind of ambivalence characterizes Smil's picture of Wenceslas IV in *The New Council*.

CHAPTER 9

Writing and the Female Body

The Weaver, the Wycliffite Woman, and
The Dispute between Prague and
Kutná Hora

The prose dispute *Tkadleček* (The weaver) (1407/9) is an example of a genre that was extremely popular in the medieval schools.[1] It consists of two disputants, the Weaver—whose name is disclosed through cryptogram as the lover Ludvík—and Misfortune. As the plaintiff, Ludvík instigates the dispute by complaining to the defendant, Misfortune, that he has recently been jilted by his lover, whose name is revealed by cryptogram as Adlička. This dialogue between two warring parties is characteristic of the medieval debate form; in similar medieval Czech examples of the same genre we find disputes between water and wine, soul and the body, death and man.[2] Since there are traditionally only two speakers involved, the problem that faces the dispute may be said to mirror its mimetic dilemma as allegorical form: torn between two mutually antagonistic parties, each representing a distinct point of view, the work cannot achieve its intended goal of presenting a stable, truthful picture of reality without tilting the balance in favor of one side or the other. As Roman Jakobson reminds us, medieval disputes have an a priori known result.[3] In fact, the binaries we find in the dispute—soul/body, wine/water, death/man, reason/emotion—are all predicated on the assumed superiority of one element over its opposite: the "soul," for example, prevails over the "body," "death" over "man," and so on. To achieve closure and allow the truth to be revealed, medieval writers were sometimes compelled to interfere with the dialogue. In *The Dispute between the Soul and the Body* (*Spor duše s tělem*), for instance, the argument between the parties is so unrelenting on both sides that a third party—in the guise of the traditional mediator between God and man, the Virgin Mary—is required to intervene and provide a fitting conclusion.[4] This tripartite variation on the standard bipartite form is a clear example of the coercive intentionality that underlies the dispute as a whole. Each work is programmed to conclude in a particular way so that the arguments proffered in the course of the work are mere formalities geared toward a predetermined outcome. The need to stack the cards in favor of one point of view and the occasional further need to impose a third mediating element to ensure a desired result only serve to underline the instability facing any written work that purports to possess the absolute authority of philosophical truth. In *The Weaver* it is Misfortune who has the last word, and it is he who embodies the text's ideological message against Ludvík's advocacy of the courtly ethic.

This chapter will explore how the dispute genre is profoundly gendered in the way it promotes its argument. In *The Weaver*, for example, Misfortune's male-connoted discourse is aligned with absolute truth while the Weaver's courtly discourse is equated with the distraction of the female body. As the text unravels, however, its closure is undermined by its inability to preserve the Aristotelian distinction between true/false and soul/body as, respectively, male and female. The arbitrariness of the textual gendering of truth also characterizes *The Dispute between Prague and Kutná Hora*, where instead of male versus female we have a conflict between a beautiful virgin (Prague) and a harridan (Kutná Hora). Here truth is equated with the virgin, untruth with the harridan. As Stephen Greenblatt has argued, works of allegory are particularly common at times of theological, political, and ideological uncertainty, when the very status of truth is at stake.[5] The dispute's mimetic instability may be said to mirror the larger epistemological crisis of truth in a society torn between the claims and counterclaims of orthodox belief and religious dissent. As we have already seen in previous chapters and will continue to see in this one, anxiety about the female body is inseparable from the late medieval crisis of truth.

The Weaver

The anonymous author of *The Weaver*—almost certainly a graduate of Prague University and like the German author of *Der Ackermann aus Böhmen*, Johannes von Tepl, probably a member of the imperial chancellery—exemplifies the new generation of clerk-courtiers. It has been suggested that *The Weaver* was written for the king's consort, Queen Sophie, at her regional court of Hradec Králové.[6] As a scholar-courtier, the author would have encountered a conflict of interest between his clerical training at the university and his courtly vocation. It is this conflict between clerical and courtly writing, I suggest, that is acted out between Misfortune and Tkadleček. If we compare *The Weaver* with an earlier work of Czech literature on a similar theme and with a similar form—*The Dispute between the Groom and the Scholar* (c. 1380s)—what distinguishes these two works is precisely the social transformation of the court during the reign of Wenceslas IV. In *The Dispute between the Groom and the Scholar*, the two disputing protagonists are both members of the growing impoverished underclass, in spite of their differing backgrounds as (respectively) university and court affiliates. In *The Weaver*, the principle of the dispute is not higher or lower social status but the status of writing itself.

The tension between the clerk and the lover was not new to the later Middle Ages. We see it in the work of Machaut, Froissart, and Petrarch.

But in the works of these authors, there is a desire to reconcile the conflict, since as functionaries of powerful courts themselves, it was in their interest to find a rapprochement between their training as clerks and their professional duties as court writers. The political situation in early-fifteenth-century Bohemia was rather different from the royal courts of England and France. Many Czech university masters and preachers railed against the excesses of the court and the church. It is against this social backdrop that we should seek to make sense of the antagonism between the lover Ludvík and the clerk Misfortune. The anonymous writer of our text chose to express the conflict between his clerk's training and his courtly vocation in the form of a traditional Scholastic dispute representing the age-old conflict between the soul and the body, since this was the only form available to him to articulate division and discord. But, as we shall see, the real debate in *The Weaver* is about the pros and cons of courtly love. In this respect, too, it is typical of the early fifteenth century. In France, at the court of Charles V, an intense debate raged about the role of courtly love. Jean de Montreuil, the provost of Lille, had instigated the debate by writing an enthusiastic commentary on *Le Roman de la Rose*. He sent a copy of his treatise to the Franco-Italian poet Christine de Pisan, who replied by attacking the famous work for its misogynist invective.[7] Although there were some similarities between the French and Czech cultural situations (Wenceslas and Charles V were both pleasure-loving kings, in distinction to their more humanist-scholarly fathers), the actual terms of the debate were different. Whereas Christine attacks courtly love for its inherent misogyny, our Czech author attacks it *in the name of misogyny*. This difference of emphasis signals the very different associations that courtly love held for both cultures. For Christine, courtly love was inextricably identified with the antifeminist animus of Jean de Meun's *Roman de la Rose* and Scholastic misogyny; for the author of *The Weaver*, it was identified with profeminism and its alleged denial of Scholastic reasoning. In Bohemia, courtly love was virtually synonymous with the profeminist animus of the royal court. As a relatively new discourse in Czech literature, courtly love posed a threat to the moral-minded Czech writers of the time. The author of *The Weaver* shared this antagonism toward courtly discourse, and the whole point of his work is to undermine the traditional power of its influence over the royal audience.

The Weaver has been shown to be an analogue of a German work of Bohemian provenance, *Der Ackermann aus Böhmen*, which takes the form of a dispute between Death and the Plowman, whose wife has recently died. According to Antonín Hrubý, *The Weaver* and *Der Ackermann* must have had the same model, a Scholastic work written sometime before 1378.[8] Scholasticism, which originated around 1100 and was centered in the universities of Paris, Oxford, and (later) Prague, was one of the most important schools of medieval thought. It sought to reconcile theology with philosophy, the Bible with Aristotle, faith with reason. Both *The Weaver* and *Der Ackermann* translate the ideals of Scholasticism into literary form. Although both works are rooted in the principles of Scholasticism, *Der Ackermann*, which is only one-quarter the length of the Czech work, sheds more of its Scholastic features than does *The Weaver*. Both the German appellation "plowman" and the Czech "weaver" are metaphorical designations for a writer. Both authors use quotations from the ancients that are contained in the popular medieval collections, Walter Burley's *Liber de vita ac moribus Philosophorum*, Valerius Maximus's *Factorum et dictorum memorabilium libri novem* (first century A.D.) and *Speculum sapientiae beati Cyrilli*. The Czech author quotes more accurately and more usually cites his sources than does the German author. Antonín Hrubý contends that the author of their mutual model was a true Schoolman, unlike the Czech and German authors. *The Weaver* contains more than 250 exempla and quotations (90 from Aristotle alone). The Czech author goes further than his German counterpart in displaying his scholarly erudition. His work is characterized by a rhetorical excess, as illustrated by the devices of repetition, anaphora, homoeoteleuton, and triad patterns.[9]

While the Plowman and Death discourse largely on eschatological and metaphysical issues arising from the demise of the Plowman's wife, Ludvík and Misfortune argue over the merits and faults of courtly writing and courtly love. Ludvík is a self-styled courtly writer steeped in the literary conventions of the time. When he introduces himself to Misfortune in chapter 3, he presents himself in allegorical terms as a weaver or writer:

> I am a weaver of a learned rank; I know how to weave without wood, frame, or iron. My shuttle, with which I thread the woof and weft, is made from bird down; my yarn is made from the clothing of various animals. The dew with which I sprinkle my field is neither plain water nor pure in form, but mixed with plain water... which I scatter here and there, up and down.[10]

In chapter 14, Misfortune also presents himself as a weaver/writer:

> We act as you do, Weaver. The tools of our trade are prepared for all men, and with our power we apply them to all men and weave.[11]

Although both Ludvík and Misfortune style themselves as writers, they proceed from diametrically opposite points of view. Ludvík is a poet of courtly love in the manner of Machaut, whereas Misfortune is a clerical writer in the mold of Augustine and the early church fathers. In this learned capacity, he abrogates to himself the power of jurisdiction over the kind of secular writing undertaken by Ludvík, especially the courtly code of which the latter is a proud practitioner:

The violet will not hide from us even with its luxuriant color, which denotes permanence. The lily with its beauty and whiteness will not fell us even in bright hope. The red rose with its scarlet color will not be veiled from us in burning love. The clover, the ivy, the juniper, the periwinkle, which is the leader in all conceived favor, cannot hide from us. The field rose with its russet color, sign of all mystery, cannot escape us. Even the invented, stolen color of grey, ingeniously composed from many colors, will not escape us. The blue cornflower of evil hope or perfection will not resist us. The dandelion with its vigor and its yellow color, a flower much abused, will not profit against us.[12]

Here Misfortune is presenting himself both as the Great Leveler (a motif appropriated from *Der Ackermann*) and as a critic of courtly love intimate with its repertoire of secret codes and meanings (as the above passage of courtly flower and color symbolism suggests). Thus the dispute is less a metaphysical *cri du coeur* in the style of *Der Ackermann* than a discursive dispute about the pros and cons of didactic and courtly writing. The whole argument begins with and hinges on the kinds of "speeches" (*řeči*) that the two speakers employ to advance their arguments. In chapter 2, Misfortune responds to Ludvík's opening harangue by mocking his opponent's novel courtly discourse/speech: "Harken, harken, harken to these new discourses."[13] In chapter 9 Ludvík reprimands his interlocutor for trying to lead him astray with "lovely discourse" and "diverse discourses," all allusions to Misfortune's ostentatious love of rhetorical clerkly language. Writing is thus the real object of contention between the speakers: Ludvík undertakes to defend courtly discourse from Misfortune's constant assaults on the courtly code.

Whereas Ludvík defines writing as a positive medium in the service of secular courtliness, Misfortune represents the patristic tradition of the schools established by early church exegetes Augustine and Jerome, who perceived the written, secular text as a dangerous distraction from the truth of Christian teaching.[14] They likened the surface meaning or letter of the text to the female body, which the (male) writer must pass through and discard to reach the truth beyond.[15] Similarly, Misfortune's speeches are intended to reinforce the moral insight that courtly allegory cannot provide the unity and stability of truth sought by the reader. Ludvík's positive view of courtly allegory figures truth as an alluringly female body concealed below the layers of language.[16] These gendered figurings of truth as male and female respectively, and the metaphor of the female body implicit in both, explain the central role of Adlička as the object of bitter contention between the disputants.

By taking turns to vilify and idealize Adlička, Ludvík and Misfortune identify her with their respective amatory and moral discourses. For Misfortune, the negative allure of the secular text is akin to the labyrinthine, female body; for Ludvík, the courtly text is fascinatingly polyvalent and multifaceted, like the veiled body of his beloved. The connection between the female body and the art of writing is central to the pivotal role of Adlička in the dispute. In chapter 9, Ludvík conducts an extended defense of his beloved in the face of Misfortune's misogynistic onslaught. He claims that the supreme virtue of Adlička is her ability to avoid false and flattering speeches. In chapter 10, Misfortune launches into a vicious assault on her allegedly spotless reputation. Responding to Ludvík's assertion that she is a noblewoman who lives in a great castle, Misfortune insinuates that she is really just a chambermaid who is responsible for stoking the oven.

Misfortune now introduces a variety of mock-courtly epithets to describe Adlička, all synonyms for a stoker or a generator of heat. In the same chapter (10), Misfortune expresses amazement that Ludvík should choose to be involved with such a common woman. As early as chapter 4 he had referred to Adlička as a *pernikářka* ("a gingerbread maker"). The stoker heats the oven and, figuratively speaking, enflames men's genitalia by arousing their passion; analogously, the gingerbread maker lights the oven to bake her goods, that is, she ignites men's desire. The various synonyms for "stoker" point metonymically to the metaphor of the oven in which the gingerbread maker bakes her goods: the vagina. In addition to its primary meaning of "gingerbread," the Old Czech *perník* can also mean "sheath for pens or quills," which would be consistent with the self-referential conceit of writing (plowing, weaving) discussed earlier. In addition, the word would appear to be another instance of obscene sexual punning, since "sheath" also designates the female genitalia or the vagina. In this sense, the derivational noun *pernikářka* would literally signify a female maker or seller of quill sheaths, a reference to Adlička's alleged reputation, not only as a prostitute, but as a procuress of prostitutes or the madam of a brothel. The same pun also alludes to Adlička's figuring as the written text into which Ludvík inserts his pen as he undertakes his craft of writing.

The conceit of the vagina implicit in these epithets of opprobrium as applied by Misfortune to Adlička signifies not only the sexual heat and promiscuity conventionally attributed to women, but also the *horror vacui*, or horrifying emptiness of meaning lurking beneath the alluring and seductive surface of writing, which the moral clerk's phallic pen must penetrate to reach the true meaning of the text. The equation of the text with the female body and the pen with the phallus was a commonplace in medieval hermeneutic theories.[17] The allegorical designation of Ludvík as a plowman, cited earlier, implies a metaphorical association between the plow/pen and the phallus, the field/page and the female body, and the seed/ink with the semen released during coitus. In her study of Chaucer's "sexual poetics," Carolyn Dinshaw provides many examples of this hermeneutic equation between the text and the female body from Chaucer to Boccaccio and Jean de Meun's *Roman de la Rose,* where the female body and the female genitalia in particular are presented as a horrifying void, a maze of disgusting passageways, a labyrinth at the center of which is concealed a monster or a fiend.[18]

The obscene sexual punning fundamental to *The Weaver* is an intrinsic feature of the medieval and patristic tendency to gender the secular or courtly text as a female body. For Misfortune the esoteric code of courtly love language is a distraction akin to the lure of the female body itself, which diverts the writer from his rigorous pursuit of truth. In chapter 12, for example, Misfortune attacks the cult of courtly love (*milost*) as a secret discourse devoted to concealing meaning and truth: "Love has its special signs, its special slogans, its special hidden speeches."[19] Adlička is identified by Misfortune as secretive and concealed in her illicit capacity as a stoker or prostitute. The relentless association of Adlička's body with this amatory discourse is continued in chapter 10, when Misfortune claims that Ludvík's good intentions are lost once he expresses his meaning in words, for then he is ensnared by the superficiality of his own speech, just as he is seduced by the lure of Adlička's wanton body.[20] Pursuant upon this jibe, Misfortune engages in more sexual punning in the form of a triad of synonyms for "oven" (*pec, kamna, vápenice*). The close proximity between Ludvík's denigrated amatory discourse and the sexual image of the vagina underscores the metonymic association between the moral threat of a woman's body and the corrupting power of courtly literature.

The misogyny expressed by Misfortune, which prevailed well into the modern era, was fixed by Aristotle in the fourth century B.C. As a Scholastic dispute, *The Weaver* seeks to reconcile reason with emotion, Aristotle with the Bible. According to Aristotle—the most heavily cited authority in the work—the physical universe was composed of form and matter; women constituted matter, chaotic and formless, while men provided the life-giving principle of form. As matter deprived of form, the female was an imperfect and incomplete version of the male, related to the opposite sex as mere receiver and inferior instrument.[21] The masculine unity of form corresponds to the universal medieval equation of man with reason/soul and woman with emotion/body: patristic exegetes, for example, maintained that woman (or Eve) represents the appetite, while man (or Adam) represents soul or intellect.[22] Extrapolating from this equation, medieval writers saw woman as naturally subject to man, because, in the words of Aquinas, "in man the discernment of reason predominates."[23]

Whereas Misfortune envisages the courtly or secular text as a whore, Ludvík idealizes it as a lady concealed beneath the multiple layers of elusive meaning. Adlička is for him the personification of that epistemological certainty and stability of truth that he seeks in writing. This defense of Adlička leads Misfortune to mock Ludvík himself as female in his hysterical comportment and compares him with flawed women of the past: "Do not act as Helen."[24] At such moments of extreme deprivation, Ludvík's language begins to approximate—and parody—the language of religious desolation, the Virgin's lamentations over the body of the crucified Christ in the medieval *Planctae*: "Gone, gone, gone my bright star."[25] Similarly, Misfortune's speeches become more histrionic in inverse proportion to their assertion of authority. In the final chapter, which extends to sixteen pages of anaphora and repetition bordering on liturgical chant, Misfortune's programmatic conclusion seems to get mired in the very medium it aspires to transcend—rhetorical language itself. As Howard Bloch illuminatingly points out, "One of the salient ironies of misogynistic discourse is that it often becomes rhetorical or ornamental in direct proportion to the extent to which it denounces woman as ornament."[26] For all his professions of Aristotelian common sense and male-associated moral rectitude, Misfortune's discourse is curiously ornate and "feminine." In spite of the neutrality suggested by the gender of his name in Czech (*Neštěstie*), Misfortune does not transcend the gendered ascriptions of medieval hermeneutics. Veiled in his own ornamental language, his words are contingent on the very rhetoricity he disparages as female.[27]

In spite of the writer's programmatic intention to undermine the cult of courtly love discourse and steer the audience toward a greater appreciation of moral writing, *The Weaver* exposes his inability to prise apart the didactic and the aesthetic aspects of his work.[28] As the text unravels, it exposes its most precious assumptions about the moral function of writing to be a generative process—a rhetorical effect of language—and its author's identity to be contingent upon this effect.[29] The writer's aspiration to realize a moral message that would transcend the rhetoricity of writing is undermined by the text's division, difference, and derivation.[30]

The Wycliffite Woman and *The Dispute between Prague and Kutná Hora*

In the last years of Charles IV's reign, Prague witnessed an alarming increase in urban poverty, a statistic echoed in the mock dispute *The Groom and the Scholar*, which realistically exposes the plight of two members of the *Lumpenproletariat* engaged in a protracted to-and-fro of one-upmanship.[31] As Graus has shown, this widespread poverty helped to fuel the Hussite reform movement, especially the Prague uprising of 1419.[32] Like his namesake Charlemagne, Charles had divided his vast inheritance among his sons. Wenceslas received the lion's share, including the kingdom of Bohemia and the title king of the Romans. For most of his reign, the hapless king was forced to deal not only with the resentment of the nobility but also with the rivalrous machinations of his younger brothers, Jošt, margrave of Moravia, and Sigismund, his successor as king of Bohemia. In spite of his personal orthodox views on religion, Charles IV had tolerated to some extent the reformist trends at work in his kingdom and—in the case of the fiery preacher Waldhauser—had even encouraged them.[33]

These religious and social burdens proved too much for the young and inexperienced Wenceslas when he ascended his father's throne in 1378. By the early years of the fifteenth century, the reputation that Bohemia had enjoyed as an international center of learning, art, and culture was in steady decline, largely as a consequence of Wenceslas's inability to control the ethnic tensions and reformist conflicts within his kingdom. Just as in the England of Henry V (r. 1413–22) nationalist policies were beginning to supplant the Ricardian policy of peace, so was Bohemia plunged into a calamitous civil war between the reformers, led by disaffected elements of the lower nobility and Hussite preachers, on the one hand, and the Catholics, led by the papacy and Sigismund of Luxembourg, on the other. Outmaneuvered by the Czech masters at the University of Prague, the German students had left the city in 1409 to establish a new seat of learning at Leipzig.[34] Under increasing pressure from the Council of Constance and from his younger brother, Sigismund, to eradicate the heretical elements at the university and in the churches of Prague, Wenceslas attempted to make some feeble concessions to the Catholic party, such as handing over control of Saint Stephen's Church—a major center of the reformed faith—to the Catholics. These events triggered a violent backlash from the reformers. Led by the preacher John of Želiv, an ardent advocate of the Hussites' demand for Holy Communion in both kinds (*sub utraque specie*), a mob stormed the Old Town Hall and defenestrated the Catholic aldermen. A few days later, the king died of a heart attack, probably brought on by the increasing political turmoil in which he found himself. With the death of Wenceslas in 1419, power passed into the hands of the Hussites for the next seventeen years. Sigismund was prevented from ascending to his brother's throne because he was blamed for betraying Hus at Constance and because he attempted to enforce religious orthodoxy on the kingdom of Bohemia.

As we have already seen in chapter 2, women played an important role in the reform movement and in the revolution that followed it. Popular in late medieval Bohemia were the Beguines, women gathered together in lay communities for a life of prayer and good works. The Beguines of Bohemia had at least eighteen houses in Prague by 1415.[35] The widespread association of Beguines with heresy and vernacular writing can be dated to the beginning of the fourteenth century, when Beghards and Beguines in Languedoc and Catalonia were exposed to radical works written in the local languages of the regions.[36] The Czech poem *The Beguines* (*Bekyně*) is a pro-Catholic satirical poem written in Czech that mocks reform-minded women in characteristically misogynistic terms for their hypocrisy and loquaciousness (lines 9–10), their ignorance of

Latin and their gossipy natures (lines 15–16), and their mock modesty and secret arrogance (lines 21–24). It inevitably betrays considerable anxiety about women's access to vernacular literacy and their ability to read and interpret the Gospels without the mediation of sacerdotal authority.[37]

Another misogynistic poem that satirizes female reformers is *The Wycliffite Woman* (*Viklefice*), from the beginning of the fifteenth century. The poem relates how a female follower of the Oxford theologian John Wyclif (1320–84) lures a young, inexperienced squire to her house at nightfall on the pretext of teaching him the true faith but with the clear intention of seducing him. Central to this witty satire is the identification of heresy with the snares of the female body. In a clever display of double entendre, the Old and New Testaments are likened to the pear-shaped breasts of the seductress. The roundness of the breasts ironizes the medieval image of the pearl as a symbol of female purity and immortality. The poem is also a clever parody of the courtly love dawn-poem—the aubade—in which two illicit lovers meet, sleep together, and part at dawn. Drawing an implied parallel between divine service and lovemaking, the poem equates the reading of the Gospels with foreplay, the actual celebration of the Mass with coitus, and the final *Te Deum* with an erotic valedictory before the male lover slips away.[38]

In spite of its satirical tone, *The Wycliffite Woman*—like *The Beguines*—reveals considerable anxiety about the perceived threat of women not only reading and preaching the vernacular Gospels but also consecrating the Host. References to the celebration of the Mass and the singing of the *Te Deum* make this fear all too clear. It is significant that the female reformer should be dubbed a Wycliffite (*viklefice*), since some of the Lollard followers of the Oxford theologian had already propounded the belief that women could be priests. According to Walter Brut or Brit, who was arrested in 1391 and submitted in October 1393, "Women have power and authority to preach and make the body of Christ, and they have the power of the keys of the church, of binding and loosing."[39] Whether such radical theory led to radical practice, with Lollard women assuming priestly responsibilities, is uncertain and contingent on anecdote and gossip. But as Margaret Aston reminds us, "Gossip is also a part of history."[40] Hence it was a short step for the Czech author of *The Wycliffite Woman* to extrapolate from the imaginary prospect of a woman consecrating the body of Christ to presenting it as a social fait accompli.

As we have witnessed elsewhere in this book in connection with women, Jews, and sodomites, the Catholic fear of the female body tends to manifest itself as a phantasmatic "projective inversion" of its own sacred beliefs. Just as (in chapter 4) Matthew Paris's anecdote of the Jew Abraham of Berkhamstead defecating repeatedly upon a statue of the Virgin Mary can be seen as an obscene inversion of the devotional scene of a female saint excreting devotional tears before a holy image (whereby the anus and the eyes become reversible body parts), so too is the Wycliffite woman's seduction of the lover-knight a phantasmatic inversion of the orthodox motif, derived from the Song of Songs, of Christ as Lover-Knight wooing his beloved, the female-associated soul (*anima*). Moreover, if late medieval women identified in a very somatic manner with the eucharistic body of Christ, this was not the consequence of any innately female quality but the cultural product of the church's obsession with female spirituality as essentially corporeal. It is this selfsame obsession that provides the common denominator between the literal female *imitatio Christi*, as endorsed by the author of *The Life of Saint Catherine*, and the lust of female sexuality depicted in *The Wycliffite Woman*. The fantasy at work in this Czech poem is thus at once heterosexual and heterodox: the perverse prospect of a man being physically seduced by a woman and receiving the Host at her sacerdotal hands.

The satirical skill of *The Wycliffite Woman* was the exception rather than the rule in the Hussite period. The years of interregnum following the extraordinary events of 1419 (1419–36) witnessed a diminution of cultural range in Bohemia, much as in contemporary England, where, in the words of Paul Strohm, there was a distinct "narrowing of the Chaucer tradition."[41] The proliferation of the Bohemian dispute genre at this period mirrored the political and religious polarization of the age, in which the voices of orthodoxy and reform were becoming ever more shrill. In *The Dispute between Prague and Kutná Hora* (c. 1420), written by an anonymous Hussite propagandist, the two warring camps are represented by Prague, whose university sided with the Hussites, and Kutná Hora, a royal mining town that remained papist.[42] Although disputes had been common in fourteenth-century Bohemia, what is new about *The Dispute between Prague and Kutná Hora* is the fact that the disputants are towns rather than individuals (as in *The Weaver*) or things (as in *The Dispute between Wine and Water*). By this time a great deal of power had shifted from the church to the urban centers.

A fixed feature of all this political turmoil is the allegorical gendering of the terms of the debate. But whereas most fourteenth-century debates are predicated on the Aristotelian distinction between male/soul and female/body, *The Dispute between Prague and Kutná Hora* consists of two female personifications. The fact that a woman, however idealized, has a positive role to play in the dispute clearly reflects the prominence of women in the Hussite reform movement. The anonymous author, who from the outset favors Hussite Prague against Catholic Kutná Hora, presents the former as a beautiful virgin and the latter as a hunchbacked harridan. The female personification of the towns derives in part from the fact that the grammatical gender of these nouns is feminine in Czech, but the typology of virgin and old woman in the medieval religious tradition also has its part to play in the debate. The allegorical conceit of Prague as a beautiful young woman clearly draws upon the Catholic tradition of the virgin-martyrs of the early church whose bodily purity matched their staunch commitment to truth. We have seen in chapter 6 how the virgin-martyr Saint Catherine of Alexandria defends Christian truth against the defamations and errors of the pagans. In his famous letter from Constance dated June 26, 1415 ("To the Faithful Czechs"), John Hus compares his own commitment to truth with Saint Catherine's repudiation of the pagan scholars: "So St Catherine would have had to recant the faith and truth of the Lord Jesus Christ simply because some fifty masters opposed her."[43]

The personification of Kutná Hora as a superstitious, backward, and stupid harridan also exploits a long-established Christian typology that originates in the allegorization of *Synagoga* as an old, frightened woman in medieval art and literature.[44] In medieval Czech literature we have several examples of the negative representation of old women in *The Wycliffite Woman*, where the Wycliffite is referred to as a "hag" (*bába*, 36); *The Decalogue*; and *The Ointment Seller* (see chapter 4). As in *The Ointment Seller*, xenophobia and misogyny coincide in *The Dispute between Prague and Kutná Hora* when Prague, responding to her opponent's objection that she has refused to accept Wenceslas IV's younger brother Sigismund as king, equates his invading Hungarians and Germans (*Šváby*) with "rotten hags" (*hnilé báby*) in a rhyming couplet (lines 2075–76), which underlines the fact that Kutná Hora was primarily a town of German settlers employed in the mining of gold, silver, and copper.[45]

Not surprisingly, Prague has the lion's share of the dispute, citing liberally the Old and New Testaments to promote her cause: the Hussite principles of receiving Holy Communion in both kinds, the corruption of the Roman Church and its practices (veneration for images and the cult of the saints), and the invalidity of papal power. Kutná Hora, who has much shorter speeches than her interlocutor, expresses the religious, social, and political views of the Roman Church and the Council of Constance, which condemned Hus to the stake in 1415. Kutná Hora tends to make the accusations against Prague, to which the latter replies at great and tedious length. One of the objections made by Kutná Hora is the Hussites' destruction of religious images. She cites the example of Saint Luke, who, according to Catholic tradition, painted a portrait of the Blessed Virgin and child. Prague replies with close reference to the Scriptures and to the first commandment, which strictly forbids the making of graven images. Like the English Lollards, the Hussites' rejection of the conventional devotion to images derived from a strict adherence to the Decalogue, which figured prominently in their vernacular reading.[46] But Wyclif's beliefs were also influential in the formation of the Hussite position. The treatise *De ymaginibus*, extant in the Prague University Library, was written by an English Wycliffite at about the same time that Jakoubek of Stříbro began preaching against the misuses of images in 1417.[47] Kutná Hora's defense of images would have seemed perfectly apt to the audience of the text, for old women were regarded as particularly susceptible to the lure of superstitous images. In *The Dispute between the Groom and the Scholar*, the clerical scholar boasts that peasant women drop to their knees to kiss the religious images that he carried in procession through the villages.[48] In her lengthy response to Kutná Hora, Prague refers three times to the "blindness" of those who venerate images, thus drawing a parallel between the latter's religious shortsightedness and her literal myopia as an old woman.

In the final speech, Christ interrupts Kutná Hora as she is about to speak in order to make his judgment in the dispute (lines 2908–82). Although it seems superfluous to impose a third mediating character in a debate so clearly dominated by one speaker, his intervention probably stems from the author's need for a male authority figure to impose patriarchal closure on the all-female discussion. Not surprisingly therefore, Christ proceeds to find fault with both cities, although his true censure is reserved for the harridan Kutná Hora. It is, of course, because of their essential "female" weaknesses that both cities are admonished: Prague is rebuked for wearing garments of gold and silver, a dangerous sign of sacerdotal pride but also a traditional complaint leveled against female vanity (lines 2940–42); Kutná Hora is referred to explicitly as "this sinful woman" (line 2953) and accused of pride, lechery, avarice, and cruelty (lines 2955–56). Although Prague is demonstrably the victor in the dispute, the reader is left in no doubt that both cities have their faults, sharing principally the vice of pride, *superbia*. Ideologically, then, the anonymous author of the dispute must have been a member of the radical Hussites, since even reformist Prague is criticized for not having relinquished all the vestiges of popishness, such as rich priestly garments.

Conclusion

Our study of three works of early-fifteenth-century Czech literature has shown clearly, I hope, that all the writers of the texts in question, regardless of their political and religious affiliation, deploy the metaphor of the female body to advance their truth claims. In *The Weaver* the body of the lovely Adlička, who has jilted her lover Tkadleček, is the site of epistemological contestation between the disputants: for Misfortune, as for the church fathers, the surface of the text is like an alluring female body whose blandishments must be resisted to discover the truth at the heart of writing; for Tkadleček, truth is figured not as that which lies beyond the female body but as that body itself, seductively veiled from view by rhetorical ornament. In *The Wycliffite Woman*, written by a pro-Catholic propagandist, the female body of the eponymous follower of Wyclif is equated with the vernacular translations of the Gospels with which she seeks to corrupt and seduce the young squire. Here the dangers of sexual promiscuity and unsupervised literacy dovetail in a brilliant series of double entendres: the Gospels, which she displays at chest level in a mock-sacerdotal gesture, are pear-shaped and delightful to the sight of the eager novice, and their subsequent devotions last through the night until they part at dawn, in a skillful parody of the dawn-poem. In the third text, *The Dispute between Prague and Kutná Hora,* the two towns are personified as a beautiful virgin and an old hag, respectively, the former standing for the reformist creed based on the written word of the Gospels, the latter for Catholic orthodoxy, with its preference for orally and visually communicated piety.[49]

The widespread use of the female body as a metaphor for good and bad, truthful and mendacious, writing signals the extent to which sexual politics were inseparable from questions of hermeneutics and truth in the Middle Ages. This connection between gender and writing goes all the way back to the church fathers and is clearly evident in Czech writing of the early fifteenth century, when virtually all tenets of orthodox belief—from the veneration of images to the sacerdotal control of the Eucharist—were coming under assault from the Hussite heretics. The threat to male well-being traditionally associated with the female body as a locus of corruption, decay, and sexual desire was a convenient, ready-made metaphor to represent the spiritual and political crisis of Bohemian society. At the heart of this crisis was the disputed status of the Body of Christ as a metaphor both for societal stability and for the doctrinal unity of church teaching. By the late Middle Ages, as Sarah Beckwith has cogently put it, "the Aristotelian notion of the body as representation of society is sacralized in the notion of Christ's body, simultaneously the consecrated host which emerges to consolidate the function of the priesthood, and Christian society."[50] The Eucharist was one of the central features of the struggle between the Hussites and the traditionalists precisely because the sacerdotal control of Christ's body was also the key to power and dominion. Since Christ's body as a metaphor for the sacrament and for society in general was at the heart of the struggle for power between the Catholic Church and its critics in early-fifteenth-century Bohemia, we might interpret the presence of the female body and the discursive conflict to define and control it in the works examined in this chapter as a displacement from the male, sacred body onto the female, secular body. In both cases, the body serves as a symbol or metaphor for power and truth in late medieval society.

At the same time, the constant recycling of this narrow repertoire of misogynistic clichés also reveals a great deal not only about the female as a symbol or metaphor but also about the political situation of women in fifteenth-century Bohemia. Although the Hussite revolution in the heady years of 1419–22 gave women rights they had never received before—primarily the right to receive Communion in both kinds and even to preach the word of God themselves—the overall picture of these years is of continuity rather than transformation, subordination rather than enfranchisement.[51] By 1436, when the Hussite Wars were formerly brought to an end by the *Compactata* of Basel, the social and political rights of women were much the same as they had been in the previous century.[52] Surely there can be no greater indicator of this continuum than the persistence of the female body as a misogynistic metaphor for bad writing on both sides of the religious divide.

✛

CHAPTER 10

Epilogue

Continuity and Change in Fifteenth-Century Czech Literature

Asecond uprising broke out in Prague in 1422 following the sudden execution of John of Želiv and several of his followers. Many of the more moderate reformers were put to the sword, and power passed into the hands of the religious extremists. At the same time, other religious radicals established a second power base at Tábor in southern Bohemia. Their military leader was John Žižka, who had sided with Želiv in the first Prague uprising. Žižka organized an efficient army of resistance to the Catholic crusaders sent to crush the Bohemian "heretics." Consisting mainly of peasants armed with flails and pitchforks, Žižka's troops inflicted one humiliating defeat after another on the numerically superior foe. The ardent spirit of the Táborite armies can still be felt in the famous Hussite song "Ye Who Are the Warriors of God,"[1] which, as František Šmahel puts it, defined "the ABC of the Hussite military code of conduct."[2] Apart from its obvious religious concern to invoke God's help and intervention in human affairs—a theme it shares with the oldest Czech hymn *Hospodine, pomiluj ny!*—the words of this song are interesting for specifying their heterogeneous audience of knights, archers, pikesmen, and flailsmen united by one religious creed and a resolve to repel the Catholic foe.

An accurate barometer of the increasingly polarized situation in Bohemia after the Prague uprising of 1422 is the pro-Catholic dispute *Václav, Havel, and Tábor*, an anonymous satirical poem of 1,185 lines written in 1424.[3] In his introduction, the author of the dispute summarizes the current religious and political situation. In addition to those who remained true to Rome, the supremacy of the pope, and the heritage of Saint Wenceslas (Václav), there are two heretical groups. One is composed of those who merely follow the teachings of Hus, while the other consists of the Táborites, who are murderers, arsonists, and plunderers. Apart from all these there remain those who sway between changing sympathies according to their greed for material gain. The three disputants—Wenceslas, representing the Roman Catholics; Havel, the waverers; and Tábor, the militant Hussites—meet on a Friday in a burned-out church. Tábor has brought some pork; the greedy Havel hesitates to eat pork on a Friday but is willing to accept it. Wenceslas scolds him, however; since they are in a church, they should pray there and not have a picnic. In the tripartite dispute that ensues, Wenceslas defends the unity of the church and reproaches the Táborites for the confiscation of ecclesiastical property; the murders of priests, monks, and nuns; and the destruction of churches and the burning of books. Tábor asserts that they are acting in accordance with the will of God; if God were against their killing, burning, and plundering they would be prevented from doing so. Havel remains noncommittal. Tábor becomes enraged and threatens the others with his club, but the dispute ends peacefully.

This work accurately reflects a society ruined by war (symbolized by the burned-out church in which the dispute takes place) and divided by religious opinion (represented by the three speakers). Hussite Bohemia became a fortress against the outside world, a bastion of heretical rebellion in Catholic Europe. The deep cultural links it had forged with Italy, France, and England in the previous century were severed; its churches were gutted, religious statues smashed, and precious manuscripts destroyed by religious zealots. But in the next few years this extremism began to lose momentum. Only the preacher and writer Peter of Chelčice, author of *The Net of Faith* (*Siet' viery*, 1440–43) and founder of the Bohemian Brethren, remained an eloquently defiant voice among the radical Táborites of southern Bohemia. At the battle of Lipany (1434), the Táborites were decisively defeated by an army consisting of the moderate wing of the Hussites (the Utraquists) in league with the Catholics. The victors signed the *Compactata* of Basel in 1436, a compromise that permitted the Bohemian reformers to receive Holy Communion in both kinds, a unique accommodation within the Church universal.

The literary and social situation in the Bohemian Lands between 1310 and 1420 was as momentous for the Czechs as the equivalent period in England was for the English.[4] The late Přemyslid rulers had looked to the German Empire for their cultural and political models but rarely beyond its western boundaries to the rest of Europe. When John of Luxembourg ascended the Bohemian throne in 1310, his French education and cosmopolitan pedigree forced the introspective Czech nobility to recognize the existence of an international court culture and a centralizing monarchy along French lines. John's attempts to sow the seeds of westernization in the soil of his new kingdom fell on the barren ground of cultural and political resistance. Yet for a time, under his dynamic son Charles IV, Bohemia not only acquiesced in its newfound role as the capital of the Holy Roman Empire and center of avant-garde European art and culture; it actually seemed poised to surpass the achievements of its most advanced neighbors. The international prestige of Bohemia was so great that foreign luminaries like Petrarch came to Prague to pay homage to the new Augustus, artists and architects flocked to the city on the Vltava to find employment in the erection and embellishment of its monuments, and foreign rulers began to look to Bohemia as the cultural and spiritual heart of the continent. In the 1390s the emperor-designate Richard II of England sought to emulate Charles IV's mode of peaceful governance, his sacral model of kingship, and his international court culture.[5]

But in the long run the centripetal political forces that had enabled the powerful Bohemian nobility to resist the late Přemyslids' and John of Luxembourg's centralizing policies proved too strong to be reversed by one man, however astute his policies, however apocalyptic his personal vision of a *Bohemia sancta*. In spite of Charles's diplomatic skills, political acumen, and harnessing of the Czech language to forge a strong Luxembourg monarchy, the nationalism and xenophobic distrust advocated by the anonymous authors of *The First Cycle of Legends*, *The Dalimil Chronicle*, *The Verse Legend of Saint Procopius*, and other works of the fourteenth century helped to define the ideology of the Czech nobility and point toward the radical politics of the next century. Although the crises of Wenceslas IV's reign were exacerbated by his vacillating policies, it would be erroneous to lay the blame for the Hussite revolution squarely at his door, just as it would be simplistic to seek its origins exclusively in the writings of John Hus or John Wyclif. One of the principal aims of this study has been to show that the momentous religious and political upheavals of fifteenth-century Bohemia predated the Hussite Revolution and were thus beyond the powers of one single individual or one group to support or resist. Diverse issues of religion, ethnicity, gender, and class combined to create a unique phenomenon in the history of the European late Middle Ages. It has been my aim to trace the presence of these issues in a series of writings in the Czech language produced between 1310 and 1420.

On balance, the revolution had its positive as well as its negative aspects. On the positive side, the Czech moderates known as the Utraquists acquired by the terms of the *Compactata* of Basel a unique position of tolerance within the universal Church: they alone were permitted to receive Holy Communion in both kinds (*sub utraque specie*). Czech became the language of their reformed faith and the medium of their political agenda in the future. Out of this nonconformist tradition would emerge the glories of the *Kralice Bible* in the sixteenth century and, a century later, the literary genius of Jan Amos Komenský (Comenius), last bishop of the Bohemian Brethren and author of the Czech masterwork *The Labyrinth of the World and the Paradise of the Heart* (*Labyrint světa a ráj srdce*, 1623).

On the negative side, there was undoubtedly a decline in the international importance of Bohemia as a center of culture and academic excellence. Books were burned, churches and monasteries razed to the ground, and ecclesiastical art destroyed or damaged during the Hussite Wars. After peace was signed in 1436, Bohemian culture was merely a shadow of what it had been fifty years before.

As we survey the period in Bohemia between 1310 and 1420, we discover a mixture of continuity and change in a society pulled incessantly between centrifugal cosmopolitan and national forces. In spite of—or perhaps because of—Bohemia's political decline in the fifteenth century, the Czech language continued to mature into a resourceful medium of the nobility's religious and political beliefs. But, as in post-Chaucerian England, there was a distinct narrowing of cultural range; in fifteenth-century Bohemia there was little to compare with the astonishing diversity of genres produced a century earlier. This impoverishment can only partly be attributed to the material adversities created by civil war. A lack of vitality, a diminution of artistry, and a loss of creativity characterized most fifteenth-century writings on both sides of the religious divides. By contrast, Czech literature of the fourteenth century had produced works like the *Alexandreida* and *The Life of Saint Catherine*, whose artistic accomplishment invites comparison with the finest works of English Ricardian literature. We might well wonder whether the efflorescence of literature in Anne's Bohemia and Chaucer's England was more than coincidental. Was it not likely that the peaceful policies promulgated and promoted by both Charles IV and his impressionable, sensitive son-in-law, Richard II, engendered the same favorable climate within which not just great court culture like *Troilus and Criseyde* or the Czech *Life of Saint Catherine* could thrive but also art of a more universal human appeal like *The Canterbury Tales* and *Sir Gawain and the Green Knight*? And was it not because of such a relatively pacifist climate that intellectual dissent could also prosper, providing common ground between English Lollards and Bohemian Hussites? And if these speculations bear some truth, must we not accept that the much overlooked figure of Anne of Bohemia was a key player in the creation of this intellectually propitious climate?

Perhaps it was because of the extraordinary advances that had been made in the previous century that Czech literature of the post-Hussite period was able to regain some of its former powers. From the 1460s on, modest manuscripts containing verse and prose romances reflected the gentry's renewed interest in entertainment as well as edifying literature; a court art of sorts revived when Prince Hynek of Poděbrady (1452–92), son of the first Hussite king George of Poděbrady, composed erotic verse and translated a selection of Boccaccio's stories from *The Decameron* (albeit from the German).[6] The sundered cultural links with Italy were also being reestablished by the 1460s. Catholic noblemen like the brothers Henry and John of Rožmberk studied at Italian universities where they imbibed the humanist spirit of Bologna, Mantua, Padua, and other great centers of learning. After the completion of their studies, many brought back to Bohemia humanist books of their own.[7] By the time the Rožmberk dynasty died out in 1611, their family library had become the most impressive private collection of humanist learning north of the Alps.

Notes

Introduction

1. Constantin Höfler, *Anna von Luxemburg*, pp. 135–36; Nigel Saul, *Richard II*, pp. 89–90.

2. See Gervase Mathew, *The Court of Richard II*, pp. 16–17; also Nigel Wilkins, "A Pattern of Patronage: Machaut, Froissart, and the Houses of Luxembourg and Bohemia in the Fourteenth Century."

3. See Höfler, *Anna von Luxemburg*, pp. 133–34. For relevant bibliographical data on Wyclif's claim, see Anne Hudson, *The Premature Reformation: Wycliffite Texts and Lollard History*, p. 30 and note 127. For its exploitation by Lollard propagandists, see ibid., pp. 248–49, and David J. Wallace, *Chaucerian Polity: Absolutist Lineages and Associational Forms in England and Italy*, p. 361.

4. Winfried Baumann, *Die Literatur des Mittelalters in Böhmen: Deutsch-Lateinisch-Tschechische Literatur vom 10. bis zum 15. Jahrhundert*; Walter Schamschula, *Geschichte der tschechischen Literatur*, 1:36.

5. See Maurice Keen, *English Society in the Later Middle Ages, 1348–1500*, p. 217.

6. See, for example, Ferdinand Seibt, *Karl IV: Ein Kaiser in Europa (1346 bis 1378)*, and Seibt, ed., *Kaiser Karl IV: Staatsmann und Mäzen*.

7. Eduard Petrů, "Literatura doby Karla IV. a Václava IV. v mimopražském prostředí," pp. 135–43.

8. See Jan Květ, *Iluminované rukopisy Královny Rejčky*, p. 26. See also Karel Stloukal, "Královna Rejčka," in *Královny, kněžny a velké ženy české*, ed. Stloukal, pp. 116–27, esp. p. 124).

9. A recent claim that *The Dalimil Chronicle* was composed by Peter I (d.1347) remains no more than a hypothesis. See Radko Šťastný, *Tajemství jména Dalimil*.

10. See Jaroslav Kadlec, "Petr II z Rožmberka."

11. See Anna Skýbová, ed., *Listy bílé paní Rožmberské*.

12. Michael J. Bennett, "The Court of Richard II and the Promotion of Literature," pp. 3–20. See also Bennett, *Community, Class, and Careerism*, pp. 233–35.

13. See Elizabeth Salter, "Chaucer and Internationalism," pp. 239–44.

14. For the Lollard connection with the University of Prague, see Karl Schnith,"Zu Wesen und Bedeutung des Lollardentums im Zeitraum von 1382 bis 1414," pp. 135–46.

15. See Karel Brušák, "The Meaning of Czech History: Pekař versus Masaryk," pp. 92–106.

16. See Eva Schmidt-Hartmann, "Forty Years of Historiography under Socialism in Czechoslovakia."

17. For the English Peasant Uprising of 1381 and the Prague uprisings of 1419 and 1422, respectively, see Steven Justice, *Writing and Rebellion: England in 1381*, and František Graus, *Struktur und Geschichte: Drei Volksaufstände im mittelalterlichen Prag*, pp. 60–73.

18. Anne Hudson, "Lollardy: The English Heresy?" in *Lollards and Their Books*, pp. 141–64, at p. 143. For Hussitism and nationalism, see František Šmahel, *Idea národa v husitských Čechách*.

19. See Paul Strohm, *Social Chaucer*, p. 36.
20. For a short life of this important pre-Hussite reformer, see Miloslav Kaňák, *Milíč z Kroměříže.*
21. David Aers and Lynn Staley, *The Powers of the Holy: Religion, Politics, and Gender in Late Medieval English Culture*, pp. 15–42.
22. For the complexity of this situation in England, see Richard Firth Green, "John Ball's Letters: Literary History and Historical Literature," pp. 191–92.
23. For the *Invectio* and its link to women Hussites, see Rudolf Urbánek, "Královny Johana a Žofie," pp. 161–62. For Peter of Úničov, see Howard Kaminsky, *A History of the Hussite Revolution*, pp. 237–38.
24. See Susan Crane, "The Writing Lesson of 1381." For the use of the vernacular to promote and contain heresy in England, see Anne Hudson, "The Context of Vernacular Wycliffism," in *The Premature Reformation*, pp. 390–445.
25. Chris Given-Wilson, *The Royal Household and the King's Affinity: Service, Politics, and Finance in England, 1360–1413*, pp. 177 (Rushook) and 179 (Burghill). On the Dominican presence at Richard's court, see Saul, *Richard II*, pp. 320–21.
26. See John H. Harvey, "Richard II and York," p. 203.
27. Anne Hudson, "*Laicus litteratus*: The Paradox of Lollardy," pp. 234–35.
28. See Anežka Vidmanová, "Latinské spisy Mistra Klareta," pp. 144–57.
29. See Vladimír Kyas, "Vznik staročeského biblického překladu," p. 49.
30. Emil Skála, "Německý jazyk v českých zemích ve 14. století," p. 76.
31. This is the conclusion of R. R. Betts in "English and Czech Influences on the Hussite Movement," in *Essays in Czech History*, 132–59, esp. p. 140.
32. Dillian Gordon, *Making and Meaning: The Wilton Diptych*, pp. 71–72.
33. For the cult of dynastic saints in central Europe, see Gábor Klaniczay, *The Uses of Supernatural Power: The Transformation of Popular Religion in Medieval and Early-Modern Europe*, pp. 111–28.
34. See David J. Wallace, "Anne of Bohemia, Queen of England, and Chaucer's Emperice," pp. 15–16.
35. "Ex radice et stirpe beatissimi Wenczeslai patris, Bohemorum quondam ducis et patronis" (quoted from Klaniczay, *Uses of Supernatural Power*, p. 122).
36. See Hans-Joachim Behr, *Literatur als Machtlegitimation: Studien zur Funktion der deutschsprachigen Dichtung am böhmischen Königshof im 13. Jahrhundert.*
37. See Aers and Staley, *Powers of the Holy*, pp. 70–71.
38. See Caroline M. Barron, "William Langland: A London poet," p. 96. For the impact of the poem on the Peasant Uprising of 1381, see Justice, *Writing and Rebellion*, pp. 102–39.
39. See, for example, Jan Lehár's introduction to a modern translation of the legend: *Legenda o svaté Kateřině*, trans. Jiří Pelán (Prague, 1988), pp. 9–27.
40. For a valuable discussion of the ideological ramifications of medieval mysticism, see Grace M. Jantzen, *Power, Gender, and Christian Mysticism*, pp. 12–18.
41. Wallace, *Chaucerian Polity*, pp. 349–78.
42. "Adde quod nec partu tantum, sed ingenio et virtute multiplici et rebus gestis et regni gloria sexus est nobilis" (Francesco Petrarch, *Le Familiari*, book 21.8, p. 62). For information about Petrarch's correspondence with Empress Anne, I am indebted to David J. Wallace, who allowed me to read in advance of publication chapter 12 of his *Chaucerian Polity: Absolutist Lineages and Associational Forms in England and Italy.*
43. For the term "hagiographic romance," see Brigitte Cazelles, ed., *The Lady as Saint: A Collection of French Hagiographic Romances of the Thirteenth Century*, p. 31.
44. Richard Firth Green, *Poets and Princepleasers: Literature and the English Court in the Late Middle Ages*, p. 54.
45. See Lee Patterson, *Chaucer and the Subject of History.*
46. See John M. Bowers, "*Pearl* in Its Royal Setting: Ricardian Poetry Revisited." For the link between courtliness and politics, see Patricia J. Eberle, "The Politics of Courtly Style at the Court of Richard II."

1. Prologue

1. For the early Slavs in the Bohemian Lands, see Ivan Rada, ed., *Dějiny zemí koruny české*, vol. 1 (Prague, 1992), pp. 24ff; Dušan Třeštík, "Příchod prvních Slovanů do českých zemí v letech 510–535," pp. 245–80 (with German summary, 279–80). For the early Slavs in general, see Francis Dvorník, *The Slavs: Their Early History and Civilization*, and A. P. Vlasto, *The Entry of the Slavs into Christendom: An Introduction to the Medieval History of the Slavs*, p. 86.

2. Vlasto, *Entry of the Slavs*, p. 86. For the early Bohemian state, see Dušan Třeštík, *Počátky Přemyslovců*.

3. The original location of the Great Moravian Empire has become a source of intense, if unresolved, scholarly debate. See Martin Eggers, *Das "Großmährische Reich": Realität oder Fiktion? Eine Neuinterpretation der Quellen zur Geschichte des mittleren Donauraumes im 9. Jahrhundert*, and Charles Bowlus, *Franks, Moravians, and Magyars: The Struggle for the Middle Danube, 788–907*.

4. Vlasto, *Entry of the Slavs*, p. 109.

5. See Karl Bittner, *Deutsche und Tschechen: Zur Geistesgeschichte des böhmischen Raumes*, vol 1, and Ferdinand Tadra, *Kulturní styky Čech s cizinou až do válek husitských* (Prague, 1897).

6. For the origins of the Slavic liturgy and literature in the Bohemian Lands, see František Graus, "Slovanská liturgie a písemnictví v přemyslovských Čechách 10. století," pp. 473–495; and John M. Clifton-Everest, "Slawisches Schriftum im 10. und 11. Jahrhundert in Böhmen."

7. Vlasto, *Entry of the Slavs*, p. 107.

8. Francis Dvorník, *The Slavs in European History and Civilization*, pp. 152–54; Josef Pekař, *Die Wenzels- und Ludmilalegenden und die Echtheit Christians*. For English translations of Old Church Slavonic and Latin Bohemian texts, see Marvin Kantor, *The Origins of Christianity in Bohemia: Sources and Commentary*.

9. Cosmas, *Chronik der Böhmen des Cosmas von Prag*, ed. Bertold Bretholz.

10. Antonín Škarka, ed., *Nejstarší česká duchovní lyrika*, p. 67.

11. Richard W. Southern, *The Making of the Middle Ages*, p. 236.

12. See Caroline Walker Bynum, *Jesus as Mother: Studies in the Spirituality of the High Middle Ages*.

13. Škarka, ed., *Nejstarší*, pp. 68–69.

14. Ibid., p. 70.

15. Ibid., pp. 76–81.

16. For *The Passional of the Abbess Kunigunde*, see Emma Urbánková and Karel Stejskal, *Pasionál Přemyslovny Kunhuty*.

17. Jiří Cejnar, ed., *Nejstarší české veršované legendy*.

18. František Svejkovský, ed., *Alexandreida*.

19. George Cary, *The Medieval Alexander*.

20. Albert Pražák, *Staročeská báseň o Alexandru velikém*.

21. Ulrich von Etzenbach, *Alexander*, ed. Wendelin Toischer.

22. "Zlé kolo najviece skřípá, / maly had najviece sípá, / a chlápě najviece chlípá." Unless otherwise noted, translations are my own.

2. A Literature of Their Own

1. See the pioneering volume of essays in Stloukal, ed., *Královny* and, more recently, Božena Kopičková, *Historické prameny k studiu postavení ženy v české a moravské středověké společnosti*. For general studies of women in the Middle Ages, see Joan M. Ferrante, *Woman as Image in Medieval Literature from the Twelfth Century to Dante*; Susan Mosher Stuard, ed., *Women in Medieval Society*; Patricia H. Labalme, ed., *Beyond their Sex: Learned Women of the European Past*; Shulamith Shahar, *The Fourth Estate: A History of Women*

in the Middle Ages, trans. Chaya Galai; Katharina M. Wilson, ed., *Medieval Women Writers;* Edith Ennen, *The Medieval Woman,* trans. Edmund Jephcott; Christiane Klapisch-Zuber, ed., *A History of Women in the West: II. Silences of the Middle Ages;* Emilia Amt, ed., *Women's Lives in Medieval Europe: A Sourcebook;* Herbert Grundmann, *Religious Movements in the Middle Ages.*

2. Jaroslav Čechura, Milan Hlaváčka, and Eduard Maur, *Ženy a milenky českých králů.*

3. See Karen Cherewatuk and Ulrike Wiethaus, eds., *Dear Sister: Medieval Women and the Epistolary Genre.*

4. Quoted from Merry E. Wiesner, *Women and Gender in Early Modern Europe,* p. 12.

5. See Klapisch-Zuber, ed., *A History of Women in the West,* pp. 427–82.

6. André Vauchez, *The Laity in the Middle Ages: Religious Beliefs and Devotional Practices,* pp. 171–83.

7. See Marina Warner, *Alone of All Her Sex: The Myth and the Cult of the Virgin Mary.*

8. Vauchez, *Laity in the Middle Ages,* p. 174.

9. Ibid., p. 172.

10. See Čechura et al., *Ženy a milenky,* pp. 31–41.

11. For the vita of Saint Ludmilla in English, see Kantor, ed., *Origins of Christianity in Bohemia,* pp. 103–4 ("Old Church Slavonic Prologue, Life of Saint Ludmilla"); pp. 156–62 (*Fuit in provincia Boemorum*); pp. 165–203 (*Legenda Christiani*); and pp. 207–13 (*Factum est,* [Homily for the Feast of Saint Ludmilla]).

12. For the life of Saint Agnes, see Jaroslav Polc, *Agnes von Böhmen 1211–1282: Königstochter, Äbtissin, Heilige.*

13. For a Latin edition and Czech translations of the letters and the anonymous medieval *Legend of the Blessed Agnes,* see Jan Kapistrán Vyskočil, ed., *Legenda blahoslavené Anežky a čtyři listy sv. Kláry,* 2 vols. For an English translation of the letters, see *Francis and Clare: The Complete Works,* pp. 189–206. The third letter is reprinted in Carolyne Larrington, ed., *Women and Writing in Medieval Europe,* pp. 149–52.

14. See Emanuela Nohejlová, "Královna Emma," in *Královny,* ed. Karel Stloukal, p. 65; see also Miloslav Bohatec, *Illuminated Manuscripts,* p. 47.

15. Eleonora Mendlová-Mráčková, "Královna Kunhuta," p. 97.

16. Škarka, ed., *Nejstarší,* pp. 50–53.

17. Pavel Spunar, *Kultura českého středověku,* p. 250.

18. See the introduction to Urbánková and Stejskal, *Pasionál.* For an older study of the *Passional of the Abbess Kunigunde,* see also Antonín Matějček, *Pasionál Abatyše Kunhuty.*

19. Jan Vilikovský, *Písemnictví českého středověku,* pp. 26–40.

20. See Elizabeth Robertson, *Early English Prose and the Female Audience,* p. 70.

21. Caroline Walker Bynum, "Women Mystics and Eucharistic Devotion in the Thirteenth Century," in *Fragmentation and Redemption,* pp. 119–50.

22. "Na to svědka slunce jmámy, / když na ně vzpomínámy, / mnoho poprskóv vídámy, / avšak jedno slunce známy" (Škarka, ed., *Nejstarší,* p. 78).

23. "V chlebnéj tváři ty sě skrýváš, / božskú světlost tu pokrýváš" (ibid., p. 77).

24. Karel Stloukal, "Královna Rejčka," p. 124.

25. Bohatec, *Illuminated Manuscripts,* p. 47.

26. Květ, *Iluminované,* p. 34.

27. Wiesner, *Women and Gender,* p. 15.

28. Francesco Petrarch, *Le Familiari,* book 21.8, p. 62.

29. See Vilikovský, *Písemnictví,* pp. 141–60.

30. Adolf Patera, "O umučení sv. Jiří," *ČČM* 61 (1887): 77–105, esp. p. 99.

31. For the Czech verse *Life of Saint Catherine,* see Josef Hrabák, ed., *Dvě legendy z doby Karlovy.*

32. Jiří Spěváček, *Karel IV. Život a dílo (1316–78),* p. 381.

33. See Jan Vilikovský, ed., *Staročeská lyrika.*

34. Václav Černý, *Staročeská milostná lyrika.*

35. For the Czech chivalric verse romances, see Alfred Thomas, *The Czech Chivalric Romances* Vévoda Arnošt *and* Lavryn *in Their Literary Context.*
36. For Anne's books, see Höfler, *Anna von Luxemburg,* pp. 133–34. Also Susan Groag Bell, "Medieval Women Book Owners: Arbiters of Lay Piety and Ambassadors of Culture," in *Sisters and Workers in the Middle Ages,* ed. Judith M. Bennett et al., pp. 158–59.
37. Mathew, *Court of Richard II,* pp. 1–11.
38. For new insights into the relationship between Chaucer and Anne of Bohemia, see chapter 12 of Wallace's *Chaucerian Polity.*
39. For a translation of the two letters, see Anne Crawford, ed., *Letters of the Queens of England, 1100–1547,* pp. 105–6.
40. Quoted from Janet Coleman, *Medieval Readers and Writers, 1350–1400,* p. 20. See also Hudson, *Lollards and Their Books,* pp. 67–84.
41. For the links between Queen Anne and the Lollard movement, see Höfler, *Anna von Luxemburg,* pp. 133–34; Betts, "English and Czech Influences," pp. 132–59; and Katherine Walsh, "Lollardisch-hussitische Reformbestrebungen in Umkreis und Gefolgschaft der Luxembergerin Anna, Königin von England (1382–1394)" (paper delivered at the conference *Häresie und Vorseitige Reformation im Spätmittelalter,* Munich, 1995). I would like to thank Professor Šmahel for drawing this paper to my attention.
42. Quoted from William E. Harkins, ed. and trans., *Czech Prose: An Anthology,* p. 18.
43. Otakar Odložilík, "Anežka ze Štítného," in *Královny,* ed. Karel Stloukal, pp. 138–42, esp. pp. 140–42.
44. František Šmahel, *Husitská revoluce,* 2:39–40.
45. Anna Kolářová-Císařová, "Typy žen husitských a Anna z Mochova," in *Královny,* ed. Karel Stloukal, pp. 161–62.
46. Rudolf Urbánek, "Královny Johana a Žofie," in *Královny,* ed. Karel Stloukal, p. 152.
47. Ibid., p. 157.
48. Šmahel, *Husitská revoluce,* pp. 38–39.
49. See Eileen Power, *Medieval Women,* p. 31.
50. František Šmahel, "Literacy and Heresy in Hussite Bohemia," in *Heresy and Literacy,* p. 246.
51. Anna Kolářová-Císařová, *Žena v hnutí husitském.*
52. Šmahel, *Husitská,* p. 40. For *Knížky,* see F. M. Bartoš, "První česká spisovatelka."
53. Šmahel, *Husitská,* p. 40.
54. For an edition of the letters, see Skýbová, ed., *Listy.*
55. Margaret L. King, *Women of the Renaissance,* p. 211.
56. Ibid.
57. Louise Schleiner, *Tudor and Stuart Women Writers,* pp. 96–106, esp. p. 97.
58. See George Ballard, *Memoirs of Several Ladies of Great Britain Who Have Been Celebrated for Their Writing or Skill in the Learned Languages, Arts, and Sciences,* pp. 237–40. See also the entry on Jane Elizabeth Weston in *The Oxford Guide to British Women Writers,* ed. Joanne Shattock, pp. 456–57.
59. Wiesner, *Women and Gender,* p. 159.
60. Zdeněk Kalista, ed., *Korespondence Zuzany Černínové z Harasova s jejím synem Humprechtem Janem Černínem z Chudenic.*

3. The War of the Bohemian Maidens

I would like to thank Ruth Mazo Karras for providing me with helpful comments on this chapter.

1. Since the sixteenth century the chronicle has been named after "Dalimil," but this attribution has proved to be spurious. According to Radko Šťastný in his book *Tajemství jména Dalimil,* the anonymous author of the chronicle was Peter I of Rožmberk. I am skeptical about this attribution since Peter was a member of the high nobility, a status

that does not comport with the pro-*zeman* (lower noble) stance of the author of the chronicle. For this and other doubts about Šťastný's hypothesis, see my review in *Slavic Review* 53, no. 4 (Winter 1994): 1134–36. See also Jan Lehár, *Nejstarší česká epika*, pp. 30–76.

2. For the Czech text, see Jiří Daňhelka et al., eds., *Staročeská kronika tak řečeného Dalimila*: "Řěči prázdné, jelikož mohu, myšli ukrátititi, / a však mysl cělú myšli položiti, / aby sě tiem mohl každý raději učiti / a k svému sě jazyku viece snažiti."

3. "Páni, račte slyšěti! / Z chlapóv šlechtici bývají / a šlechtici často chlapy syny jmievají. / Nebo ostaralé střiebro šlechtu činí / a často šlechticě chudoba sprostenstvím viní. / Vyšli smy všichni z otcě jednoho / a ten sě čte šlechticem, jehož otec jměl střiebra mnoho. / A když jest tak šlechta s chlapstvem smiešena, / budeť Božena má žena. / Raději sě chci s šlechetnú sedlkú českú smieti / než králevú německú za ženu jmieti. / Vřeť každému srdce po jazyku svému, / a pro to Němkyně méně bude přieti lidu mému. / Němkyni německú čeled' bude jmieti / a německy bude učiti mé děti. / Pro to bude jazyka rozdělenie / a inhed zemi jisté zkaženie. / Páni, neviete dobra svého, / lajíce mi z manželstva mého. / Kde byste řěčníky bráli, / když byste přěd německú knění stáli?"

4. See chapter 2 in this volume for a discussion of the beautiful Latin *Passional* that is named for Abbess Kunigunde.

5. See Robert Bartlett, *The Making of Europe: Conquest, Colonization, and Cultural Change, 950–1350*, p. 198.

6. See Jan Gebauer, ed., *Staročeský slovník* (Prague, 1903), vol. 1.

7. Marianne Shapiro, *De vulgari eloquentia: Dante's Book of Exile*, p. 48.

8. Saint Augustine, *On Christian Doctrine*.

9. For the Latin source, see Cosmas, *Chronik der Böhmen des Cosmas von Prag*, ed. Bretholz, pp. 19–21.

10. Vladimir Karbusicky, *Anfänge der historischen Überlieferung in Böhmen: Ostmitteleuropa in Vergangenheit und Gegenwart*, pp. 57–59.

11. "Chtiece své řěči užiti, / jechu sě hradu staviti."

12. Stephen G. Nichols, "An Intellectual Anthropology of Marriage in the Middle Ages," p. 72.

13. Ibid.

14. For a general discussion of women's enforced silence in the Middle Ages, see Klapisch-Zuber, ed., *A History of Women*, p. 425: "The voices of women were stifled, imprisoned by an ethic that treated sins of the tongue as gluttony and harbingers of worse, of lust and pride."

15. "Jako holubi letie z svých kotcóv, / takéž sě dievky bráchu ot svých otcóv."

16. "Krašším sě káza líčiti, / a chytréj řěči užiti."

17. For the standard misogynistic view of women as cunning and deceitful in the Latin lyrics of medieval Bohemia, see Jan Vilikovský, *Latinská poesie žákovská v Čechách*, pp. 76–83.

18. Tertullian, "The Apparel of Women," pp. 135–36.

19. "Uzřevše, že na Vyšehradě veliký hlad, / za přímiřím pozvachu jich na svój hrad. / Tu s nimi krašie panny posadichu, / jež chytré řěči mnoho umiechu."

20. See R. Howard Bloch, "Medieval Misogyny," p. 19. Compare also the antifeminist Czech lyric "Píseň o ženách" (The song of women) in *Staročeská lyrika*, ed. Jan Vilikovský, pp. 114–117, esp. p. 116. Compare also the reference to female cunning in the Old Czech *Desatero* (Decalogue), in Josef Hrabák, ed., *Staročeské satiry Smilovy školy*, p. 64 (lines 301–8).

21. Karbusicky, *Anfänge*, p. 59.

22. See Svejkovský, ed., *Alexandreida*.

23. Albert Pražák, *Staročeská píseň o Alexandru velikém*, p. 117.

24. "Některé přěd nimi klekáchu, / některé sě k nim lísáchu. / A což kolivěk činiechu, / mužských srdec neobměkčichu."

25. Nathaniel Edward Griffin, ed., *Guido de Columnis Historia Destructionis Troiae*.

26. "Et Pirrus in sue uindicte satisfaccionem totum corpus eius per frustra truncauit" (ibid., p. 217).

27. Svejkovský, ed., *Alexandreida*, 773–828.

28. "And Pirrus In his greuaunce Toke on hir a foule vengaunce, For he lefft not of hir a spot That he ne hit hewe as flesch to pot" (J. Ernst Wülfing, ed., *The Laud Book of Troy*, p. 505, lines 17135–38).

29. For the fruitful application for the same term to the medieval blood libel legend, see Alan Dundes, "The Ritual Murder or Blood Libel Legend: A Study of Anti-Semitic Victimization through Projective Inversion."

4. Alien Bodies

1. Jarmila F. Veltrusky, *Mastičkář: A Sacred Farce from Medieval Bohemia*, pp. 328–29. For the Czech-English parallel text of the play, see ibid., pp. 332–76. All page references are to this edition.

2. Mikhail Bakhtin, *Rabelais and His World*. See also E. Jane Burns, *Bodytalk: When Women Speak in Old French Literature*.

3. See František Graus, *Pest- Geissler- Judenmorde: Das 14. Jahrhundert als Krisenzeit*, and Richard E. Lerner, *The Age of Adversity: The Fourteenth Century*.

4. "Straka na stracě přeletěla řěku, / maso bez kosti provrtělo dievku, / okolo turneje, hoho, / i vrazi sě mezi nohy to mnoho."

5. Bernd-Ulrich Hergemöller, ed., *Maiestas Carolina: Das Kodifikationsentwurf Karls IV. für das Königreich Böhmen von 1355*, pp. 216–17.

6. Gottlieb Bondy and Franz Dworsky, *Zur Geschichte der Juden in Böhmen, Mähren und Schlesien von 906 bis 1620*, 1:7–8.

7. Ibid., p. 51.

8. Ibid., pp. 80–81.

9. Ibid., pp. 82–84.

10. Kantor, ed., *Origins of Christianity in Bohemia*, pp. 62–63.

11. Škarka, ed., *Nejstarší*, p. 70.

12. See Urbánková and Stejskal, *Pasionál Přemyslovny Kunhuty*.

13. See Alfred Thomas, "Czech-German Relations as Reflected in Old Czech Literature," pp. 200–201.

14. Miri Rubin, "The Eucharist and the Construction of Medieval Identities," p. 57.

15. For late medieval society as the sacralized Body of Christ, see Sarah Beckwith, *Christ's Body: Identity, Culture, and Society in Late Medieval Writings*, p. 32.

16. Thomas, "Czech-German Relations," pp. 201–2.

17. For this insight I am indebted to Jan Ziolkowski's paper, "The Obscenities of Old Women: Vetularity and Vernacularity" (delivered at the conference "Obscenity: Social Control and Artistic Creation in the European Middle Ages," Harvard University, May 13–15, 1995).

18. "Mistře, v onomno biech počal l'udi léčiti, / tu mi počěchu staré baby pod nos pzdieti."

19. See Josef Hrabák, ed., *Staročeské satiry Hradeckého rukopisu a Smilovy školy*, pp. 91–95.

20. See Jan Gebauer, ed., *Slovník Staročeský*, vol. 1 (A-J) (Prague, 1903), p. 39.

21. See John Bossy, *Christianity in the West, 1400–1700*, p. 85.

22. Wolfgang S. Seiferth, *Synagogue and Church in the Middle Ages: Two Symbols in Art and Literature*, p. 28.

23. "Známy tě, kteréhos rodu: / však biřicóv syn z Českého Brodu."

24. See Roman Jakobson, "Medieval Mock Mystery: The Old Czech *Unguentarius*," pp. 254–55.

25. Joshua Trachtenberg, *The Devil and the Jews: The Medieval Conception of the Jew and Its Relation to Modern Anti-Semitism*, pp. 109–23.

26. "Jiní mistři po svém právu / maží svými mastmi hlavu; / ale tys mi, mistře, dobře zhodil, / ež mi všichni řit mast'ú oblil."

27. See R. I. Moore, *The Formation of a Persecuting Society: Power and Deviance in Western Europe, 950–1250*, p. 38.

28. Matthew Paris, *Chronicles of Matthew Paris: Monastic Life in the Thirteenth Century*, ed. trans. Richard Vaughan, pp. 214–15.

29. See Franz Spina, ed. *Die altčechsiche Katharinenlegende der Stockholm-Brünner Handschrift*, p. 24.

30. See Caroline Walker Bynum, "The Female Body and Religious Practice in the Later Middle Ages," in *Fragmentation and Redemption*, pp. 181–238.

31. For a similar psychological approach to the blood libel legend (the accusation that Jews killed Christian children and mixed their blood with the matzah), see Dundes, "Ritual Murder," pp. 336–76.

32. Trachtenberg, *Devil and the Jews*, p. 149.

33. Seiferth, *Synagogue and Church*, p. 28.

34. Ibid., p. 9.

35. Ibid., p. 11.

36. Roman Jakobson, *Moudrost starých Čechů: Odvěké základy národního odboje*, pp. 118–19.

37. See "Articuli contra Hieronym de Praga," in *Rerum Concilii Constantiensis*, vol. 4 (Frankfurt and Leipzig, 1699), column 675.

38. Trachtenberg, *Devil and the Jews*, p. 50.

39. For the association of Jews with homosexuality, see Steven F. Kruger, "The Bodies of Jews in the Late Middle Ages," p. 303.

40. Seiferth, *Synagogue and Church*, p. 29.

41. Jakobson, "Medieval Mock Mystery," p. 256 n. 14.

42. Seiferth, *Synagogue and Church*, p. 85.

43. Robert S. Gottfried, *The Black Death: Natural and Human Disaster in Medieval Europe*, pp. 52–53. For the association of Jews with the Black Death, see also Seiferth, *Synagogue and Church*, p. 73.

44. Bondy and Dworsky, *Zur Geschichte*, p. 60.

45. Robert B. Pynsent, *Conceptions of Enemy: Three Essays on Czech and Slovak Literature*, pp. 9–10.

46. See Michael Camille, "The Image and the Self: Unwriting Late Medieval Bodies," p. 68.

47. See Richard Kieckhefer, *Repression of Heresy in Medieval Germany*, p. 68.

48. Gail McMurray Gibson, *The Theatre of Devotion: East Anglian Drama and Society in the Late Middle Ages*, pp. 36–37.

49. Jonathan Goldenberg, *Sodometries: Renaissance Texts, Modern Sexualities*, pp. 1–2.

50. For a related discussion, see Kathleen Biddick, "Genders, Bodies, Borders: Technologies of the Visible," p. 415.

51. For the connection between sex and minorities in medieval society, see Jeffrey Richards, *Sex, Dissidence, and Damnation: Minority Groups in the Middle Ages*.

5. A Bohemian *Imitatio Christi*

1. Karel Stejskal, *European Art in the Fourteenth Century*, p. 147.

2. Aers and Staley, *Powers of the Holy*, p. 67.

3. See Alfred Thomas, "*Imitatio Christi*: A New Perspective on the Fourteenth-Century Czech Verse *Legend of St Procopius*," pp. 344–55. For the Marxist position, see the introduction to Hrabák, ed., *Dvě legendy*, p. 37. All quotations from the text of the verse legend refer to this edition.

4. Thomas, "*Imitatio Christi*," p. 355.

5. Bossy, *Christianity in the West*, pp. 81–82.

6. For the Latin and Czech texts of the legend, see Václav Chaloupecký and Bohumil Ryba, *Středověké legendy prokopské: Jejich historický rozbor a texty*.

7. Ibid., pp. 11–14.

8. See William E. Harkins, ed. and trans., *Czech Prose: An Anthology*, pp. 9–15, quote at p. 10. For the Czech text, see Chaloupecký and Ryba, *Středověké legendy*, pp. 162–68.

9. Quoted from Harkins, ed., *Czech Prose*, p. 14.

10. For the whole text, see Chaloupecký and Ryba, *Středověké legendy*, pp. 271–73.

11. "Prosmy jeho, at' nás ráčí obrániti a naše nepřátely z země vyhnati a mier a pokoj nám uprositi, nebo jest on náš obránce a dědic českéj země. A dávno by Čechy zahynuly, protože mají němečské země okolo sebe, by jě s. Prokop a s. Václav nebránili" (ibid., p. 273).

12. See Evelyn Birge Vitz, "From the Oral to the Written in Medieval and Renaissance Saints' Lives," in *Images of Sainthood in Medieval Europe*, p. 99.

13. For the phenomenon of medieval minstrels, see Walter Salmen, *Der Fahrende Musiker im Europäischen Mittelalter*. For the descendants of these minstrels in the early modern period, see Peter Burke, *Popular Culture in Early Modern Europe*, p. 94.

14. "Slyšte, staří, i vy, děti, / co jáz vám chci pověděti / o dědicěvi slovenském."

15. See Adolf Patera, ed., *Hradecký rukopis* (Prague, 1881).

16. See Hrabák, ed., *Dvě legendy*, p. 70.

17. Peter Burke discusses the frequent coincidence of popular and aristocratic taste in the early modern period, citing the example of a Norman squire who read the romance *Amadis de Gaule* aloud to his peasants when it rained (see Burke, *Popular Culture*, p. 26).

18. For the edition of *The Decalogue, The Satires of the Artisans*, and *The Fable of the Fox and the Jug*, see Hrabák, ed., *Staročeské satiry*.

19. See Vilikovský, *Písemnictví*, p. 141.

20. For the Latin exemplum on which the Czech fable is based, see Jan Vilikovský, ed., *Staročeské satiry z Hradeckého rukopisu*, p. 93.

21. Ibid., introduction, v.

22. "Poslúchajte, hostákové, / k tomu všichni lejchéřěvé, / kteří po světu blúdíte / a na lidech k tomu lúdíte, / ješto rádi béřete cuzie / chovajte sě duše ztracenie / otkadž nenie vykúpenie, / jedno tam věčné bydlenie."

23. See Donald Weinstein and Rudolph M. Bell, *Saints and Society: The Two Worlds of Western Christendom, 1000–1700*, p. 167.

24. For information on the reformers, see Spěváček, *Karel IV*, pp. 522–26. For the theme of the Antichrist in western thought, see Bernard McGinn, ed., *Antichrist: Two Thousand Years of the Human Fascination with Evil*.

25. For the intimate relation of social unrest to religious ideals in the second half of the fourteenth century in England, see Coleman, *Medieval Readers and Writers, 1350–1400*, p. 60.

26. Weinstein and Bell, *Saints and Society*, p. 206.

27. See Magdalena Carrasco, "Sanctity and Experience in Pictorial Hagiography: Two Illustrated Lives of Saints from Romanesque France," p. 34.

28. "Non lusit cum aliis pueris, sed semper cum matre ecclesiam frequentabat" (Chaloupecký and Ryba, *Středověké legendy*, p. 105).

29. "Nikdy neviděli, by smál, / ani kdy s dietkami več jhrál, / jedno pěl hodiny nebo páteře / někde súkromie nebo v kóře."

30. "Stupebant autem omnes qui eium audiebant super prudentia et responsis eius" (Robert Weber, ed., *Biblia sacra iuxta vulgatem versionem*, 2:1610).

31. This detail occurs only in the *Vita maior* and the Czech verse legend. According to Chaloupecký and Ryba, *Středověké legendy* (pp. 96–97), it probably alludes to Charles IV's foundation of the Emauzy Monastery in 1347.

32. See Weinstein and Bell, *Saints and Society*, p. 154.

33. "Secessit ad provinciam suam, non ut parentes suos videre vellet, sed ut heremi secreciorem locum quereret" (Chaloupecký and Ryba, *Středověké legendy*, p. 103).

34. Hrabák, ed., *Dvě legendy*, p. 27, note 11.
35. "Hierusalem, Hierusalem quae occidis prophetas et lapidas eos qui ad te missi sunt quotiens volui congregare filios tuos quemadmodum gallina congregat pullos suos sub alas et noluisti" (Weber, ed., *Biblia sacra*, 2:1563).
36. "Hrniechu k němu nebožátka, / právě jako k slepici kuřátka."
37. "Choval sem vás ot počátka / jako slepicě svá kuřátka."
38. "Tot' smy po tobě ošiřeli nebožátka, / auvech, jako po slepici kuřátka."
39. Hrabák, ed., *Staročeské satiry*, p. 9.
40. See Karel Brušák, "Some Notes on *Tandariáš a Floribella*, a Czech Fourteenth-Century Chivalrous Romance," pp. 44–56.
41. Bynum, *Jesus as Mother*, p. 114.
42. "Vy siemě proklaté, / vy jste hadového roda."
43. "Serpentes genimina viperarum quomodo fugietis a iudicio gehenae?" (Weber, ed., *Biblia sacra*, 2:1563).
44. For comparison with saints in late medieval England, see Eamon Duffy, *The Stripping of the Altars: Traditional Religion in England, 1400–1580*, pp. 186–88.
45. See Klaus P. Janofsky, "National Characteristics in the Portrayal of English Saints in the *South English Legendary*," p. 84.
46. Weinstein and Bell, *Saints and Society*, p. 147.
47. "České země osvěta."
48. "O vy nevěrní sokové, / vy jste diáblovi poslové."
49. "V rucě berlu držieše, / jíž nemilostivě Němce tepieše. / Němci ijedné otpovědi nejmiechu, / jedno druh před druhem běžiechu; / nic na cestu netázáchu, / jedno jako kozlové skákáchu."
50. John Klassen, *The Nobility and the Making of the Hussite Revolution*, p. 17.
51. Hrabák, ed., *Dvě legendy*, p. 23.
52. See Erich Auerbach, *Scenes from the Drama of European Literature*, p. 72.

6. The Radiant Rose

1. Bynum, *Fragmentation and Redemption*, p. 122.
2. See Henri Brémond, *Saint Catherine d'Alexandrie*, p. 10.
3. Spina, *Die altčechische Katharinenlegende*, xii.
4. Jacobus de Voragine, *The Golden Legend*, pp. 708–16.
5. See Clemence of Barking, *The Life of Saint Catherine*, xiii.
6. See Eamon Duffy, "Holy Maydens, Holy Wyfes: The Cult of Women Saints in Fifteenth- and Sixteenth-Century England," p. 185.
7. See *Seinte Katherine*, ed. S. R. T. O. d'Ardenne and E. J. Dobson; for an anthology of the so-called Katherine-Group, see Bella Millet and Jocelyn Wogan-Browne, eds., *Medieval English Prose for Women: The Katherine Group and Ancrene Wisse*; see also Osbern Bokenham, *Legendys of Hooly Wummen*, ed. Mary S. Serjeantson.
8. See Franz Machílek, "Privatsfrömmigkeit und Staatsfrömmigkeit," p. 88.
9. For the emperor's life and work, see Seibt, ed., *Kaiser Karl IV*.
10. See Vladimír J. Koudelka, "Zur Geschichte der böhmischen Domikanerprovinz im Mittelalter: I—Provinzialprioren, Inquisitoren, Apost. Ponitentiare," in *AFP* 25 (1955): 75–79.
11. For the Dominicans' association with female piety, see Ennen, *Medieval Woman*, pp. 133–36.
12. See Friedrich Prinz, *Böhmen im mittelalterlichen Europa: Frühzeit, Hochmittelalter, Kolonisationsepoche*, p. 169.
13. Ibid., p. 169.
14. Ennen, *Medieval Woman*, p. 135.
15. Škarka, ed., *Nejstarší*, pp. 76–81.
16. See Josef Hemmerle, "Karl IV. und die Orden," p. 304.

17. For the Dominican authorship of the prose *Life of Christ,* see Vladimir J. Koudelka, "Zur Geschichte der böhmischen Dominikanerprovinz im Mittelalter: III- Bischöfe und Schriftsteller," pp. 57–59. For the Czech translation of the Vulgate, see František Kavka, "Die Hofgelehrten," p. 250.

18. See Jan Vilikovský, *Próza z doby Karla IV,* p. 256.

19. Vilikovský, *Písemnictví,* pp. 154–55.

20. Ibid., p. 154.

21. For the so-called "Vulgate" (the Latin source of the dispute and the passion), see Jan Urban Jarník, *Dvě verse starofrancouzské legendy o sv. Kateřině Alexandrijské.* For the Latin source of the conversion (*Fuit in insula Cypri rex quidam, nomine Costus*), see Franz Spina, ed., *Die altčechische Katharinenlegende der Stockholm-Brunner Handschrift;* for the edition of the unique Czech version (III F 6, Brno), see Josef Hrabák, ed., *Dvě legendy.* For a modern Czech translation of the Czech text, see *Legenda o svaté Kateřině,* trans. Jiří Pelán, with an introduction by Jan Lehár (Prague, 1988).

22. George M. Cummins, *The Language of the Old Czech Legenda o sv. Kateřině,* p. 363.

23. Harkins, ed. and trans., *Czech Prose,* pp. 13–14. For the Czech original, see Chaloupecký and Ryba, eds., *Středověké,* p. 166.

24. "Když z dětiných let vystúpi, / urozomě dobře tomu, / ž' zlo v porobě býti komu."

25. "Neb v svém rozumě znajieše, / že zle v porobenstvě žíti, / i nerodi za muž jíti."

26. Cazelles, *The Lady as Saint,* pp. 30–38.

27. Vilikovský, *Písemnictví,* p. 181.

28. "Po jejie bělúcí líčku / slzy potóčkem sě valéchu, / její oči sě kaléchu / ve krvi velikú žádostí."

29. Ferrante, *Woman as Image,* p. 6.

30. "Cuius ineffabilem pulchritudinem ex splendore (cervicis et) capillorum aureorum cognoscens nec non ex candore niueo suorum vestimentorum" (Spina, ed., *Die altčechische Katharinenlegende,* p. 26).

31. "Maria, ta vzkvetlá panna, jiež matka jest svatá Anna, / drží švého jedináčka, / Krista, milého synáčka, / kochajíc jej myslú čilú. / A nad jeho pleckú milú / šijka bielá svietí lsknúci, / jako lilium bělúcí / lskne kdy z najsvětlejší lásky. / A jeho žádúcie vlásky / svietie, všie poskvrny nahé, / jako ryzé zlato drahé / lskne nad jiné zlato draží; / V těch vlasiech nad jeho paží / zatáčeli sě pupenci / jakožto zlatí prstenci / zdělaní ot pomyšlenie."

32. See Kathleen Ashley and Pamela Sheingorn, eds., *Interpreting Cultural Symbols: Saint Anne in Late Medieval Society,* pp. 25–26, esp. p. 17.

33. Bynum, *Fragmentation and Redemption,* p. 198.

34. Ashley and Sheingorn, eds., *Interpreting Cultural Symbols,* p. 2.

35. See Gail McMurray Gibson, "Saint Anne and the Religion of Childbed: Some East Anglian Texts and Talismans," pp. 95–110.

36. See Wiesner, *Women and Gender,* p. 184. It is interesting to compare the role of Saint Anne with the domestic, down-to-earth Virgin Mary in the Czech *Life of Christ,* where the Mother of God performs the domestic tasks of sewing and cooking. For the domestication of sacred scenes in the context of late medieval female piety, see Diana M. Webb, "Woman and Home: The Domestic Setting of Late Medieval Spirituality," pp. 159–74.

37. See Emanuel Poche et al., eds., *Praha středověká,* p. 202.

38. Jan Menšík, ed., *Počátky staročeské mystiky,* p. 80.

39. Burke, *Popular Culture,* p. 35.

40. Significantly, Tommaso da Modena had Dominican connections in Italy, where he painted the murals of Dominican saints now housed in the Museo Civico in Treviso. It would be interesting to explore a possible Dominican link in Tommaso's connections with the court of Charles IV. For Tommaso's connections to the Bohemian court painters, see Albert Kutal, *Gothic Art in Bohemia and Moravia,* p. 63.

41. See Ulrika Rublack, "Female Spirituality and the Infant Jesus in Late Medieval Dominican Convents," p. 43. For medieval religious dolls in general, see Christiane Klapisch-

Zuber, "Holy Dolls: Play and Piety in Florence in the Quattrocento," in *Women, Family and Ritual in Renaissance Italy*, pp. 310–29.

42. For the lily as a symbol of the Annunciation, see Marina Warner, *Alone of All Her Sex: The Myth and Cult of the Virgin Mary*, p. 99.

43. The Czech art historian Jaroslav Pešina regards the coronation of the emperor and Blanche of Valois in 1347 as the source for the golden fleur-de-lis embossed on the cape of the angel Gabriel in the Annunciation panel of the Vyšší Brod Altar (see Jaroslav Pešina, *Mistr vyšebrodského cyklu*, p. 18).

44. Spina, ed., *Die altčechische Katharinenlegende*, xviii.

45. Dante Alighieri, *The Divine Comedy*. Vol. 3, *Paradiso*, p. 466.

46. See the introduction to Cazelles, *The Lady as Saint*.

47. Warner, *Alone of All Her Sex*, 126.

48. See Pauline Matarasso, ed., *The Cistercian World: Monastic Writings of the Twelfth Century*, p. 65.

49. For Kunigunde and her *Passional*, see Vilikovský, *Písemnictví*, pp. 26–40.

50. "Veni, virgo electa et filia mea delecta" (Spina, ed., *Die altčechische Katharinenlegende*, p. 35).

51. "Vítaj, má přežádná! / Vítaj, mojě choti ladná / Pod' sem, vzvolené líčko, / ke mně, milá holubičko!"

52. Thomas, *The Czech Chivalric Romances*, p. 136.

53. Peter Brown, *The Body and Society: Men, Women and Sexual Renunciation in Early Christianity*, p. 299.

54. Ibid.

55. Derek A. Pearsall and Elizabeth Salter, *Landscapes and Seasons of the Medieval World*, p. 147.

56. Spina, ed., *Die altčechische Katharinenlegende*, xxi.

57. Vilikovský, *Písemnictví*, pp. 186–87.

58. See Vlasta Dvořáková, "Karlštejn a dvorské malířství doby Karla IV."

59. See Richard K. Emmerson, "The Apocalypse in Medieval Culture," in *The Apocalypse in the Middle Ages*, ed. Richard K. Emmerson and Bernard McGinn, pp. 293–332, esp. p. 313.

60. See Michael Levey, *Painting at Court*, p. 31.

61. Eugen Hillenbrand, ed. and trans., *Vita Caroli Quarti (Die Autobiographie Karls IV.)*, p. 66.

62. See Eduard Petrů, "Symbolika drahokamů a barev v Životě svaté Kateřiny," *Slavia* 64, no. 4 (1995): 381–86, quote at p. 384. Petrů discerns a parallel between the colors of the jewels and the colors of Catherine's body in the later flagellation scene, but omits to explore how the metaphor of the virginal, resurrected body gives significance to this parallelism.

63. Emmerson, "Apocalypse," p. 322.

64. Ibid., p. 326.

65. Ibid., p. 328.

66. See E. V. Gordon, ed., *Pearl*, xxvii.

67. Jaroslav Ludvíkovský, ed., *Kristiánova legenda*, p. 30.

68. Millet and Wogan-Browne, eds., *Medieval English Prose for Women*, p. 48.

69. "Il bel zaffiro / del quale il ciel più chiaro s'inzaffira."

70. Spina, ed., *Die altčechische Katharinenlegende*, vxiii.

71. Compare a similar mode of adaptation in the early-thirteenth-century prose life of Saint Catherine written for an audience of anchoresses. See Anne Savage and Nicholas Watson, ed. and trans., *Anchoritic Spirituality: Ancrene Wisse and Associated Works* (New York, 1991), p. 261.

72. "Kateřina tu udatně / jide tam, kdež tiesar stáše, / i vece k němu: 'Co páše / tvá bludná moc, zlý tiesaři? / Pro něžto sě s tebú sváři, / v tom sem já práva, ty to vieš. / I proč ten blud činiti smieš?' "

73. Bohuslav Havránek et al., eds., *Výbor z české literatury*, 1:525.

74. Ibid., p. 529.

75. See John Murray, ed., *Le Château d'Amour de Robert Grosseteste, évêque de Lincoln*, lines 605–28.

76. See Jan Vilikovský, *Latinská poesie žákovská v Čechách*, pp. 122–24. For the love lyric "Píseň o barvách," see Vilikovský, ed., *Staročeská lyrika*, pp. 63–64.

77. See J. Pelikán, "Příspěvky ke kritice a výkladu štokholmské legendy o sv. Kateřině," esp. pp. 66–73. The citations of German *Minnesang* color symbolism are taken from this essay.

78. See Peter Ochsenbein, "Leidensmystik in dominikanischen Frauenklöstern des 14. Jahrhundert am Beispiel der Elsbeth von Oye," p. 362.

79. See Ovid, *Metamorphoses*, Book X.1 (p. 225).

80. Brown, *Body and Society*, pp. 167–68.

81. R. W. Southern, *Western Society and the Church in the Middle Ages*, p. 307.

82. Miri Rubin, *Corpus Christi: The Eucharist in Late Medieval Culture*, p. 142.

83. Ibid.

84. See William A. Hinnebusch, *The Early English Friars Preachers*, pp. 279–96.

85. See the introduction to Gottfried von Strassburg, *Tristan*, pp. 14–15.

86. Bynum, "Women Mystics and Eucharistic Devotion in the Thirteenth Century," in *Fragmentation and Redemption*, pp. 119–50.

87. "Úrazy i jejie rány / mažít' mastmi nebeskými; / tak lékaři andělskými / Kristus svú chot tu kojieše."

88. Bynum, *Jesus as Mother*, p. 117.

89. Ibid., p. 122.

90. "Věz, ežt' sem ot nikohého / ztrávy tělesnéj nejměla, / ale jenž skrze anděla / krmil Daniele spoře, / kdyžto ve lvovéj oboře / vězal u krále z Babylona, / ten mě sčedře z svého lóna / krmil, pojil i uzdravil / i svú milostí oslavil."

91. Compare also the rural simile in lines 13–14 of the legend.

92. See Bynum, *Fragmentation and Redemption*, pp. 231–32.

93. Compare the fresco of Catherine with her wheel and sword on the north wall of the Church of Saint Vitus in Český Krumlov, southern Bohemia (c. 1420), where we see the green of the saint's mantle and her golden hair and crown, the first and last of the six colors enumerated in the description of the flagellation in our legend.

94. V. Vondrák, ed., *Kremsmünsterská legenda o 10,000 rytířích*, in *LF* 16 (1889): 21–45, esp. pp. 38–39, lines 305–29.

95. Vilikovský, *Písemnictví*, pp. 184–85.

96. And if pregnant women be cured through her [the saint's] intercession, God should quickly send them succor. And no house in which her passion is painted should ever suffer damage from fire or lightning. (Bokenham, *Legendys of Hooly Wummen*, p. 134).

97. See Duffy, "Holy Maydens," p. 189. For virgins as powerful protectors in early Christianity, see Brown, *Body and Society*, pp. 156–59.

98. Anneliese Schröder, *St. Catherine: Text of Story and Legend*, p. 18.

99. Ibid., p. 21.

100. Bynum, *Fragmentation and Redemption*, p. 269.

101. Ibid., p. 214.

102. "Rači ny dens nakrmiti, / živé krmě nasytiti, / jejé silú posíliti, / jejé rozkoš v dušu vlíti" (strophe 25, lines 1–4).

7. Bohemian Knights

1. Erich Auerbach, *Mimesis: Dargestellte Wirklichkeit in der abendländischen Literatur*, pp. 134–35.

2. See Susan Crane, *Insular Romance: Politics, Faith, and Culture in Anglo-Norman and Middle English Literature*; for German *mise-en-prose*, see Helmut Melzer, *Trivialisierungstendenzen im Volksbuch*.

3. Jane H. M. Taylor, "The Significance of the Insignificant: Reading Reception in the Burgundian *Erec* and *Cligès.*" I would like to thank Dr. Taylor for allowing me to read and quote from the written version of her paper.

4. See Jan Lehár, *Nejstarší česká epika*, pp. 81–82; see also Eduard Petrů, ed., *Rytířské srdce majíce*, p. 12. All page references of Czech quotations from *Duke Ernest* refer to this edition.

5. Václav Janouch, "K pramenům a stilu Alexandreidy staročeské," pp. 376–77.

6. Ulrich von Etzenbach, *Wilhelm von Wenden*, ed. Wendelin Toischer, line 1271.

7. "Ustalý rád pitie sáhá, / zeschlým lukám časná vláha, / čstná žena muži předráha."

8. For a biblical analogue to this imagery, see Leopold Zatočil, "K staročeské Alexandreidě," p. 447.

9. Ferrante, *Woman as Image*, pp. 6–7.

10. "Řiedko jest kdy pochváleno: / bez trávy lúka sečená, / bez příslovie krásná žena."

11. Janouch, "K pramenům," p. 283.

12. "Nejedna slovutná žena / nedóstojně obnažena."

13. Ferrante, *Woman as Image*, p. 30.

14. "Vzpoměňtež, že ste svobodni, / a tito hostie nehodní' již sú porobeni vámi."

15. Peter of Zittau, *Kronika zbraslavská*, ed. J. Emler, FRB, 8 vols. (Prague, 1884), 4:17.

16. Jan Loriš, ed., *Sborník hraběte Baworowského*, pp. 146–300.

17. See David Blamires, *Herzog Ernst and the Other-World Voyage: A Comparative Study*, p. 70.

18. For Marian features in the German version B, see ibid., p. 73.

19. Ferrante, *Woman as Image*, p. 65.

20. "Tu by tepruv mátě plakala, / když by svého syna viděla...."

21. Loriš, *Sborník*, p. 19.

22. "A ta bieše podobná k luně, / když světlost najvětší jmievá / a v slunečnost se odievá."

23. For this conceit, and other Marian formulae, in secular love poetry, see Peter Kesting, *Maria-Frouwe: Über den Einfluß der Marienverehrung auf den Minnesang bis Walther von der Vogelweide*, p. 99.

24. For the relationship between literature and the visual arts, see Karel Stejskal's afterword to his edition of *Tkadleček*, p. 215; see also Stejskal, *The Monastery Na Slovanech.*

25. "Ant' sě dvoří, ant' sě chanie / před ní nosem sem i tam klanie."

26. Rada, ed., *Dějiny zemí*, p. 124.

27. For editions of *Lavrin*, see Loriš, ed., *Sborník*, pp. 353–406 (a direct transcription of the manuscript); and Petrů, ed., *Rytířské srdce majíce*, pp. 197–256 (modernized spelling).

28. Georg Holz, ed., *Laurin und der kleine Rosengarten*. For the complex transmission of the German text, see Joachim Heinzle, "Überlieferungsgeschichte als Literaturgeschichte zur Textentwicklung des Laurin," pp. 172–91.

29. See Alfred Thomas, "*Pych* and *pýcha*: The Old Czech *Lavryn* as Exemplum," pp. 53–58. On a historical note, it is tempting to see a parallel between Lavrin's theft and transgression and Wenceslas IV's encroachments on the property of the higher nobility. For more on these territorial conflicts, see chapter 8 in this volume.

30. See Peter Kern, *Die Artusromane des Pleier: Untersuchungen über den Zusammenhang von Dichtung und literarischer Situation*, p. 217. For the Czech text, see Ulrich Bamborschke, ed., *Der altčechische Tandariuš*. All page references are to this edition.

31. Kern, *Die Artusromane*, pp. 41–42.

32. Here I find myself in disagreement with Petrů's view of this romance as the only true western-style romance in medieval Czech literature. See Eduard Petrů, "Specifičnost rytířské epiky ve slovanských literaturách," p. 255. See also Petrů, ed., *Rytířské srdce majíce*, p. 20.

33. See Brušák, "Some Notes," p. 47.

34. Kern, *Die Artusromane*, pp. 225.
35. Brušák, "Some Notes," p. 49.
36. Ibid., p. 48.
37. Josef Hrabák, ed., "O ženě zlobivé," in *Staročeské satiry Smilovy školy*, pp. 146–48.
38. Brušák, "Some Notes," p. 48.
39. Ibid.
40. A. Mc. I. Trounce, ed., *Athelston*, lines 639–41.
41. Václav Nebeský, "Tristram welký rek," p. 297. See also Jan Gebauer, "Tristram," pp. 108–39; and Zdeňka Tichá, ed., *Tristram a Izalda*, pp. 5–20.
42. For the relationship to Eilhart, see Ulrich Bamborschke, ed., *Das altčechische Tristan-Epos*, 1:127.
43. For these and other details, see Alfred Thomas, "The Treatment of the Love Theme in the Old Czech *Tristram*."
44. Bamborschke, ed., *Tristan Epos*, 1:83.
45. "Ty jsi jako vlk, ješto béře ovcě / i neumieš svého mužě plakati. / Ját' po něm umiem lépe lkáti."
46. Compare Danielle Buschinger, "La légende de *Tristan* en Allemagne au moyen âge après Eilhart et Gottfried: Quelques jalons," p. 37. See also Melzer, *Trivialisierungstendenzen*.

8. From Courtier to Rebel

1. Smil Flaška z Pardubic, *Nová rada*, ed. Jiří Daňhelka. All page references are to this edition.
2. Ibid., pp. 5–16.
3. *Rada otce synovi*, in *Výbor z české literatury*, ed. Karel J. Erben, 1:910–28.
4. See Richard Firth Green, "An Adviser to Princes," in *Poets and Princepleasers*, pp. 135–67. For advice literature in late medieval England, compare Judith Ferster, *Fictions of Advice: The Literature and Politics of Counsel in Late Medieval England*.
5. See the standard twelfth-century bestiary translated by T. H. White in *The Book of Beasts*.
6. For the earliest examples of beast poetry in medieval Latin, see Jan Ziolkowski, *Talking Animals: Medieval Latin Beast Poetry, 750–1150*.
7. Derek Pearsall and Elizabeth Salter, *The Life of Geoffrey Chaucer*, pp. 121–27.
8. Donald R. Howard, *Chaucer: His Life, His Works, His World*, pp. 314–15. For the improbable thesis that Chaucer may have read *The New Council*, see V. Langhans, "Altes und Neues zu Chaucers Parlement of Foules."
9. Gervais du Bus, *Le Roman de Fauvel*.
10. See Jan B. Čapek, "Alegorie Nové rady a Theriobulie"; Čapek, "Die Ironie des Smil Flaška"; and Čapek, "Vznik a funkce Nové rady."
11. See Joyce E. Salisbury, *The Beast Within: Animals in the Middle Ages*, p. 114.
12. Josef Tříška, ed., *Předhusitské bajky*, p. 90.
13. Gregorius de Hungaricali Broda, *Quadripartitus (Speculum sapiencie)*, MS Prague UK XI F10. For the edition, see J. G. Th. Grässe, ed., *Die beiden ältesten lateinischen Fabelbücher des Mittelalters des Bischofs Cyrillus Speculum sapientiae und des Nicolaus Pergamenus Dialogus creatrarum*.
14. Bartholomeus Claretus de Solencia, *Klaret a jeho družina*, ed. Václav Flajšhans.
15. For the life of Wenceslas IV, see Jiří Spěváček, *Václav IV, 1361–1419. K předpokladům Husitské revoluce*. For the life of Richard II, see Saul, *Richard II*.
16. Images of the king with female bath attendants became a favorite motif in the margins of manuscripts commissioned for the king. Compare *The Astronomical Anthology of Wenceslas IV*, Vienna, Österreichische Staatsbibliothek, cod. 2352, fol. 34v.
17. See Rada, ed., *Dějiny zemí*, p. 121.

18. See Ivan Hlaváček, "Aktivita české šlechty na dvoře Václava IV," pp. 205–16.
19. Klassen, *The Nobility*, chap. 4.
20. Tříška, ed., *Bajky*, pp. 90–91.
21. See Daňhelka, ed., *Nová rada*, p. 6.
22. "Neb to, králi, slušie na tě, / aby chodil v ryzém zlatě. / Nad to tobě pravi cele, / měj sě vždy rád vesele: tanec, turnej, časté klánie,/ szuova krásné panny, panie / at' sě tiem tvé srdce kojí.'"
23. "Pak sě silně sběhnú roty. / Tu mnohý na tom potkání / letění sě neobrání / a tak těžce bude ztlačen. / Ty pro to nebud' rozpačen, / když sě tak rytieřsky sberú, / tepút' sě i v tvář sě zderú,/ křičiec: 'Reta! Reta!' v hluku. / Ihned nejednoho ztluků / opáčivše jej na ruby, / mnohémut' vytepú zuby. / Tut' mnozí svú vuóli zdějí / v takém rytieřském turneji."
24. Grässe, ed., *Die Fabelbücher*, pp. 40–41.
25. See Maurice Keen, *Chivalry*, pp. 94–95.
26. Josef Krása, ed., *The Travels of Sir John Mandeville: A Manuscript in the British Library*, plate 20.
27. For a study of the semantic function of "knight" (*rytieř*) and "nobleman" (*pán*) in fourteenth-century Bohemia, see Wojciech Iwańczak, *Tropem rycerskiej przygody: wzorzec rycerski w pismiennictwie czeskim XIV wieku*. For social rituals like hunting and jousting at the Luxembourg court, see Iwańczak, "Dwór jako centrum kultury v Czechach Luksemburskich," pp. 145–84.
28. Čapek, "Die Ironie," 68–79.
29. Ziolkowski, *Talking Animals*, pp. 213–18.
30. Flajšhans, ed., *Klaret*, 2:49.
31. See Mathew, *Court of Richard II*, pp. 33–34.
32. "Dulcia carmina fert sua vernea plus philomena" (Grässe, ed., *Die Fabelbücher*, p. 63).
33. "Etsi laris regii philomena vernacula, que tuo ore insita citharizat" (Tříška, ed., *Bajky*, p. 39).
34. See Morton W. Bloomfield, "The Problem of the Hero in the Later Medieval Period," esp. pp. 29–30.
35. Quoted from Paul Strohm, *Social Chaucer*, p. 36.
36. Patterson, *Chaucer and the Subject of History*, p. 39.
37. See Alfred Thomas, " 'A Mirror for Princes': Literature and Ideology in Pre-Hussite Bohemia."

9. Writing and the Female Body

1. František Šimek, ed., *Tkadleček, hádka milence s Neštěstím*. All subsequent page numbers refer to this edition. The 1974 edition (with modernized spelling) is substantially the same as the earlier, unmodernized version edited by Hynek Hrubý and František Šimek (Prague, 1923). English translations of the text are my own.
2. See *Svár vody s vínem*, in *Staročeské satiry*, ed. Josef Hrabák, pp. 131–45; Roman Jakobson, ed., *Spor duše stělem*; and *O Rozmlouvání člověka se smrtí*, in *Veršované skladby doby husitské*, ed. František Svejkovský, pp. 49–89.
3. Jakobson, ed., *Spor duše*, p. 23.
4. See ibid., n. 6.
5. See Stephen Greenblatt, ed., *Allegory and Representation*. Baltimore, Md., and London, 1981), pp. 1–25, esp. p. 2.
6. See Helmut Rosenfeld, "Der alttschechische *Tkadleček* in neuer Sicht: Ackermann-Vorlage, Waldenserallegorie oder höfische Dichtung?"
7. For a lucid summary of the debate about *Le Roman de la Rose*, see Charity Cannon Willard, "The Franco-Italian Professional Writer: Christine de Pisan," in *Medieval Women Writers*, ed. Katharina M. Wilson, pp. 336–38.
8. For the German analogue, see Willy Krogmann, ed., *Der Ackermann aus Böhmen*. For the relationship between the German and Czech texts, see Antonín Hrubý, *Der Ack-*

ermann aus Böhmen und seine Vorlage. See also Helmut Rosenfeld, "Johannes de Šitbor, der *Tkadleček* und die beiden *Ackermann*-Fassungen von 1370 und 1401"; and Walter Schamschula, "*Der Ackermann aus Böhmen* und "Tkadlecek"—ihr Verhältnis in neuer Sicht."

9. For the question of rhetorical style in *The Weaver*, see Vilikovský, *Písemnictví*, pp. 220–36. See also the introduction to *Tkadleček*, ed. Šimek, p. 15.

10. "Ját' jsem tkadlec učeným řádem, bez dřievie, bez rámu a bez železa tkáti uměji. Člunek mój, jímžto osnuji, jest z ptačie vlny; přiezie má z rozličných zvieřat oděvu jest. Rosa, jenž rolí mú skropuje, nenie obecná voda, ani sama o sobě, ale jest s obecnú vodú smiešena, jížto v svú potřebu jednak nahoru, jednak dolóv i sem i tam krópěje podávám" (p. 32).

11. "Myt' činíme, jakto ty, Tkadlečku, činíš. Naše brdo ke všem lidem připraveno jest; všechno, což jest na světě, to my svú mocí snošujem a zosnujem" (p. 140).

12. "Tut' fiola své moci před námi neskryje svú rozkošnú barvú všie ustavičnosti. Tut' lilium krású svú a bělostí před námi neuteče svú dobrú nádějí. Tu ruože červená svú šarlatnú barvú v hořící milostí nám se neopne, tut' dětelík, ni břčtan, ni chvojka, ni barvínek, jenž jest všie počaté milosti vuodce, nám sé neskryje. Tut' ruože polská svú brunátnú barvú všeho tajemstvie utéci se nás nemuož. Tut' vymyšlená a kradená barva šerá z mnohých složená svú vysokú myslí nad nám se nevyzdvihuje. Tut' blankytný charpený neboli čakankový květ svú zlú nádějí neboli svú dokonalostí nám se neprotiví. Tut' také pléška svú miezhú, svú žlutú barvú, jenž na haně vydána jest, proti nám nezíšče" (p. 140).

13. "Slyš, slyš těchto nových řečí" (p. 27).

14. Carolyn Dinshaw, *Chaucer's Sexual Poetics*, p. 22.

15. Ibid.

16. Ibid., p. 21.

17. For the association of writing with sexual intercourse implicit in this patristic image of passing through the "female" text, see Alain de Lille, *The Plaint of Nature*, p. 156.

18. Dinshaw, *Chaucer's Sexual Poetics*, p. 79.

19. "Milost má svá zvlášcie znamenie, svá zvláštie hesla, své zvláštnie řeči skryté" (p. 121).

20. Dinshaw, *Chaucer's Sexual Poetics*, p. 22.

21. Aristotle, *Historia animalium (On the Generation of Animals)*, pp. 728–30.

22. Caroline Walker Bynum, "The Female Body and Religious Practice," in *Fragmentation and Redemption*, pp. 181–238, esp. p. 202.

23. Thomas Aquinas, *Summa Theologica*, 1:466.

24. "Neciň jako Elena" (p. 124).

25. "Preč jest se brala má světlá hvězda" (p. 39).

26. Bloch, "Medieval Misogyny," p. 22, note 29.

27. Compare Dinshaw on Chaucer's rhetoric-loving homosexual Pardoner, in *Chaucer's Sexual Poetics*, p. 157.

28. Bloch, "Medieval Misogyny," pp. 10–11.

29. Compare Roland Barthes, *The Pleasure of the Text*, p. 64: "Text means Tissue; but whereas hitherto we have always taken this tissue as a product, a ready-made veil behind which lies, more or less hidden, meaning (truth), we are now emphasizing the tissue, the generative idea that the text is made, is worked out in perpetual interweaving; lost in his tissue—this texture—the subject unmasks himself, like a spider dissolving in the constructive secretions of (her) web."

30. Bloch, "Medieval Misogyny," p. 14.

31. For this text, see Hrabák, ed., *Staročeské satiry*, pp. 115–31.

32. For the Prague uprisings of 1419 and 1422, see František Graus, *Struktur und Geschichte*, pp. 60–73.

33. See Howard Kaminsky, *A History of the Hussite Revolution*, p. 8.

34. Ferdinand Seibt, "Johannes Hus und der Abzug der deutschen Studenten aus Prag 1409," in *Hussitenstudien: Personen, Ereignisse, Ideen einer frühen Revolution*, pp. 1–15.

35. John Klassen,"Women and Religious Reform in Late Medieval Bohemia," p. 205.
36. See Robert E. Lerner, "Writing and Resistance among Beguins of Languedoc and Catalonia," pp. 186–204.
37. For the text of *The Beguine*, see Vilikovský, ed., *Staročeská lyrika*, pp. 118–19.
38. For *The Wycliffite Woman*, see ibid., pp. 120–22. For an English translation of *The Wycliffite Woman* (with the somewhat misleading, freely translated title of *The Lollard Lady*), see Alfred French, ed., *An Anthology of Czech Poetry*, pp. 75–79.
39. Quoted from Margaret Aston, *Lollards and Reformers: Images and Literacy in Late Medieval Religion*, p. 52.
40. Ibid., p. 69.
41. Paul Strohm, "Chaucer's Fifteenth-Century Audience and the Narrowing of the Chaucer Tradition."
42. See Jiří Daňhelka, ed., *Husitské skladby Budyšínského rukopisu*, pp. 80–165.
43. Quoted from Harkins, ed. and trans., *Czech Prose*, pp. 38–39. For the Czech text, see Bohuslav Havránek et al. eds., *Výbor z české literatury doby husitské*, 1:197: "Tak by svatá Kateřina, dievka mladá, měla byla ustúpiti pravdy a viery pána Jezukrista proto, že padesát mistróv proti ní stálo aneb bylo."
44. Seiferth, *Synagogue and Church*, p. 11.
45. "S svými Uhry, Němci, Šváby. / Dosti na něm hnilé báby!" (Daňhelka, ed., *Husitské*, p. 139).
46. See Margaret Aston, "Lollards and Images," p. 105.
47. Ibid., p. 144.
48. Hrabák, ed., *Staročeské satiry*, p. 122, lines 255–59.
49. For the equation of the feminine with oral and popular culture, see Biddick, "Gender, Bodies, Borders," p. 413.
50. Sarah Beckwith, *Christ's Body: Identity, Culture, and Society in Late Medieval Writings*, p. 32.
51. Klassen, "Women, " p. 203.
52. For a similar conclusion with respect to Lollard women in England, see Shannon McSheffrey, *Gender and Heresy: Women and Men in Lollard Communities, 1420–1530*.

10. Epilogue

1. Printed in Havránek et al., eds., *Výbor z české doby husitské literatury*, 1:324–25.
2. Šmahel, "Literacy and Heresy," p. 250.
3. See Svejkovský, ed., *Veršované skladby doby husitské*, pp. 116–50.
4. Keen, *English Society*, pp. 301–2.
5. Mathew, *Court of Richard II*, p. 17.
6. For Czech literary contacts with the western Renaissance, see Josef Macek, "Bohemia and Moravia."
7. Hans-Bernd Harder, "Zentren des Humanismus in Böhmen und Mähren."

Bibliography

✣

Primary texts are listed under the name of the author if this is known; anonymous texts and anthologies of works by more than one writer are listed under the editor's name.

Aers, David, ed. *Culture and History, 1350–1600: Essays on English Communities, Identities, and Writing.* Detroit, Mich., 1992.

Aers, David, and Lynn Staley. *The Powers of the Holy: Religion, Politics, and Gender in Late Medieval English Culture.* University Park, Pa., 1996.

Amt, Emilie, ed. *Women's Lives in Medieval Europe: A Sourcebook.* New York and London, 1993.

Aquinas, Saint Thomas. *Summa theologica.* Ed. and trans. Fathers of the English Dominican Province. 3 vols. New York, 1947.

Aristotle. *Historia animalium (On the Generation of Animals).* Trans. A. L. Peck. Cambridge, Mass., 1953.

Ashley, Kathleen, and Pamela Sheingorn, eds. *Interpreting Cultural Symbols: Saint Anne in Late Medieval Society.* Athens and London, 1990.

Aston, Margaret. *Lollards and Reformers: Images and Literacy in Late Medieval Religion.* London, 1984.

———. "Lollards and Images." In *England's Iconoclasts.* Vol. 1, *Laws against Images,* pp. 96–159. Oxford, 1988.

Auerbach, Erich. *Mimesis: Dargestellte Wirklichkeit in der abendländischen Literatur.* Bern, 1948.

———. *Scenes from the Drama of European Literature.* New York, 1959.

Augustine, Saint. *On Christian Doctrine.* Trans. D. W. Robertson. Indianapolis and New York, 1958.

Bakhtin, Mikhail. *Rabelais and His World.* Trans. Helen Iswolsky. Cambridge, Mass., and London, 1968.

Ballard, George. *Memoirs of Several Ladies of Great Britain Who Have Been Celebrated for Their Writing or Skill in the Learned Languages, Arts, and Sciences.* Ed. Ruth Perry. Detroit, Mich., 1985.

Bamborschke, Ulrich, ed. *Das altčechische Tristan-Epos.* 2 vols. Wiesbaden, 1968–69.

———. *Der altčechische Tandariuš.* Berlin, 1982.

Barking, Clemence of. *The Life of Saint Catherine.* Ed. William McBain. ANTS, 18. Oxford, 1984.

Barron, Caroline J. "William Langland: A London Poet." In *Chaucer's England,* ed. Barbara Hanawalt, pp. 91–109. Minneapolis, 1992.

Barthes, Roland. *The Pleasure of the Text.* Trans. Richard Howard. London, 1976.

Bartlett, Robert. *The Making of Europe: Conquest, Colonization, and Cultural Change, 950–1300.* Princeton, N.J., 1993.

Bartlett, Robert and Angus Mackay, eds. *Medieval Frontier Societies.* Oxford, 1989.

Bartoš, F. M. "První česká spisovatelka." *Krešt'anská revue* 24 (1957): 119–22.

Baumann, Winfried. *Die Literatur des Mittelalters in Böhmen: Deutsch-Lateinisch-Tschechische Literatur vom 10. bis zum 15. Jahrhundert.* Veröffentlichungen des Collegium Carolinum, 37. Munich and Vienna, 1978.

Beckwith, Sarah. *Christ's Body: Identity, Culture, and Society in Late Medieval Writings.* London, 1993.

Behr, Hans-Joachim. *Literatur als Machtlegitimation: Studien zur Funktion der deutschsprachigen Dichtung am böhmischen Königshof im 13. Jahrhundert.* Munich, 1989.

Bell, Susan Groag. "Medieval Women Book Owners: Arbiters of Lay Piety and Ambassadors of Culture." In *Sisters and Workers in the Middle Ages,* ed. Judith M. Bennett et al., pp. 135–61. Chicago, 1989.

Bennett, Judith M. et al., eds. *Sisters and Workers in the Middle Ages.* Chicago and London, 1989.

Bennett, Michael J. *Community, Class, and Careerism: Cheshire and Lancashire in the Age of "Sir Gawain and the Green Knight."* Cambridge, 1983.

———. "The Court of Richard II and the Promotion of Literature." In *Chaucer's England,* ed. Barbara Hanawalt, pp. 3–20. Minneapolis, 1992.

Betts, R. R. *Essays in Czech History.* London, 1969.

Biddick, Kathleen. "Genders, Bodies, Borders: Technologies of the Visible." *Speculum* 68 (1993): 389–418.

Biller, Peter, and Anne Hudson, eds. *Heresy and Literacy, 1000–1530.* Cambridge Studies in Medieval Literature, 23. Cambridge, 1994.

Bittner, Karl. *Deutsche und Tschechen: Zur Geistesgeschichte des böhmischen Raumes.* Vol 1. Prague, 1936.

Blamires, David. *Herzog Ernst and the Otherworld Voyage: A Comparative Study.* Manchester, 1979.

Blaschke, A. "Zu den Anfängen der Literatur in Böhmen unter den Přemysliden." *ZfSl* 1 (1962): 276–82.

Bloch, R. Howard. "Medieval Misogyny." In *Misogyny, Misandry, and Misanthropy,* ed. R. Howard Bloch and Frances Ferguson, pp 1–24. Berkeley, Los Angeles, and London, 1989.

———. *Medieval Misogyny and the Invention of Western Romantic Love.* Chicago and London, 1991.

Bloomfield, Morton W. "The Problem of the Hero in the Later Medieval Period." In *Concepts of the Hero in the Middle Ages and the Renaissance,* ed. Norman T. Burns and Christopher J. Reagan. Albany, 1975, pp. 27–48.

Blumenfeld-Kosinski, Renate, and Timea Szell, eds. *Images of Sainthood in Medieval Europe.* Ithaca and London, 1991.

Bohatec, Miloslav. *Illuminated Manuscripts.* Trans. Till Gottheinerová. Prague, 1970.

Bokenham, Osbern. *Legendys of Hooly Wummen.* Ed. Mary S. Serjeantson. EETS. London, 1938.

Bondy, Gottlieb, and Franz Dworsky. *Zur Geschichte der Juden in Böhmen, Mähren und Schlesien von 906 bis 1620.* Prague, 1906.

Bossy, John. *Christianity in the West, 1400–1700.* Oxford, 1985.

Boulay, F. R. H. du, and Caroline M. Barron, eds. *The Reign of Richard II: Essays in Honor of May McKisack.* London, 1971.

Bowers, John M. "*Pearl* in Its Royal Setting: Ricardian Poetry Revisited." *Studies in the Age of Chaucer* 17 (1995): 111–55.

Bowlus, Charles. *Franks, Moravians, and Magyars: The Struggle for the Middle Danube, 788–907.* Philadelphia, 1995.

Brémond, Henri. *Saint Catherine d'Alexandrie.* Paris, 1923.

Brown, Peter. *The Cult of the Saints: Its Rise and Function in Latin Christianity.* Chicago, 1981.

———. *The Body and Society: Men, Women, and Sexual Renunciation in Early Christianity.* New York, 1988.

Brownlee, Marina S., et al., eds. *The New Medievalism.* Baltimore, Md., and London, 1991.

Brückner, Alexander. "Böhmische Studien." *AfSlPh* 11 (1888): 81–82, 189–90; 12 (1889): 321–22; 13 (1890): 1–2.

Brušák, Karel. "The Meaning of Czech History: Pekař versus Masaryk." In *Intelluctuals and the Future in the Habsburg Monarchy, 1890–1914,* ed. László Péter and Robert B. Pynsent, pp. 92–106. London, 1988.

———. "Some Notes on *Tandariáš a Floribella,* a Czech Fourteenth-Century Chivalrous Romance." In *Gorski vijenac: A Garland of Essays Offered to Professor Elizabeth Mary Hill,* ed. Robert Auty et al., pp. 44–56. Cambridge, 1970.

Burke, Peter. *Popular Culture in Early Modern Europe.* New York, 1978.

Burns, E. Jane. *Bodytalk: When Women Speak in Old French Literature.* Philadelphia, 1993.

Bus, Gervais du. *Le Roman de Fauvel.* Ed. John Murray. SATF. Paris, 1914; reprint, 1968.

Buschinger, Danielle. "La légende de *Tristan* en Allemagne au moyen âge après Eilhart et Gottfried: Quelques jalons." *Actes du colloque des 5. et 6. mai 1978: Littérature et société au moyen âge,* pp. 35–49. Picardy, 1978.

Bynum, Caroline Walker. *Jesus as Mother: Studies in the Spirituality of the High Middle Ages.* Berkeley, Los Angeles, and London, 1982.

———. *Holy Feast and Holy Fast: The Religious Significance of Food to Medieval Women.* Berkeley, Los Angeles, and London, 1987.

———. *Fragmentation and Redemption: Essays on Gender and the Human Body in Medieval Religion.* New York, 1991.

Camille, Michael. *The Gothic Idol: Ideology and Image-Making in Medieval Art.* Cambridge, 1989.

———. "The Image and the Self: Unwriting Late Medieval Bodies." In *Framing Medieval Bodies,* ed. Sarah Kay and Miri Rubin, pp. 62–99. Manchester, 1994.

Čapek, Jan B. "Alegorie Nové rady a Theriobulie." *VKČSN* 2 (1936): 1–53.

———. "Die Ironie des Smil Flaška." *SlR* 10 (1936): 68–79.

———. "Vznik a funkce Nové rady." *VKČSN* 1 (1938): 1–100.

———. "Dalimilův *hlahol jasný.*" *LF* 68 (1941): 36–47.

Carrasco, Magdalena. "Sanctity and Experience in Pictorial Hagiography: Two Illustrated Lives of Saints from Romanesque France." In *Images of Sainthood in Medieval Europe,* ed. Renate Blumenfeld-Kosinski and Timea Szell, pp. 33–66. Ithaca and London, 1991.

Cary, George. *The Medieval Alexander.* Cambridge, 1956.

Cazelles, Brigitte, ed. *The Lady as Saint: A Collection of French Hagiographic Romances of the Thirteenth Century.* Philadelphia, 1991.

Čechura, Jaroslav, Milan Hlaváčka, and Eduard Maur. *Ženy a milenky českých králů.* Prague, 1994.

Cejnar, Jiří, ed. *Nejstarší české veršované legendy.* Prague, 1964.

Černý, Karel J. *Staročeská báseň o Laurinovi a její originál.* Pardubice, 1893.

Černý, Václav. *Staročeská milostná lyrika.* Prague, 1948.

———. *Staročeský Mastičkář.* Rozpravy české akademie věd, 65, 7. Prague, 1955.

Chaloupecký, Václav, and Bohumil Ryba, eds. *Středověké legendy prokopské: Jejich historický rozbor a texty.* Prague, 1953.

Charles IV. *Vita Caroli Quarti.* Ed. and trans. Eugen Hillenbrand. Stuttgart, 1979.

Cherewatuk, Karen, and Ulrike Wiethaus, eds. *Dear Sister: Medieval Women and the Epistolary Genre.* Philadelphia, 1993.

Chytil, Karel. *Antikrist v naukách a umění středověku a husitské obrazové antiteze.* Prague, 1918.

Clifton-Everest, John M. "Slawisches Schrifttum im 10. und 11. Jahrhundert in Böhmen." *Bohemia* 37, no. 2 (1996): 257–70.

Coakley, John. "Friars, Sanctity, and Gender: Mendicant Encounters with Saints, 1250–1325." In *Medieval Masculinities,* ed. Clare A. Lees, pp. 91–110. Minneapolis, 1994.

Coleman, Janet. *Medieval Readers and Writers, 1350–1400.* New York, 1981.

Constable, Giles. *Three Studies in Medieval Religious and Social Thought.* Cambridge, 1995.

Cosmas. *Chronik der Böhmen des Cosmas von Prag.* Ed. Bertold Bretholz. MGH, 2. Berlin, 1923.

Crane, Susan. *Insular Romance: Politics, Faith, and Culture in Anglo-Norman and Middle English Literature.* Berkeley, Los Angeles, and London, 1986.

———. "The Writing Lesson of 1381." In *Chaucer's England,* ed. Barbara Hanawalt, pp. 201–21. Minneapolis, 1992.

Crawford, Anne, ed. *Letters of the Queens of England, 1100–1547.* Stroud, England, and Dover, N.H., 1994.

Culler, Jonathan. *The Pursuit of Signs: Semiotics, Literature, Deconstruction.* Ithaca and New York, 1981.

Cummins, George M. *The Language of the Old Czech* Legenda o sv. Kateřině. Slavistische Beiträge, 87. Munich, 1975.

Daňhelka, Jiří. "Die ältere tschechische Literatur und die Probleme ihrer Gliederung." *WdSl* 13 (1968): 1–16.

Daňhelka, Jiří, ed. *Husitské skladby Budyšínského rukopisu.* Prague, 1952.

———. *Staročeská kronika tak řečeného Dalimila.* 2 vols. Texty a studie k dějinám českého jazyka a literatury 4. Prague, 1988.

Dante Alighieri. *The Divine Comedy.* Vol. 3, *Paradiso,* trans. John D. Sinclair. Oxford, 1961.

d'Ardenne, S. R. T. O., and E. J. Dobson, eds. *Seinte Katherine.* EETS. Oxford, 1981.

Dinshaw, Carolyn. *Chaucer's Sexual Poetics.* Madison, Wis., 1989.

Dinzelbacher, Peter, and Dieter R. Bauer, eds. *Frauenmystik im Mittelalter.* Stuttgart, 1985.

———. *Religiöse Frauenbewegung und mystische Frömmigkeit im Mittelalter.* Cologne and Vienna, 1988.

Du Boulay, F. R. H., and Caroline M. Barron, eds. *The Reign of Richard II: Essays in Honor of May McKisack.* London, 1971.

Duffy, Eamon. "Holy Maydens, Holy Wyfes: The Cult of Women Saints in Fifteenth- and Sixteenth-Century England." In *Women in the Church,* ed. W. J. Sheils and Diana Wood, pp. 175–96. Studies in Church History, 27. Oxford, 1990.

———. *The Stripping of the Altars: Traditional Religion in England, 1400–1580.* New Haven and London, 1992.

Dundes, Alan. "The Ritual Murder or Blood Libel Legend: A Study of Anti-Semitic Victimization through Projective Inversion." In *The Blood Libel Legend: A Casebook in Anti-Semitic Folklore,* ed. Alan Dundes, pp. 336–76. Madison, Wis., 1991.

Dvořáková, Vlasta. "Karlštejn a dvorské malířství doby Karla IV." In *Dějiny českého výtvarného umění od počátků do konce středověku,* ed. Rudolf Chadraba et al. 2 vols. 1:310–27. Prague, 1984.

Dvořáková, Vlasta, et al. *Gothic Mural Painting in Bohemia and Moravia, 1300–78.* Oxford, 1964.

Dvorník, Francis. *The Slavs: Their Early History and Civilization.* Boston, 1959.

———. *The Slavs in European History and Civilization.* New Brunswick, N.J., 1962.

Eberle, Patricia J. "The Politics of Courtly Style at the Court of Richard II." In *The Spirit of the Court: Selected Proceedings of the Fourth Congress of the International Courtly Literature Society,* ed. Glyn S. Burgess and Robert A. Taylor, pp. 168–78. Suffolk, England, 1985.

Eggers, Martin. *Das "Großmährische Reich": Realität oder Fiktion? Eine Neuinterpretation der Quellen zur Geschichte des mittleren Donauraumes im 9. Jahrhundert.* Monographien zur Geschichte des Mittelalters, 40. Stuttgart, 1995.

Emmerson, Richard K., and Bernard McGinn, eds. *The Apocalypse in the Middle Ages.* Ithaca, N.Y., and London, 1992.

Ennen, Edith. *The Medieval Woman.* Trans. Edmund Jephcott. Oxford, 1989.

Erben, Karel J., ed. *Výbor z literatury české.* Prague, 1845–68.

Etzenbach, Ulrich von. *Alexander.* Ed. Wendelin Toischer. Tübingen, 1888.

———. *Wilhelm von Wenden.* Ed. Wendelin Toischer. Bibliothek der mittelhochdeutschen Literatur in Böhmen, 1. Prague, 1876.

Feifalik, Julius. *Studien zur Geschichte der altböhmischen Literatur.* 2 vols. Prague, 1860.
Ferrante, Joan M. *Woman as Image in Medieval Literature from the Twelfth Century to Dante.* New York and London 1975.
Ferster, Judith. *Fictions of Advice: The Literature and Politics of Counsel in Late Medieval England.* Philadelphia, 1996.
Flajšhans, Václav, ed. *Klaret a jeho družina.* 2 vols. Prague, 1926–28.
Francis and Clare: The Complete Works. Trans. Regis J. Armstrong and Ignatius C. Brady. London, 1982.
French, Alfred, ed. *An Anthology of Czech Poetry.* Ann Arbor, Mich.: 1973.
Geary, Patrick J. *Living with the Dead in the Middle Ages.* Ithaca, N.Y., and London, 1994.
Gebauer, Jan. "Tristram." *LF* 6 (1879): 108–39.
Gibson, Gail McMurray. *The Theater of Devotion: East Anglian Drama and Society in the Late Middle Ages.* Chicago and London, 1989.
———. "Saint Anne and the Religion of Childbed: Some East Anglian Texts and Talismans." In *Interpreting Cultural Symbols,* ed. Kathleen Ashley and Pamela Sheingorn, pp. 95–110. Athens and London, 1990.
Given-Wilson, Chris. *The Royal Household and the King's Affinity: Service, Politics, and Finance in England, 1360–1413.* New Haven and London, 1986.
———. *The English Nobility in the Late Middle Ages: The Fourteenth-Century Political Community.* London, 1987.
Goldberg, Jonathan. *Sodometries: Renaissance Texts, Modern Sexualities.* Stanford, Calif., 1992.
Gordon, Dillian. *Making and Meaning: The Wilton Diptych.* London, 1993.
Gordon, E. V., ed. *Pearl.* Oxford, 1980.
Gottfried, Robert S. *The Black Death: Natural and Human Disaster in Medieval Europe.* New York, 1983.
Gottfried von Strassburg. *Tristan.* Trans. A. T. Hatto. Harmondsworth, 1960.
Grässe, J. G. Th., ed. *Die beiden ältesten lateinischen Fabelbücher des Mittelalters des Bischofs Cyrillus Speculum sapientiae und des Nicolaus Pergamenus Dialogus creatrarum.* Tübingen, 1880.
Graus, František. *Struktur und Geschichte: Drei Volksaufstände im mittelalterlichen Prag.* Sigmaringen, 1971.
———. *Die Nationenbildung der Westslawen im Mittelalter.* Sigmaringen, 1980.
———. *Pest- Geissler- Judenmorde: Das 14. Jahrhundert als Krisenzeit.* Göttingen, 1987.
———. "Slovanská liturgie a písemnictví v přemyslovských Čechách 10. století." *ČČH* 14, no. 4 (1966): 473–95.
Green, Dennis H. *Irony in the Medieval Romance.* Cambridge, 1979.
Green, Richard Firth. *Poets and Princepleasers: Literature and the English Court in the Late Middle Ages.* Toronto, Buffalo, and London, 1980.
———. "John Ball's Letters: Literary History and Historical Literature." In *Chaucer's England,* ed. Barbara Hanawalt, pp. 176–200. Minneapolis, 1992.
Griffin, Nathaniel Edward, ed. *Guido de Columnis Historia Destructionis Troiae.* Cambridge, Mass., 1936.
Grosseteste, Robert. *Le Château d'Amour de Robert Grosseteste, évêque de Lincoln.* Ed. John Murray. Paris, 1918.
Grundmann, Herbert. *Religious Movements in the Middle Ages.* Trans. Steven Rowan. Notre Dame and London, 1995.
Hanawalt, Barbara, ed. *Chaucer's England: Literature in Historical Context.* Medieval Studies at Minnesota, 4. Minneapolis, 1992.
Harder, Hans-Bernd, et al., eds. *Studien zum Humanismus in den böhmischen Ländern.* Cologne and Vienna, 1988.
———. "Zentren des Humanismus in Böhmen und Mähren." In *Studien zum Humanismus in den böhmischen Ländern,* ed. Hans-Bernd Harder et al., pp. 21–38. Cologne and Vienna, 1988.

Harkins, William E., ed. and trans. *Czech Prose: An Anthology.* Ann Arbor, Mich., 1983.

Harvey, John H. "Richard II and York." In *The Reign of Richard II: Essays in Honour of May McKisack,* ed. F. R. H. du Boulay and Caroline M. Barron, pp. 202–17. London, 1971.

Havránek, Bohuslav, et al., eds. *Výbor z české literatury od počátků po dubu Husovu I.* Prague, 1957.

——. *Výbor z české literatury doby husitské I.* Prague, 1963.

Hay, Denys. *Europe in the Fourteenth and Fifteenth Centuries.* 2nd ed. London and New York, 1989.

Heffernan, Thomas J. *Sacred Biography: Saints and Their Biographers in the Middle Ages.* New York and Oxford, 1988.

Heinzle, Joachim. "Überlieferungsgeschichte als Literaturgeschichte zur Textentwicklung des Laurin." In *Deutsche Heldenepik in Tirol: König Laurin und Dietrich von Bern in der Dichtung des Mittelalters,* ed. Egon Kühebacher, pp. 172–91. Bolzano, 1977.

Hemmerle, Josef. "Karl IV. und die Orden." In *Kaiser Karl IV,* ed. Ferdinand Seibt, pp. 301–5. Munich, 1987.

Hergemöller, Bernd-Ulrich, ed. *Maiestas Carolina: Das Kodifikationsentwurf Karls IV. für das Königreich Böhmen von 1355.* Veröffentlichungen des Collegium Carolinum, 74. Munich, 1995.

Hillenbrand, Eugen, ed. and trans. *Vita Caroli Quarti (Die Autobiographie Karls IV).* Stuttgart, 1979.

Hinnebusch, William A. *The Early English Friars Preachers.* Rome, 1951.

Hlaváček, Ivan. "Aktivita české šlechty na dvoře Václava IV." *MHB* (Prague) 1 (1991): 205–16.

Höfler, Constantin. *Anna von Luxemburg.* Denkschriften der königlichen Akademie der Wissenschaften, Philosophisch-Historische Classe, 20, pp. 89–240. Vienna, 1871.

Holz, Georg, ed. *Laurin und der kleine Rosengarten.* Halle, 1897.

Howard, Donald R. *Chaucer: His Life, His Works, His World.* New York, 1987.

Hrabák, Josef. *Studie ze starší české literatury.* Prague, 1956.

——. *Ze starší české literatury.* Prague, 1964.

Hrabák, Josef, ed. *Dvě legendy z doby Karlovy.* Prague, 1959.

——. *Staročeské satiry Hradeckého rukopisu a Smilovy školy.* Prague, 1962.

Hrubý, Antonín. *Der Ackermann aus Böhmen und seine Vorlage.* Münchener Texte und Untersuchungen zur deutschen Literatur des Mittelalters, 35. Munich, 1971.

Hudson, Anne. *Lollards and Their Books.* London and Ronceverte, 1985.

——. *The Premature Reformation: Wycliffite Texts and Lollard History.* Oxford, 1988.

——. "Laicus litteratus: The Paradox of Lollardy." In *Heresy and Literacy, 1000–1530,* ed. Peter Biller and Anne Hudson, pp. 222–236. Cambridge, 1994.

Iwańczak, Wojciech. *Tropem rycerskiej przygody: Wzorec rycerski w piśmiennictwie czeskim 14. wieku.* Warsaw, 1985.

——. "Tomáš Štítný, Esquisse pour un portrait de la sociologie médiévale." *Revue historique* 113 (1989): 3–28.

——. "Dwór jako centrum kultury v Czechach Luksemburskich." *MHB* (Prague) 1 (1991): 145–84.

Jacobus de Voragine. *The Golden Legend.* Trans. Granger Ryan and Helmet Ripperger. New York, London, and Toronto, 1941.

Jakobson, Roman. "Medieval Mock Mystery: The Old Czech *Unguentarius.*" In *Studia philologica et litteraria in honorem L. Spitzer,* pp. 245–65. Bern, 1958.

——. *Moudrost starých Čechů: Odvěké základy národního odboje.* New York, 1943.

——, ed. *Spor duše s tělem.* Prague, 1927.

Janofsky, Klaus P. "National Characteristics in the Portrayal of English Saints in the *South English Legendary.* " In *Images of Sainthood in Medieval Europe,* ed. Renate Blumenfeld-Kosinski and Timea Szell, pp. 81–93. Ithaca, N.Y., 1991.

Janouch, Václav. "K pramenům a stilu Alexandreidy staročeské." *LF* 63 (1936): 273–88; *LF* 68 (1941): 374–82.

Jantzen, Grace M. *Power, Gender, and Christian Mysticism.* Cambridge, 1995.

Jarník, Jan Urban, ed. *Dvě verse starofrancouzské legendy o sv. Kateřině Alexandrijské.* Prague, 1895.

Johanssen, Ulrich. *Die alttschechische Alexandreis in ihrem Verhältnis zum Gualterus.* Munich, 1930.

Justice, Steven. *Writing and Rebellion: England in 1381.* Berkeley, Los Angeles, and London, 1994.

Kadlec, Jaroslav. "Petr II z Rožmberka." *Strahovská knihovna* 5–6, no. 1 (1970–71): 89–98.

Kalista, Zdeněk, ed. *Korespondence Zuzany Černínové z Harasova s jejím synem Humprechtem Janem Černínem z Chudenic.* Prague, 1941.

Kaminsky, Howard. *A History of the Hussite Revolution.* Berkeley and Los Angeles, 1967.

Kaňák, Miloslav. *Milíč z Kroměříže.* Prague and Blahoslav, 1975.

Kantor, Marvin. *The Origins of Christianity in Bohemia: Sources and Commentary.* Evanston, Ill., 1990.

Karbusicky, Vladimir. *Anfänge der historischen Überlieferung in Böhmen: Ostmitteleuropa in Vergangenheit und Gegenwart.* Cologne and Vienna, 1980.

Kavka, František. "Die Hofgelehrten." In *Kaiser Karl IV.*, ed. Ferdinand Seibt, pp. 249–53. Munich, 1978.

———. *Život na dvoře Karla IV.* Prague, 1993.

———. "Bohemia." In *The Reformation in National Context*, ed. B. Scribner et al., pp. 131–54. Cambridge, 1994.

Keen, Maurice. *Chivalry.* New Haven, Conn., and London, 1984.

———. *English Society in the Later Middle Ages, 1348–1500.* Harmondsworth, 1990.

Kern, Peter. *Die Artusromane des Pleier: Untersuchungen über den Zusammenhang von Dichtung und literarischer Situation.* Philologische Studien und Quellen, 100. Berlin, 1981.

Kesting, Peter. *Maria-Frouwe: Über den Einfluß der Marienverehrung auf den Minnesang bis Walther von der Vogelweide.* Medium Aevum, 5. Munich, 1965.

Kieckhefer, Richard. *Repression of Heresy in Medieval Germany.* Liverpool, 1979.

———. *Magic in the Middle Ages.* Cambridge, 1989.

King, Margaret L. *Women of the Renaissance.* Chicago and London, 1991.

Klaniczay, Gábor. *The Uses of Supernatural Power: The Transformation of Popular Religion in Medieval and Early-Modern Europe.* Trans. Susan Singerman. Princeton, N.J., 1990.

Klapisch-Zuber, Christiane. *Women, Family, and Ritual in Renaissance Italy.* Trans. Lydia G. Cochrane. Chicago and London, 1985.

———, ed. *Silences of the Middle Ages.* Vol. 2 of *A History of Women in the West*, ed. Georges Duby and Michelle Perrot. Cambridge, Mass., and London, 1992.

Klassen, John. *The Nobility and the Making of the Hussite Revolution.* Boulder, Colo., 1978.

———. "Women and Religious Reform in Late Medieval Bohemia." *Renaissance and Reformation* 5, no. 4 (1981): 203–21.

Köhler, Erich. *Ideal und Wirklichkeit in der höfischen Epik.* 2nd ed. Tübingen, 1970.

Kolářová-Císařová, Anna. *Žena v hnutí husitském.* Prague, 1915.

———. *Žena v Jednotě bratrské.* Prague, 1942.

Kopecký, M. *Úvod do studia staročeských rukopisů a tisků.* Prague, 1978.

Kopičková, Božena. *Historické prameny k studiu postavení ženy v české a moravské středověké společnosti.* Prague, 1992.

Koudelka, Vladimír J. "Zur Geschichte der böhmischen Dominikanerprovinz im Mittelalter: I- Provinzialprioren, Inquisitoren, Apost. Ponitentiare." *AFP* 25 (1955): 75–79.

———. "Zur Geschichte der böhmischen Dominikanerprovinz im Mittelalter: III- Bischöfe und Schriftsteller." *AFP* 17 (1957): 39–110.

Krása, Josef, ed. *The Travels of Sir John Mandeville: A Manuscript in the British Library.* Trans. Peter Kussi. New York, 1983.

Krogmann, Willy, ed. *Der Ackermann aus Böhmen.* Deutsche Klassiker des Mittelalters, 1. Wiesbaden, 1964.

Kruger. Steven F. "The Bodies of Jews in the Late Middle Ages." In *The Idea of Medieval Literature: New Essays on Chaucer and Medieval Culture in Honor of Donald R. Howard*, ed. James M. Dean and Christian K. Zacher, pp. 301–23. Newark, Delaware, 1992.

Kutal, Albert. *Gothic Art in Bohemia and Moravia*. Trans. Till Gottheinerová. London, 1971.

Květ, Jan. *Iluminované rukopisy Královny Rejčky*. Prague, 1931.

Kyas, Vladimír. *První český překlad bible*. Prague, 1971.

———. "Vznik staročeského biblického překladu." In *Mezinárodní vědecká konference*, ed. J. Porák, pp. 48–53.

———. "Die alttschechische Bibelübersetzung des 14. Jahrhundert und ihre Entwicklung im 15. Jahrhundert." In *Kutnohorská Bible*, ed. R. Olesch and H. Rothe, pp. 9–32.

Labalme, Patricia H., ed. *Beyond Their Sex: Learned Women of the European Past*. New York and London, 1980.

Lambert, Malcolm. *Medieval Heresy: Popular Movements from the Gregorian Reform to the Reformation*. 2nd ed. Oxford and Cambridge, Mass., 1992.

Langhans, Václav. "Altes und Neues zu Chaucers Parlement of Fowles." *Anglia* 54 (1930): 25–66.

Larrington, Carolyne. *Women and Writing in Medieval Europe: A Sourcebook*. London, 1995.

Lawrence, Christopher H. *The Friars: The Impact of the Early Mendicant Movement on Western Society*. London and New York, 1994.

Lees, Clare A., ed. *Medieval Masculinities: Regarding Men in the Middle Ages*. Medieval Cultures at Minnesota, 7. Minneapolis, 1994.

Lehár, Jan. *Nejstarší česká epika*. Prague, 1983.

———, ed. *Středověká česká lyrika*. Prague, 1990.

Lerner, Robert E. *The Age of Adversity: The Fourteenth Century*. Ithaca, N.Y., 1968.

———. *The Heresy of the Free Spirit in the Later Middle Ages*. Berkeley and Los Angeles, 1972.

———. "Writing and Resistance among Beguins of Languedoc and Catalonia." In *Heresy and Literacy, 1000–1530*, ed. Peter Biller and Anne Hudson, pp. 186–204. Cambridge, 1994.

Levey, Michael. *Painting at Court*. London, 1971.

Lille, Alain de. *The Plaint of Nature*. Trans. James J. Sheridan. Toronto, 1980.

Loriš, Jan, ed. *Sborník hraběte Baworowského*. Prague, 1903.

Ludvíkovský, Jaroslav, ed. *Kristánova legenda*. Prague, 1978.

Lunt, Horace G. "Skimpy Evidence, Nationalism and Closed Minds: The Case of Methodius, Morava, and the 'Moravian King.'" In *O Rus! Studia litteraria slavica in honorem Hugh McLean*, ed. Simon Karlinsky, James L. Rice, and Barry P. Scherr, pp. 142–52. Berkeley Slavic Specialties, 1995.

Macek, Josef. "Bohemia and Moravia." In *The Renaissance in National Context*, ed. Roy Porter and Mikuláš Teich, pp. 197–220. Cambridge, 1992.

Machílek, Franz. "Privatsfrömmigkeit und Staatsfrömmigkeit." In *Kaiser Karl IV*, ed. Ferdinand Seibt, pp. 87–101. Munich, 1978.

Matarasso, Pauline, ed. *The Cistercian World: Monastic Writings of the Twelfth Century*. Harmondsworth, 1993.

Matějček, Antonín. *Pasionál Abatyše Kunhuty*. Prague, 1922.

Mathew, Gervase. *The Court of Richard II*. New York, 1968.

McGinn, Bernard, ed. *Meister Eckhart and the Beguine Mystics*. New York, 1994.

———. *Antichrist: Two Thousand Years of the Human Fascination with Evil*. San Francisco, 1994.

McSheffrey, Shannon. *Gender and Heresy: Women and Men in Lollard Communities, 1420–1530*. Philadelphia, 1995.

Melzer, Helmut. *Trivialisierungstendenzen im Volksbuch*. Hildesheim and New York, 1972.

Mendlová-Mráčková, Eleonora. "Královna Kunhuta." In *Královny*, ed. Karel Stloukal, pp. 95–103. Prague, 1940.

Menšík, Jan, ed. *Počátky staročeské mystiky*. Prague, 1948.

Millet, Bella, and Wogan-Browne, Jocelyn, eds. *Medieval English Prose for Women: Selections from the Katherine Group and Ancrene Wisse.* Oxford, 1990.

Moore, Robert I. *The Formation of a Persecuting Society: Power and Deviance in Western Europe, 950–1250.* Oxford and Cambridge, Mass., 1987.

Morris, Colin. *The Discovery of the Individual, 1050–1200.* Medieval Academy Reprints for Teaching, 19. Toronto, Buffalo, and London, 1987.

Murray, John, ed. *Le Château d'Amour de Robert Grosseteste, évêque de Lincoln.* Paris, 1918.

Nebeský, Václav. "Tristram welký rek." *ČČM* (1846): 277–300.

Nechutová, Jana. "Ženy v Husově okolí. K protiženským satirám husitské doby." In *Jan Hus mezi epochami, národy a konfesemi,* ed. Jan Blâhoslav Lášek, pp. 68–73. Prague, 1995.

Nejedlý, Zdeněk. *Dějiny předhusitského zpěvu v Čechách.* Prague, 1904.

———. *Počátky husitského zpěvu.* Prague, 1907.

Nichols, Stephen G. "An Intellectual Anthropology of Marriage in the Middle Ages." In *The New Medievalism,* ed. Marina S. Brownlee et al., pp. 70–95. Baltimore, Md., 1991.

Nohejlová, Emanuela. "Královna Emma." In *Královny,* ed. Karel Stloukal, pp. 63–65. Prague, 1940.

Novotný, Václav., ed. *M. Jana Husi korespondence a dokumenty.* Prague, 1920.

Ochsenbein, Peter. "Leidensmystik in dominikanischen Frauenklöstern des 14. Jahrhundert am Beispiel der Elsbeth von Oye." In *Religiöse Frauenbewegung und mystische Frömmigkeit im Mittelalter,* ed. Peter Dinzelbacher and Dieter R. Bauer, pp. 353–72. Cologne and Vienna, 1988.

Olesch, Robert, and Hans Rothe, eds. *Kuttenberger Bibel- Kutnohorská Bible bei Martin von Tišnov: Kommentare.* Paderborn, 1989.

Ovid. *Metamorphoses.* Trans. Mary M. Innes. Harmondsworth, England, 1955.

Paris, Matthew. *Chronicles of Matthew Paris: Monastic Life in the Thirteenth Century.* Ed. and trans. R. Vaughan. New York, 1986.

Patschovsky, Alexander. *Die Anfänge einer ständigen Inquisition in Böhmen.* Berlin and New York, 1975.

Patterson, Lee. *Chaucer and the Subject of History.* Madison, Wis., 1991.

Pearsall, Derek A. and Elizabeth Salter. *Landscapes and Seasons of the Medieval World.* London, 1973.

———. *Old English and Middle English Poetry.* London, 1977.

———. *The Life of Geoffrey Chaucer.* Oxford, 1992.

Pekař, Josef. *Die Wenzels- und Ludmilalegenden und die Echtheit Christians.* Prague, 1906.

Pelikán, Jiří. "Příspěvky ke kritice a výkladu štokholmské legendy o sv. Kateřině." *LF* 18 (1891): 64–73.

Pešina, Jaroslav. *Mistr vyšebrodského cyklu.* Prague, 1983.

Petrarch, Francesco. *Le Familiari.* Ed. Vittorio Rosso. Vol. 4. Florence, 1942.

Petrů, Eduard. *Zašifrovaná skutečnost.* Ostrava, 1972.

———. "Literatura doby Karla IV. a Václava IV. v mimopražském prostředí." In *Mezinárodní vědecká konference,* ed. J. Porák, pp. 135–43. Prague, 1981.

———. "Specifičnost rytířské epiky ve slovanských literaturách." *Slavia* 52, nos. 3–4 (1983): 250–58.

———. "Symbolika drahokamů a barev v Životě svaté Kateřiny." *Slavia* 64, no. 4 (1995): 381–86.

———. *Vzdálené hlasy: Studie o starší české literatuře.* Prague, 1996.

———, ed. *Rytířské srdce majíce.* Živá díla minulosti, 96. Prague, 1984.

Poche, Emanuel et al., eds., *Praha středověká.* Prague, 1983.

Polc, Jaroslav. *Agnes von Böhmen 1211–1282: Königstochter, Äbtissin, Heilige.* Munich, 1989.

Porák, Jaroslav, ed. *Mezinárodní vědecká konference: "Doba Karla IV. v dějinách národů ČSSR."* Prague, 1981.

Porter, Roy, and Teich, Mikuláš, eds. *The Renaissance in National Context.* Cambridge, 1992.

Power, Eileen. *Medieval Women.* Ed. M. M. Postan. Cambridge, 1975.

Pražák, Albert. *Staročeská píseň o Alexandru velikém.* Prague, 1946.

Prinz, Friedrich. *Böhmen im mittelalterlichen Europa: Frühzeit, Hochmittelalter, Kolonisationsepoche.* Munich, 1984.

Pynsent, Robert B. "The Baroque Continuum in Czech Literature." *SEER* 62, no. 3 (1984): 321–43.

———. *Conceptions of Enemy: Three Essays on Czech and Slovak Literature.* Cambridge, 1988.

Rada, Ivan, ed. *Dějiny zemí koruny české.* Vol. 1. Prague, 1992.

Rádl, Emanuel. *Válka Čechů s Němci.* Knihovna české mysli, 5. Prague, 1928.

Repp, Ferdinand. "Textkritische Untersuchungen zur Überlieferung des *Vévoda Arnošt* im Codex Baworowský." *ZfSl* 1 (1956): 41–57.

Richards, Jeffrey. *Sex, Dissidence, and Damnation: Minority Groups in the Middle Ages.* London and New York, 1991.

Robertson, Elizabeth. *Early English Prose and the Female Audience.* Knoxville, Tenn., 1990.

Rosenfeld, Helmut. "Johannes de Šitbor, der *Tkadleček* und die beiden *Ackermann*-Fassungen von 1370 und 1401." *WdSl* 26, no. 1 (1981): 102–24.

———. "Der alttschechische *Tkadleček* in neuer Sicht: Ackermann-Vorlage, Waldenserallegorie oder höfische Dichtung?" *WdSl* 26, no. 2 (1981): 357–78.

Rubin, Miri. *Corpus Christi: The Eucharist in Late Medieval Culture.* Cambridge, 1991.

———. "The Eucharist and the Construction of Medieval Identities." In *Culture and History, 1350–1600: Essays on English Communities, Identities, and Writing,* ed. David Aers, pp. 43–63. Detroit, Mich., 1992.

Rublack, Ulrika. "Female Spirituality and the Infant Jesus in Late Medieval Dominican Convents." *Gender and History* 6, no. 1 (1994): 37–57.

Salisbury, Joyce E. *The Beast Within: Animals in the Middle Ages.* New York and London, 1994.

Salmen, Walter. *Der Fahrende Musiker im Europäischen Mittelalter.* Kassel, 1960.

Salter, Elizabeth. *English and International: Studies in the Literature, Art, and Patronage of Medieval England.* Ed. Derek Pearsall and Nicolette Zeeman. Cambridge, 1988.

Saul, Nigel. *Richard II.* New Haven, Conn., and London, 1997.

Schamschula, Walter. "Der *Ackermann aus Böhmen* und 'Tkadleček'—ihr Verhältnis in neuer Sicht." *Bohemia* 2 (1982): 307–17.

———. *Geschichte der tschechischen Literatur.* Vol. 1, *Von den Anfängen bis zur Aufklärungszeit.* Bausteine zur Geschichte der Literatur bei den Slaven, 36. Cologne and Vienna, 1990.

Schleiner, Louise. *Tudor and Stuart Women Writers.* Bloomington and Indianapolis, 1994.

Schmidt-Hartmann, Eva. "Forty Years of Historiography under Socialism in Czechoslovakia: Continuity and Change in Patterns of Thought." *Bohemia* 29, no. 2 (1988): 300–324.

Schnith, Karl. "Zu Wesen und Bedeutung des Lollardentums im Zeitraum von 1382 bis 1414." In *Die Universität zu Prag,* Schriften der Sudetendeutschen Akademie der Wissenschaften und Künste, 7, pp. 135–46. Munich, 1986.

Schröder, Anneliese. *St. Catherine: Text of Story and Legend.* Trans. Hans Hermann Rosenwald. The Saints in Legend and Art, 17. Recklinghausen, 1965.

Seibt, Ferdinand, ed. *Kaiser Karl IV: Staatsmann und Mäzen.* Munich, 1978.

———. *Hussitenstudien: Personen, Ereignisse, Ideen einer frühen Revolution.* Veröffentlichungen des Collegium Carolinum, 60. Munich, 1987.

———. "Gab es einen böhmischen Frühhumanismus?" In *Studien zum Humanismus in den böhmischen Ländern,* ed. Hans-Bernd Harder et al., pp. 1–19. Cologne, 1988.

———. *Karl IV: Ein Kaiser in Europa, 1346 bis 1378*. Munich, 1994.

Seiferth, Wolfgang S. *Synagogue and Church in the Middle Ages: Two Symbols in Art and Literature*. Trans. Lee Chadeayne and Paul Gottwald. New York, 1970.

Shahar, Shulamith. *The Fourth Estate: A History of Women in the Middle Ages*. Trans. Chaya Galai. London and New York: Routledge, 1983.

Shapiro, Marianne. *De vulgari eloquentia: Dante's Book of Exile*. Lincoln, Nebr., and London, 1990.

Shattock, Joanne, ed. *The Oxford Guide to British Women Writers*. Oxford and New York, 1993.

Šimek, František, ed. *Tkadleček, hádka milence s Neštěstím*. Prague, 1974.

Skála, Emil. "Německý jazyk v českých zemích ve 14. století." In *Mezinárodní vědecká konference*, ed. J. Porák, pp. 73–84. Prague, 1981.

Škarka, Antonín, ed. *Nejstarší česká duchovní lyrika*. Prague, 1946.

Skýbová, Anna, ed. *Listy bílé paní Rožmberské*. Prague, 1985.

Šmahel, František. *Idea národa v husitských Čechách*. České Budějovice, 1971.

———. "Husitští 'doktoři' jehly a verpánku." In *Směřování*, ed. N. Rejchrtová, pp. 89–96. Prague, 1983.

———. *Husitská revoluce*. 4 vols. Vol 2. Prague, 1993.

———. "Literacy and Heresy in Hussite Bohemia." In *Heresy and Literacy, 1000–1530*, ed. Peter Biller and Anne Hudson, pp. 237–54. Cambridge, 1994.

———. *Zur politischen Präsentation und Allegorie im 14. und 15. Jahrhundert*. Otto-von-Freising-Vorlesungen der Katholischen Universität Eichstätt, 9. Munich, 1994.

Smil Flaška z Pardubic. *Nová rada*. Ed. Jiří Daňhelka. Prague, 1950.

Southern, Richard W. *The Making of the Middle Ages*. London, 1953.

———. *Western Society and the Church in the Middle Ages*. Harmondsworth, England, 1970.

———. *Medieval Humanism and Other Studies*. Oxford, 1970.

Spěváček, Jiří. *Karel IV: Život a dílo (1316–1378)*. Prague, 1979.

———. *Václav IV, 1361–1419: K předpokladům Husitské revoluce*. Prague, 1986.

———. *Jan Lucemburský a jeho doba, 1296–1346*. Prague, 1994.

———. "Politické a státoprávní předpoklady pro rozvoj umění a kultury v epoše vlády českých Lucemburků (1310–1419)." In *Pocta Karlu Malému k 65. narozeninám*, ed. Ladislav Soukup, pp. 101–11. Prague, 1995.

Spina, Franz, ed. *Die altčechische Katharinenlegende der Stockholm-Brünner Handschrift*. Prague, 1913.

Spinka, Matthew. *John Hus's Concept of the Church*. Princeton, N.J., 1966.

———. *John Hus: A Biography*. Princeton, N.J., 1968.

Spunar, Pavel. *Kultura českého středověku*. Prague, 1985.

Šťastný, Radko. *Tajemství jména Dalimil*. Prague, 1991.

Stejskal, Karel. *European Art in the Fourteenth Century*. Trans. Till Gottheinerová. Prague, 1978.

———. *The Monastery Na Slovanech*. Prague, 1974.

Stloukal, Karel, ed. *Královny, kněžny a velké ženy české*. Prague, 1940.

Strohm, Paul. "Chaucer's Fifteenth-Century Audience and the Narrowing of the Chaucer Tradition." *Studies in the Age of Chaucer* 4 (1982): 3–32.

———. *Social Chaucer*. Cambridge, Mass., and London, 1989.

———. *Hochon's Arrow: The Social Imagination of Fourteenth-Century Texts*. Princeton, N.J., 1992.

Stuard, Susan Mosher, ed. *Women in Medieval Society*. Pennsylvania, 1976.

Svatoš, Michal, ed. *Dějiny univerzity Karlovy*, vol. 1 (1347/48-1622). Prague, 1995.

Svejkovský, František, ed. *Alexandreida*. Prague, 1963.

———. *Veršované skladby doby husitské*. Prague, 1963.

Swoboda, Karl M., ed. *Gothik in Böhmen*. Munich, 1969.

Tasker, Edward G. *Encyclopedia of Medieval Church Art*. London, 1993.

Taylor, Jane H. M. "The Significance of the Insignificant: Reading Reception in the Burgundian *Erec* and *Cligès*." Paper presented at the Eighteenth International Arthurian Congress, Garda, Italy, July 21–27, 1996.

Tepl, Johannes von. *Der Ackermann aus Böhmen.* Ed. Willy Krogmann. Deutsche Klassiker des Mittelalters 1. Wiesbaden, 1954.

Tertullian. "The Apparel of Women." Trans. Edwin A. Quain. In *Disciplinary, Moral, and Ascetical Works,* trans. Rudolph Arbesmann et al. The Fathers of the Church, 40. New York, 1959.

Thomas, Alfred. "Courtly Love in *Vévoda Arnošt.*" *SSR* 5 (1985): 3–17.

———. "*Pych* and *pýcha*: The Old Czech *Lavryn* as Exemplum." *WdSl* 30, no. 1 (1985): 53–58.

———. "The Treatment of the Love Theme in the Old Czech *Tristram.*" *WdSl* 30, no. 2 (1985): 260–68.

———. *The Czech Chivalric Romances* Vévoda Arnošt *and* Lavryn *in Their Literary Context.* Göppinger Arbeiten zur Germanistik, 504. Göppingen, 1989.

———. "Czech-German Relations as Reflected in Old Czech Literature." In *Medieval Frontier Societies,* ed. Robert Bartlett and Angus Mackay, pp. 199–216. Oxford, 1989.

———. "'A Mirror for Princes': Literature and Ideology in Pre-Hussite Bohemia." *FMLS* 25, no. 4 (October, 1989): 315–28.

———. "*Imitatio Christi*: A New Perspective on the Fourteenth-Century Czech Verse Legend of St Procopius." *WdSl* 39, no. 2 (1994): 344–55.

———. *The Labyrinth of the Word: Truth and Representation in Czech Literature.* Veröffentlichungen des Collegium Carolinum, 78. Munich, 1995.

———. "Aussenseiter: Frauen, Juden und Deutsche in dem alttschechischen *Unguentarius.*" *Bohemia* 38, no. 2 (1997): 310–18.

Thomson, S. Harrison. "Learning at the Court of Charles IV." *Speculum* 25 (1950): 1–20.

Tichá, Zdeňka, ed. *Tristram a Izalda.* Prague, 1980.

Trachtenberg, Joshua. *The Devil and the Jews: The Medieval Conception of the Jew and Its Relation to Modern Anti-Semitism.* Philadelphia, 1943.

Třešťík, Dušan. *Kosmas.* Prague, 1966.

———. *Kosmova kronika: Studie k počátkům českého dějepisectví a politického myšlení.* Prague, 1968.

———. "Příchod prvních Slovanů do českých zemí v letech 510–535." *ČČH* 94, no. 2 (1996): 245–80.

———. *Počátky Přemyslovců: Vstup Čechů do dějin (530–935).* Prague, 1997.

Tříška, Josef, ed. *Předhusitské bajky.* Prague, 1990.

Trounce, A. Mc. I., ed. *Athelston.* EETS, 224. London, 1951.

Urbánek, Rudolf. "Královny Johana a Žofie." In *Královny* ed. Karel Stloukal, pp.143–58. Prague, 1940.

Urbánková, Emma, and Karel Stejskal. *Pasionál Přemyslovny Kunhuty.* České dějiny, 48. Prague, 1975.

Vauchez, André. *The Laity in the Middle Ages: Religious Belief and Devotional Practices.* Ed. Daniel E. Bornstein and trans. Margery J. Schneider. Notre Dame and London, 1993.

Vávra, Elizabeth. "Bildmotiv und Frauenmystik—Funktion und Rezeption." In *Frauenmystik,* ed. Peter Dinzelbacher, pp. 201–230. Stuttgart, 1985.

Veltrusky, Jarmila F. *Mastičkář: A Sacred Farce from Medieval Bohemia.* Michigan Studies in the Humanities, 6. Ann Arbor, Mich., 1985.

Vidmanová, Anežka. "Latinské spisy Mistra Klareta." In *Mezinárodní vědecká konference,* ed. J. Porák, pp. 144–57. Prague, 1981.

Vilikovský, Jan. *Latinská poesie žákovská v Čechách.* Bratislava, 1932.

———. *Písemnictví českého středověku.* Prague, 1948.

———. *Próza z doby Karla IV.* Prague, 1938.

Vilikovský, Jan, ed. *Staročeská lyrika.* Prague, 1940.

———, ed. *Staročeské satiry z Hradeckého rukopisu.* Prague, 1942.

Vitz, Evelyn Birge. "From the Oral to the Written in Medieval and Renaissance Saints' Lives." In *Images of Sainthood in Medieval Europe,* ed. Renate Blumenfled-Kosinski and Timea Szell, pp. 97–114. Ithaca, N.Y., 1991.

Vlasto, A. P. *The Entry of the Slavs into Christendom: An Introduction to the Medieval History of the Slavs.* Cambridge, 1970.

Votočková-Joachimová, Jana. *Anežka Přemyslovna.* Postavy české minulosti, 2. Prague, 1940.

Vyskočil, Jan Kapistrán, ed. *Legenda blahoslavené Anežky a čtyři listy sv. Kláry.* 2 vols. Prague, 1932–33.

Wallace, David J., "Anne of Bohemia, Queen of England, and Chaucer's Emperice." *Litteraria Pragensia* 5, no. 9 (1995): 1–16.

———. *Chaucerian Polity: Absolutist Lineages and Associational Forms in England and Italy.* Stanford, 1997.

Warner, Marina. *Alone of All Her Sex: The Myth and the Cult of the Virgin Mary.* New York, 1983.

Webb, Diana M. "Woman and Home: The Domestic Setting of Late Medieval Spirituality." In *Women in the Church,* ed. W. J. Sheils and Diana Wood, pp. 159–74. Oxford, 1990.

Weber, Robert, ed. *Biblia sacra iuxta vulgatem versionem.* 2 vols. Stuttgart, 1969.

Weinstein, Donald, and Rudolph M. Bell. *Saints and Society: The Two Worlds of Western Christendom, 1000–1700.* Chicago and London, 1982.

White, Hayden B. *The Content of the Form: Narrative Discourse and Historical Representation.* Baltimore and London, 1987.

White, T. H., ed. *The Book of Beasts.* London, 1954.

Wiesner, Merry E. *Women and Gender in Early Modern Europe.* Cambridge, 1993.

Wilkins, Nigel. "A Pattern of Patronage: Machaut, Froissart, and the Houses of Luxembourg and Bohemia in the Fourteenth Century." *French Studies* 37, no. 3 (July 1983): 257–81.

Wilson, Katharina M., ed. *Medieval Women Writers.* Manchester, 1984.

Winter, Edward. *Frühhumanismus: Seine Entwicklung in Böhmen und deren Bedeutung für die Kirchenreformbestrebungen im 14. Jahrhundert.* Berlin, 1964.

Wogan-Browne, Jocelyn. "The Virgin's Tale." In *Feminist Readings in Middle English Literature: The Wife of Bath and All Her Sect,* ed. Ruth Evans and Lesley Johnson, pp. 165–94. London and New York, 1994.

Wülfing, J. Ernst, ed. *The Laud Book of Troy.* London, 1903.

Zatočil, Leopold. "K staročeské Alexandreidě." In *Sborník pocta Fr. Trávníčkovi a F. Wollmannovi,* pp. 446–59. Brno, 1948.

Ziolkowski, Jan. *Talking Animals: Medieval Latin Beast Poetry, 750–1150.* Philadelphia, 1993.

Index

✣

Compiled by Eileen Quam and Theresa Wolner

Index

MEDIEVAL CULTURES

Alfred Thomas was educated at Trinity Hall, Cambridge University, where he received both his B.A. and Ph.D. in Slavic Languages and Literatures. He currently is John L. Loeb Associate Professor of the Humanities, Harvard University. Thomas is author of *The Czech Chivalric Romances* Vévoda Arnošt *and* Lavryn *in Their Literary Context* (1989) and *The Labyrinth of the Word: Truth and Representation in Czech Literature* (1995), as well as many articles on medieval and modern Czech and Slovak literatures.

David Wallace is Judith Rodin Professor of English, University of Pennsylvania, and a coeditor of the University of Minnesota Press Medieval Cultures series. His work seeks to situate English writing within and as part of a greater European culture. Wallace's most recent book is *Chaucerian Polity* (1997).